Lyon Travel Guide 2025

Top Attractions, Best Time to Visit, Local Foods, Hotels and Essential Itinerary for First-Timers

Preston .F. Paradise

TABLE OF CONTENTS

INTRODUCTION

Are you dreaming of a journey to a city brimming with history, culture, and culinary delights? Wondering where you can experience medieval charm and modern vibrancy in one destination? Looking for a place where every street tells a story, and every meal is a celebration? Curious about a city that's less touristy yet incredibly rich in experiences? Thinking about a getaway that combines stunning architecture, beautiful parks, and a lively arts scene? Seeking a destination that's perfect for solo travelers, families, and couples alike? If any of these questions resonate with you, then Lyon should be at the top of your travel list for 2025.

Overview of Lyon

Lyon, the third-largest city in France, is a captivating blend of history, culture, and modernity. Nestled at the confluence of the Rhône and Saône rivers, this vibrant city boasts a rich heritage that dates back over 2,000 years. Known as the gastronomic capital of France, Lyon offers an unparalleled culinary experience, making it a must-visit destination for food enthusiasts. The city's charm lies in its well-preserved architecture, ranging from Roman ruins and medieval buildings to Renaissance masterpieces and contemporary designs.

A City of History and Innovation

Lyon's historical significance is reflected in its UNESCO World Heritage status, which recognizes its beautifully preserved old town, the Renaissance district of Vieux Lyon, the Fourvière hill, and the Presqu'île. These areas showcase the city's architectural and cultural evolution, providing a window into the past while still embracing modernity.

Culinary Capital of France

Renowned for its exceptional cuisine, Lyon is home to numerous Michelin-starred restaurants, traditional Lyonnaise bouchons, and bustling food markets. The city's culinary reputation is built on its rich gastronomic heritage, with local specialties like coq au vin, quenelles, and praline tarts delighting visitors' palates.

Cultural and Artistic Hub

Lyon is also a cultural and artistic hub, hosting numerous festivals, exhibitions, and performances throughout the year. The city is famous for its vibrant arts scene, with institutions like the Musée des Beaux-Arts, the Musée des Confluences, and the Opéra de Lyon offering a wealth of artistic and cultural experiences.

Geographic Beauty and Accessibility

Strategically located in southeastern France, Lyon is easily accessible by air, train, and road, making it a convenient destination for travelers. The city enjoys a temperate climate with four distinct seasons, providing a pleasant environment for visitors year-round. Lyon's picturesque setting, with its rolling hills, rivers, and parks, offers numerous opportunities for outdoor activities and scenic views.

Why Visit Lyon in 2025?

Lyon in 2025 is poised to offer an extraordinary travel experience, combining its rich historical heritage with modern innovations and vibrant cultural events. Here are compelling reasons why Lyon should be on your travel list for 2025:

1. Cultural Events and Festivals

Lyon will host a variety of cultural events and festivals in 2025, providing a unique opportunity to experience the city's lively atmosphere. From the famous Fête des Lumières (Festival of Lights) to the Biennale of Contemporary Art and the Nuits de Fourvière (Fourvière Nights), there will be no shortage of exciting activities to immerse yourself in the local culture.

2. Gastronomic Delights

As the gastronomic capital of France, Lyon offers an unparalleled culinary experience. In 2025, new restaurants and food tours will join the already thriving food scene. Indulge in traditional Lyonnaise cuisine at local bouchons, explore the bustling markets, and enjoy world-class dining at Michelin-starred establishments. The city's dedication to culinary excellence ensures that every meal will be a memorable experience.

3. Historical and Architectural Marvels

Lyon's rich history is reflected in its stunning architecture. In 2025, several historical sites and museums will feature special exhibitions and events celebrating the city's heritage. Explore the Roman ruins of Fourvière, wander through the Renaissance streets of Vieux Lyon, and marvel at the grandeur of the Basilica of Notre-Dame de Fourvière. Each visit offers a journey through time and a deeper understanding of Lyon's cultural significance.

4. Modern Developments and Innovations

Lyon is continuously evolving, with new urban developments enhancing its appeal. In 2025, visitors will benefit from improved infrastructure, including expanded public transportation options, eco-friendly initiatives, and modernized tourist facilities. These advancements make exploring the city more convenient and sustainable, ensuring a pleasant and efficient travel experience.

5. Scenic Beauty and Outdoor Activities

The city's geographical setting, nestled between two rivers and surrounded by picturesque hills, offers numerous opportunities for outdoor activities. In 2025, new parks and recreational areas will open, providing even more spaces for hiking, cycling, and boating. The Parc de la Tête d'Or, one of the largest urban parks in France, will host special events and activities, making it a perfect spot for relaxation and leisure.

6. Vibrant Neighborhoods and Local Experiences

Lyon's diverse neighborhoods each offer a unique charm and character. In 2025, enhanced walking tours and local experiences will allow you to discover the best of Vieux Lyon, the Presqu'île, La Croix-Rousse, and other vibrant districts. Whether you're exploring the traboules (hidden passageways) of Croix-Rousse or enjoying the trendy boutiques and cafes in Confluence, you'll find plenty of reasons to fall in love with Lyon.

7. Accessibility and Connectivity

Lyon's strategic location in southeastern France makes it easily accessible from major European cities. With its well-connected airport, high-speed train services, and extensive road network, getting to Lyon in 2025 will be convenient and straightforward. The city's efficient public transportation system ensures that exploring Lyon and its surrounding regions is hassle-free.

8. Unique Shopping Experiences

Lyon is a shopping paradise, offering everything from luxury boutiques to charming local markets. In 2025, new shopping districts and renovated markets will provide even more opportunities to find unique souvenirs, fashion, and local products. The city's flea markets and artisanal shops are perfect for discovering one-of-a-kind items and supporting local craftspeople.

9. Sustainability Initiatives

Lyon is committed to sustainability and green living. In 2025, the city will introduce new eco-friendly initiatives, including green transportation options, sustainable tourism practices, and environmentally conscious urban planning. These efforts make Lyon an attractive destination for eco-conscious travelers looking to reduce their carbon footprint while enjoying a vibrant city experience.

In 2025, Lyon will be a city that seamlessly blends its historic charm with modern innovation, creating a travel experience that is both enriching and unforgettable. Whether you are a history enthusiast, a foodie, an art lover, or an adventurer, Lyon has something extraordinary to offer. Plan your visit and discover why Lyon is one of the most captivating destinations in France.

History and Culture Significance

Lyon, often hailed as the "City of Lights," is a treasure trove of historical and cultural significance that spans over two millennia. Its rich past and vibrant present combine to create a city of immense charm and importance.

Historical Significance

Ancient Foundations

Lyon's origins date back to Roman times when it was known as Lugdunum. Founded in 43 BC, Lugdunum became one of the most significant cities in Roman Gaul. It served as the administrative center of the Roman province and was a major hub for trade and commerce. Remnants of this Roman heritage can still be seen today, including the ancient amphitheater on Fourvière Hill and the Roman baths.

Medieval and Renaissance Growth

During the medieval period, Lyon flourished as a key trading and banking center. Its strategic location at the confluence of the Rhône and Saône rivers made it a vital commercial hub. The city's prosperity continued into the Renaissance, when Lyon emerged as a center of silk production and cultural development. The Renaissance period left a lasting mark on Lyon's architecture, evident in the beautifully preserved buildings of Vieux Lyon (Old Lyon) and the elaborate traboules (hidden passageways) that weave through the district.

The Silk Industry

Lyon's association with the silk industry began in the 15th century and reached its peak during the 19th century. The city's silk weavers, known as canuts, played a pivotal role in Lyon's economic and cultural life. The Musée des Tissus, housed in a former silk merchant's mansion, celebrates this heritage and showcases an extensive collection of textiles.

Cultural Significance

UNESCO World Heritage

In 1998, Lyon was designated a UNESCO World Heritage site in recognition of its historical and architectural significance. The designation encompasses several key areas, including Vieux Lyon, Fourvière Hill, and the Presqu'île, each offering a glimpse into the city's diverse historical layers.

Gastronomic Excellence

Lyon's culinary reputation is unparalleled. Known as the gastronomic capital of France, the city has a rich tradition of food and wine. It is renowned for its traditional Lyonnaise cuisine, characterized by hearty and flavorful dishes. The city is also home to Les Halles de Lyon-Paul Bocuse, a famed food market that showcases the best of regional produce and gourmet delights.

Art and Culture

Lyon has a thriving cultural scene that encompasses a wide range of artistic expressions. The city is home to numerous museums, including the Musée des Beaux-Arts, which houses an impressive collection of fine art, and the Musée des Confluences, which explores natural history and anthropology. The city also hosts the Biennale of Contemporary Art, one of Europe's most important art events, and the Nuits de Fourvière, a festival of music, theater, and dance held in the Roman amphitheater.

Cinema Legacy

Lyon is closely associated with the Lumière brothers, Auguste and Louis, who are credited with inventing the cinematograph and pioneering the motion picture industry. The Musée Lumière, located in the former Lumière family home, is dedicated to their groundbreaking contributions to cinema and offers an immersive experience into the history of film.

Architectural Diversity

The architectural landscape of Lyon reflects its historical evolution. From the ancient Roman ruins and medieval buildings to Renaissance mansions and modernist constructions, Lyon's architecture offers a visual narrative of its past. The Basilica of Notre-Dame de Fourvière, perched on a hill overlooking the city, is a notable example of 19th-century religious architecture, while the contemporary designs of the Confluence district represent the city's forward-looking spirit.

Festivals and Traditions

Lyon's cultural calendar is filled with festivals and traditions that celebrate its heritage and contemporary creativity. The Fête des Lumières, held every December, transforms the city into a magical light show, while the annual Lyon Street Food Festival and various music and dance events highlight the city's dynamic cultural life.

Conclusion

Lyon's history and culture are woven into the very fabric of the city, creating a rich tapestry that attracts visitors from around the world. Its ancient roots, combined with its vibrant cultural scene and culinary excellence, make Lyon a city of profound historical significance and contemporary allure. Exploring Lyon offers a journey through time, from its Roman origins to its modern-day achievements, making it a truly captivating destination.

Geography and Climate

Lyon is strategically situated in southeastern France, at the confluence of the Rhône and Saône rivers. This advantageous location has historically made it a key center for trade and commerce, contributing to its development and prosperity.

Rivers and Hills

Rivers: The Rhône River flows from north to south, while the Saône River runs parallel to it, meandering from the east. Their confluence in Lyon creates picturesque waterfronts and offers opportunities for scenic boat rides and riverside strolls.

Hills: Lyon is set against a backdrop of hills, notably Fourvière Hill to the west and Croix-Rousse Hill to the north. Fourvière Hill is home to the Basilica of Notre-Dame de Fourvière and provides panoramic views of the city. Croix-Rousse, historically associated with the silk industry, is known for its vibrant cultural scene and traboules (hidden passageways).

Urban Layout

Lyon's urban area is divided into several distinct districts:

Presqu'île: The central peninsula between the Rhône and Saône rivers is the city's commercial and cultural heart.

Vieux Lyon: The historic old town, located on the western bank of the Saône, is renowned for its Renaissance architecture and narrow, winding streets.

La Croix-Rousse: Situated on a hill to the north, this district is known for its bohemian atmosphere and historical ties to the silk industry.

Confluence: A modern district at the confluence of the Rhône and Saône, featuring contemporary architecture and a thriving business and residential area.

Climate

Lyon experiences a temperate climate, characterized by four distinct seasons: spring, summer, autumn, and winter. The city's climate is influenced by its geographical position and proximity to the Alps and Mediterranean Sea.

Spring (March to May)

Weather: Spring in Lyon is mild and pleasant, with temperatures gradually warming up from around 10°C (50°F) in March to 18°C (64°F) in May.

Highlights: This is an ideal time to explore the city's parks and gardens, such as Parc de la Tête d'Or, as the flowers begin to bloom and outdoor activities become more enjoyable.

Summer (June to August)

Weather: Summers in Lyon are generally warm to hot, with average temperatures ranging from 20°C (68°F) to 30°C (86°F). July and August are the warmest months.

Highlights: Summer is perfect for enjoying outdoor events, festivals, and dining al fresco. The city's riversides and parks are popular spots for relaxation and leisure.

Autumn (September to November)

Weather: Autumn brings cooler temperatures, ranging from 14°C (57°F) in September to 9°C (48°F) in November. The weather can be quite variable, with a mix of sunny and rainy days.

Highlights: The fall foliage in Lyon's parks and surrounding hills provides a beautiful backdrop for exploring the city. It's also a great time to enjoy seasonal food and wine.

Winter (December to February)

Weather: Winters in Lyon are relatively mild compared to other regions of France, with temperatures ranging from 1°C (34°F) to 8°C (46°F). Snowfall is rare but possible.

Highlights: The winter season includes the famous Fête des Lumières (Festival of Lights) in December, where the city is illuminated with spectacular light displays. It's also a cozy time to enjoy Lyon's hearty cuisine and warm up in its cafes and restaurants.

Conclusion

Lyon's geographical setting and temperate climate make it an appealing destination year-round. Its scenic rivers, surrounding hills, and varied seasonal weather provide a diverse range of experiences for visitors. Whether you're exploring the city's historic sites, enjoying outdoor activities, or participating in seasonal events, Lyon's climate and geography contribute to its charm and allure.

How to Use This Guide

Welcome to your comprehensive guide to Lyon! Whether you're planning a trip, exploring the city, or seeking useful tips, this guide is designed to help you make the most of your visit. Here's a quick overview of how to navigate and utilize the information provided:

Get Started with an Overview

Begin by reading the **Overview of Lyon** to get a general sense of what the city has to offer. This section introduces you to Lyon's unique blend of history, culture, and modernity, and helps you understand why it's a must-visit destination in 2025.

Plan Your Trip

Use **Chapter 1: Travel Essentials** to gather important information on visas, currency, language, and safety. This chapter provides the foundational knowledge you need to prepare for your trip, ensuring that you have all necessary documentation and understand the local customs.

In **Chapter 2: Planning Your Trip**, you'll find practical advice on packing, budgeting, and other travel tips. This section will help you pack efficiently and plan your finances to make your stay enjoyable and stress-free.

Getting to and Around Lyon

Chapter 3: Getting to Lyon covers the various transportation options for reaching the city, including air, train, bus, and car travel. Choose the best method for your needs based on convenience and budget.

Once in Lyon, refer to **Chapter 4: Getting Around Lyon** for detailed information on public transportation, cycling, walking, and other ways to explore the city. This section will help you navigate Lyon easily and efficiently.

Explore Lyon's Attractions

Dive into **Chapter 5: Top Attractions in Lyon** to discover must-see landmarks, museums, parks, and historic sites. This chapter highlights the city's main attractions and provides insights into what makes each one special.

For a deeper understanding of Lyon's neighborhoods, check out **Chapter 6: Neighborhoods of Lyon**. This section offers an overview of various districts, helping you choose where to stay and explore based on your interests.

Find the Perfect Accommodation

In **Chapter 7: Accommodation Options in Lyon**, explore different types of lodging, from luxury hotels to budget-friendly options. This chapter will guide you in selecting accommodations that best suit your preferences and budget.

Enjoy Lyon's Unique Features

Chapter 8: Beaches in Lyon provides information on the city's man-made and natural beach spots, perfect for relaxing and enjoying the outdoors during warmer months.

Explore Lyon's historical and cultural sites in **Chapter 9: Historical and Cultural Sites**. This section delves into the city's rich past and its impact on Lyon's cultural landscape.

For outdoor enthusiasts, **Chapter 10: Outdoor Activities** offers a range of activities from hiking to cycling and boat tours, highlighting the best ways to enjoy Lyon's natural beauty.

Indulge in Local Experiences

Chapter 11: Shopping in Lyon helps you navigate the city's shopping scene, from markets and boutiques to luxury shops and flea markets.

Chapter 12: Food and Drink is a must-read for foodies, providing insights into traditional Lyonnaise cuisine, local markets, cafés, and nightlife.

Plan Day Trips

If you're interested in exploring beyond Lyon, **Chapter 13: Day Trips from Lyon** offers recommendations for nearby destinations such as the Beaujolais wine region, Pérouges, and Annecy.

Create Your Itinerary

Chapter 14: Essential Itinerary for First-Timers provides a suggested 7-day itinerary to help you make the most of your visit. This can serve as a foundation that you can customize based on your interests and time available.

Review Practical Information

Finally, **Chapter 15: Practical Information** covers safety, medical services, travel etiquette, and money-saving tips. This section ensures that you're well-prepared for any situation and helps you navigate local customs.

Wrap Up with Final Tips

Conclude your guide with **Chapter 16: Conclusion**, which includes useful apps, basic Lyonnaise phrases, and final recommendations. This will provide you with additional resources and last-minute tips to enhance your trip.

Chapter 1: Travel Essentials

Visa and Entry Requirements

When planning a trip to Lyon, it's important to be aware of the visa and entry requirements to ensure a smooth arrival. Here's a detailed guide on what you need to know:

Determine Visa Requirements

Schengen Visa: Lyon is part of France, which is a member of the Schengen Area. Depending on your nationality, you may need a Schengen visa to enter France. Citizens from countries within the Schengen Area do not require a visa. However, if you are from a non-Schengen country, you will need to apply for a Schengen visa.

Visa-Free Countries: Many countries, including the United States, Canada, Australia, Japan, and several others, do not require a visa for short stays (up to 90 days within a 180-day period) for tourism or business.

Visa-Required Countries: If you are from a country that requires a visa, you will need to apply for a Schengen visa. The list of countries requiring a visa can be found on the official Schengen visa website or the French consulate's website in your country.

Visa Application Process

If you need a Schengen visa, follow these steps to apply:

Application Form: Complete the Schengen visa application form. This can usually be done online or obtained from the French consulate or visa application center in your country.

Documents Required:

Passport: A passport valid for at least three months beyond your intended stay, with at least two blank pages.

Photographs: Recent passport-sized photographs that meet Schengen visa photo requirements.

Travel Itinerary: Proof of your travel plans, including flight reservations and accommodation bookings.

Travel Insurance: Proof of travel insurance with coverage of at least €30,000 for medical emergencies.

Proof of Financial Means: Evidence that you can support yourself during your stay, such as bank statements or a letter of employment.

Visa Fee: Payment of the visa fee, which varies depending on your nationality and age.

Submission: Submit your application form and supporting documents to the French consulate or visa application center. Some countries may require an appointment.

Processing Time: Visa processing times can vary, but it generally takes around 15 calendar days. It is advisable to apply well in advance of your planned travel dates.

Entry Requirements

Passport Control: Upon arrival in Lyon, you will go through passport control where a border officer will check your visa (if applicable) and passport. Make sure your passport is valid and matches the details on your visa.

Customs Regulations: Familiarize yourself with France's customs regulations, including restrictions on bringing certain items into the country. The French customs website provides detailed information on prohibited and restricted items.

Special Considerations

Long-Term Stays: If you plan to stay longer than 90 days or for purposes other than tourism or business (such as work or study), you may need to apply for a long-stay visa or residence permit. Check with the French consulate for specific requirements.

Travel During COVID-19: Depending on the global situation and travel restrictions related to COVID-19, additional entry requirements such as vaccination certificates, PCR tests, or quarantine may be in place. Check the latest travel advisories and entry requirements before your trip.

Additional Resources

French Consulate or Embassy: Visit the official website of the French consulate or embassy in your country for the most accurate and updated information on visa requirements and application procedures.

Visa Application Centers: Many countries have visa application centers that assist with the visa application process. Check if there is a center near you for support.

By understanding and preparing for the visa and entry requirements, you can ensure a hassle-free arrival in Lyon and focus on enjoying your trip.

Currency and Banking

Understanding the currency and banking system in Lyon is essential for a smooth and enjoyable trip. Here's what you need to know about money matters in the city:

Currency

Currency Used: The official currency in Lyon, as in the rest of France, is the Euro (€). The Euro is used across the Eurozone, which includes many European countries.

Banknotes and Coins: Euro banknotes come in denominations of €5, €10, €20, €50, €100, €200, and €500. Coins are available in €1, €2, 1 cent, 2 cents, 5 cents, 10 cents, 20 cents, and 50 cents.

Currency Exchange

Exchange Services: Currency exchange services are widely available in Lyon. You can exchange money at banks, currency exchange offices, and some hotels. Currency exchange counters at the airport and major train stations also offer these services.

ATMs: ATMs (automated teller machines) are plentiful throughout the city. They provide an easy way to withdraw Euros using your credit or debit card. ATMs typically offer competitive exchange rates, but be aware of any foreign transaction fees your bank may charge.

Banking Services

Banks: Major banks in Lyon include BNP Paribas, Société Générale, Crédit Agricole, and Crédit Lyonnais, among others. Banks generally operate Monday to Friday, with hours typically from 9:00 AM to 5:00 PM. Some branches may open on Saturdays.

Opening an Account: If you need banking services for an extended stay, you may consider opening a local bank account. Requirements for opening an account usually include proof of identity, proof of address, and a residence permit if you are staying long-term.

Credit and Debit Cards

Acceptance: Credit and debit cards are widely accepted in Lyon, including Visa, MasterCard, and American Express. Most restaurants, shops, hotels, and transportation services accept card payments.

Chip and PIN: France uses the chip-and-PIN system for card transactions. Ensure your card has a chip and that you know your PIN, as it may be required for many transactions.

Notify Your Bank: Inform your bank of your travel plans to avoid having your card flagged for suspicious activity.

Cash and Payments

Cash: While cards are widely accepted, it's a good idea to carry some cash for smaller purchases, tips, or in places that may not accept cards. You can withdraw cash from ATMs or exchange currency at banks and exchange offices.

Tipping: Tipping is not obligatory in France, as a service charge is often included in the bill. However, it's customary to leave small change (around 5-10% of the bill) if you are satisfied with the service.

Foreign Transaction Fees: Be aware that using foreign credit or debit cards may incur transaction fees. Check with your bank or card issuer regarding fees and exchange rates before traveling.

Notify Your Bank: Inform your bank of your travel plans to ensure uninterrupted access to your accounts and to avoid any issues with card usage abroad.

Online and Mobile Banking

Online Banking: Most banks offer online banking services, allowing you to manage your account, pay bills, and transfer money from anywhere with an internet connection.

Mobile Payment Apps: Mobile payment apps like Apple Pay, Google Pay, and others are becoming increasingly popular and are accepted at many establishments in Lyon.

Emergency Contacts

Lost or Stolen Cards: If your credit or debit card is lost or stolen, contact your card issuer immediately to report it and request a replacement. Most card issuers have 24/7 customer service for such emergencies.

Bank Assistance: For banking issues or questions while in Lyon, you can visit a local bank branch or contact your bank's customer service.

By understanding the currency and banking system in Lyon, you can ensure that you have the financial resources you need for a smooth and enjoyable stay.

Language and Communication

Navigating language and communication in Lyon is essential for a successful visit. While Lyon is a French-speaking city, you'll find that English is increasingly understood in tourist areas. Here's what you need to know about language and communication in Lyon:

Language Overview

Primary Language: French is the official language of Lyon. Most signs, menus, and public announcements are in French.

Regional Dialects: While the primary language is French, you may hear regional accents and dialects, though standard French is widely understood.

Basic French Phrases

Learning a few basic French phrases can enhance your experience and help you communicate more effectively. Here are some useful phrases:

Greetings and Courtesies:

Bonjour (Good morning/hello)

Bonsoir (Good evening)

Merci (Thank you)

S'il vous plaît (Please)

Excusez-moi (Excuse me)

Au revoir (Goodbye)

Asking for Help:

Parlez-vous anglais ? (Do you speak English?)

Je ne parle pas très bien français. (I don't speak French very well.)

Pouvez-vous m'aider ? (Can you help me?)

Dining and Shopping:

Je voudrais... (I would like...)

L'addition, s'il vous plaît. (The check, please.)

Combien ça coûte ? (How much does it cost?)

Je cherche... (I am looking for...)

Communication Tips

English Speakers: In major tourist areas, restaurants, hotels, and shops, you'll find that many people speak English, especially those in the service industry. However, speaking a bit of French can enhance your interactions and show respect for the local culture.

Language Apps: Consider using language translation apps like Google Translate to help with communication. These apps can translate text and speech in real-time, making it easier to understand and be understood.

Phrasebooks: Carrying a small French phrasebook can be handy for quick reference and learning essential phrases on the go.

Public Services and Signage

Public Transport: Public transportation information is generally provided in French. Stations and buses often have signs indicating routes and schedules. Some major transportation hubs may have information in English.

Tourist Information: Tourist information centers and major attractions often provide brochures and assistance in English and other languages.

Social Etiquette

Politeness: The French place a high value on politeness. Always greet people with "Bonjour" or "Bonsoir" when entering shops or restaurants and say "Merci" when receiving assistance.

Formal and Informal Speech: French has both formal (vous) and informal (tu) forms of address. Use "vous" in formal settings or when addressing strangers, and "tu" with friends or people you know well.

Digital Communication

Wi-Fi: Free Wi-Fi is commonly available in hotels, cafes, restaurants, and some public spaces. Many public places have Wi-Fi networks that you can connect to, sometimes requiring a simple registration.

SIM Cards and Roaming: If you need mobile data, consider purchasing a local SIM card or an international roaming plan. This can provide you with better connectivity and access to maps and communication apps.

Emergency Assistance

Emergency Services: In case of emergency, you can dial 112 for general emergency services. This number is valid across Europe and connects you to police, fire, and medical services.

Embassies and Consulates: For assistance related to your nationality, you can contact your country's embassy or consulate in France.

Cultural Sensitivity

Respect Local Customs: Even if you're not fluent in French, making an effort to use the local language and showing respect for cultural norms will be appreciated by locals. It helps build positive interactions and enriches your travel experience.

By understanding and using these communication strategies, you'll be better equipped to navigate Lyon with confidence, make meaningful connections, and fully enjoy your visit.

Health and Safety

Ensuring your health and safety during your trip to Lyon is crucial for a worry-free experience. Here's a comprehensive guide to help you stay healthy and safe while exploring this vibrant city:

Health Considerations

Healthcare System: France has a high-quality healthcare system with well-equipped hospitals and medical facilities. In Lyon, you'll find several reputable hospitals and clinics providing a range of medical services.

Emergency Services: For emergency medical assistance, you can dial 15 to reach the emergency services (Samu). For general emergencies, including medical, fire, and police services, dial 112, which is available throughout Europe.

Health Insurance: Ensure you have comprehensive travel insurance that covers medical expenses. European Health Insurance Cards (EHIC) or Global Health Insurance Cards (GHIC) may provide some coverage if you're a European Union or UK resident.

Vaccinations: No specific vaccinations are required for travel to Lyon unless you're coming from an area with a risk of yellow fever. It's always good to check with your healthcare provider before traveling for any updates on recommended vaccinations or health advisories.

Pharmacies: Pharmacies are widely available in Lyon. They can provide over-the-counter medications and advice on minor health issues. Look for pharmacies with a green cross symbol.

Safety Tips

Personal Safety: Lyon is generally a safe city with low crime rates. However, like any urban area, it's wise to take standard safety precautions:

Be aware of your surroundings, especially in crowded places like markets or tourist spots.

Keep your personal belongings secure and avoid displaying valuable items.

Use hotel safes for important documents and valuables when not in use.

Transport Safety: Public transportation in Lyon is safe and well-maintained. When using the metro, tram, or bus, keep an eye on your belongings and be cautious during peak hours.

If you're using taxis or ride-sharing services, ensure you use licensed and reputable companies. Avoid accepting rides from unsolicited offers.

Scams: Be cautious of common tourist scams. Avoid engaging with aggressive street vendors or individuals asking for money. Always verify the legitimacy of services or offers before making payments.

Emergency Contacts

Local Emergency Numbers:

Police: 17

Fire Department: 18

Medical Emergency: 15

General Emergency: 112

Consular Assistance: In case of any issues related to your nationality, such as lost passports or legal troubles, contact your country's embassy or consulate in Lyon.

Travel Precautions

Food and Water: Lyon is known for its culinary scene, and food safety standards are high. It is generally safe to eat at restaurants and street food stalls. However, if you have dietary restrictions or allergies, communicate them clearly.

Drink tap water in Lyon is safe, but if you prefer bottled water, it is readily available.

Weather Considerations: Lyon experiences a temperate climate. In summer, protect yourself from the sun with sunscreen and stay hydrated. In winter, be prepared for colder temperatures and potential rain. Dress appropriately for the weather and plan indoor activities if necessary.

Health Services

Hospitals: Some of the main hospitals in Lyon include:

Hôpital Edouard Herriot

Hôpital de la Croix-Rousse

Hôpital Saint-Joseph-Saint-Luc

General Practitioners: If you need a general practitioner, you can find private clinics and medical offices throughout the city. Your hotel concierge or local tourism office can assist in locating a suitable medical professional.

Insurance and Documentation

Travel Insurance: Make sure your travel insurance covers medical emergencies, trip cancellations, and lost belongings. Keep a copy of your insurance policy and emergency contact numbers with you.

Medical Documentation: If you have any pre-existing medical conditions or require specific medications, carry relevant documentation and prescriptions. It's also wise to have a list of any allergies or special medical needs.

Safety for Solo Travelers

Solo Travel Safety: Lyon is safe for solo travelers, but always use common sense. Inform someone of your itinerary and stay connected with family or friends. Utilize reputable services and avoid risky areas, especially after dark.

By staying informed about health and safety measures, you can enjoy your time in Lyon with confidence and peace of mind.

Travel Insurance

Travel insurance is a critical component of your travel preparations, ensuring you're protected against unexpected events during your trip to Lyon. Here's a guide to help you understand the importance of travel insurance and what to look for when selecting a policy:

Why Travel Insurance is Important

Travel insurance provides financial protection and peace of mind against a range of potential issues, including:

Medical Emergencies: Covers medical expenses in case of illness or injury while abroad.

Trip Cancellation or Interruption: Reimburses non-refundable expenses if you have to cancel or cut short your trip due to unforeseen circumstances.

Lost or Stolen Belongings: Provides compensation for lost, stolen, or damaged luggage and personal items.

Travel Delays: Offers coverage for additional expenses incurred due to flight cancellations or delays.

Emergency Evacuation: Covers costs related to emergency evacuation and repatriation if necessary.

Types of Coverage

When selecting travel insurance, consider the following types of coverage:

Medical Coverage: Ensure your policy covers medical expenses, including hospitalization, emergency treatment, and prescription medications. Verify that it includes coverage for pre-existing conditions if applicable.

Trip Cancellation/Interruption: Look for coverage that reimburses you for non-refundable expenses if you need to cancel or interrupt your trip due to illness, family emergencies, or other covered reasons.

Baggage and Personal Belongings: This covers lost, stolen, or damaged luggage and personal items. Check the limits and exclusions in the policy to ensure adequate protection.

Travel Delay: Provides compensation for additional expenses such as accommodation and meals if your travel is delayed due to reasons like flight cancellations or missed connections.

Emergency Evacuation and Repatriation: Covers the cost of emergency evacuation and return to your home country if necessary due to medical emergencies.

How to Choose the Right Policy

Assess Your Needs: Consider your specific needs and travel plans. If you're participating in high-risk activities, ensure your policy covers such activities.

Compare Policies: Compare different travel insurance providers and policies to find the one that offers the best coverage for your needs at a reasonable cost.

Check Policy Exclusions: Carefully review the policy exclusions and limitations. Some policies may not cover certain activities, pre-existing conditions, or specific travel scenarios.

Read the Fine Print: Understand the terms and conditions, including coverage limits, deductibles, and the process for filing claims. Ensure you are aware of how to contact your insurer in case of an emergency.

Insurance Providers: You can purchase travel insurance from insurance companies, either directly or through their websites. Many major insurers offer travel insurance policies.

Travel Agencies: Some travel agencies offer travel insurance as part of their services. This can be convenient but ensure you compare it with other options to get the best coverage.

Online Comparison Sites: Use online comparison tools to compare different insurance policies and providers. These sites allow you to see a range of options and choose the one that fits your needs.

What to Do in Case of an Emergency

Contact Your Insurer: In the event of a medical emergency, travel delay, or other covered incidents, contact your insurance provider as soon as possible. They will guide you on the next steps and how to file a claim.

Document Everything: Keep detailed records of any incidents, including receipts, medical reports, and correspondence with your insurer. This documentation will be crucial for filing claims.

Emergency Assistance: Most travel insurance providers offer 24/7 emergency assistance. Use this service for guidance on medical emergencies or other urgent situations.

General Tips

Buy Early: Purchase travel insurance as soon as you book your trip to ensure coverage for trip cancellations and other issues that may arise before you travel.

Understand the Policy: Make sure you fully understand what is covered and what is not. Ask questions if anything is unclear.

Keep a Copy: Carry a copy of your insurance policy and emergency contact information with you during your trip.

By securing appropriate travel insurance, you can enjoy your visit to Lyon with greater peace of mind, knowing that you're protected against a range of potential issues.

Best Time to Visit

Choosing the right time to visit Lyon can greatly enhance your experience. The city offers something unique throughout the year, so understanding the climate, events, and peak seasons can help you plan a memorable trip. Here's a guide to the best times to visit Lyon:

Spring (March to May)

Weather: Spring in Lyon is mild and pleasant. Temperatures range from 10°C to 20°C (50°F to 68°F), with increasing sunshine and blooming flowers. This is a great time for outdoor activities and exploring the city's parks and gardens.

Events:

Festival of Lights (Fête des Lumières): Held in early December, this is one of Lyon's most famous festivals, showcasing stunning light displays and attracting visitors from around the world.

Gastronomy Festivals: Lyon's culinary scene comes alive with various food festivals and events celebrating local cuisine.

Advantages: Spring offers fewer crowds compared to summer, making it easier to explore attractions and enjoy outdoor dining.

Summer (June to August)

Weather: Summer in Lyon is warm to hot, with temperatures ranging from 20°C to 30°C (68°F to 86°F). July and August are the hottest months, with occasional heatwaves. It's an excellent time to enjoy outdoor cafes and river cruises.

Events:

Lyon Music Festival: Held in June, this festival features a variety of musical performances and concerts.

Lyon Jazz Festival: Taking place in July, this event showcases jazz musicians from around the world.

Advantages: Summer offers a vibrant atmosphere with numerous festivals and outdoor activities. The long daylight hours are ideal for sightseeing and exploring.

Disadvantages: It can be quite crowded, especially in popular tourist areas. Accommodations may be more expensive, and some locals may be on vacation, affecting service availability.

Autumn (September to November)

Weather: Autumn in Lyon is characterized by cooler temperatures, ranging from 10°C to 20°C (50°F to 68°F), and beautiful fall foliage. It's a wonderful time to experience the city's parks and scenic views.

Events:

Lyon Contemporary Art Biennale: Held every two years in the fall, this event features contemporary art exhibitions and installations.

Beaujolais Nouveau Festival: In November, this festival celebrates the release of the new Beaujolais wine, a popular event in Lyon's nearby Beaujolais wine region.

Advantages: Autumn offers mild weather and fewer tourists compared to summer. It's a great time to enjoy cultural events and seasonal cuisine.

Weather: Winters in Lyon are cold but generally not severe. Temperatures range from 0°C to 8°C (32°F to 46°F), with occasional rain and fog. Snow is rare but possible.

Events:

Fête des Lumières (Festival of Lights): Held in early December, this is the highlight of Lyon's winter season, with stunning light displays across the city.

Christmas Markets: Lyon's Christmas markets offer festive foods, crafts, and gifts, adding to the city's holiday charm.

Advantages: Winter offers a unique festive atmosphere, especially with the Fête des Lumières and Christmas celebrations. It's a quieter time for sightseeing, with fewer tourists.

Disadvantages: The weather can be chilly and rainy, and some attractions may have shorter hours or be closed for maintenance.

Considerations

Booking in Advance: If you plan to visit during peak seasons or major events, book accommodations and tickets well in advance to secure the best rates and availability.

Local Events and Festivals: Check the local event calendar when planning your visit, as Lyon hosts numerous festivals, exhibitions, and cultural events throughout the year.

Personal Preferences: Consider your personal preferences for weather, crowds, and activities. Each season offers a different experience, so choose the one that aligns with your interests.

By selecting the best time to visit Lyon based on your preferences and the city's seasonal highlights, you can make the most of your trip and enjoy all that this captivating city has to offer.

Chapter 2: Planning Your Trip

The Essential Lyon Packing List

Having your travel documents in order is crucial for a smooth and stress-free trip to Lyon. Here's a list of essential travel documents you should bring:

1. Passport

Validity: Ensure your passport is valid for at least six months beyond your planned departure date.

Copies: Carry both physical and digital copies of your passport in case it gets lost or stolen.

2. Visa

Requirement: Check if you need a visa to enter France based on your nationality and travel plans.

Documents: If a visa is required, ensure you have the approved visa in your passport.

3. Travel Insurance

Coverage: Proof of travel insurance that covers health, accidents, theft, and cancellations.

Policy Details: Have a copy of your insurance policy number and emergency contact information.

4. Flight/Train Tickets

Confirmation: Bring printed or digital copies of your flight or train tickets.

Details: Include all relevant information such as departure and arrival times, ticket numbers, and booking references.

5. Hotel Reservations

Confirmation: Printed or digital copies of your hotel or accommodation bookings.

Details: Include reservation numbers, addresses, and contact information for your accommodation.

6. Emergency Contacts

Local Contacts: Addresses and phone numbers of local embassies or consulates.

Personal Contacts: Contact information for friends or family who may need to be reached in an emergency.

7. Itinerary

Plans: A copy of your travel itinerary, including key dates, planned activities, and important locations.

Notes: Any reservations or special arrangements you have made.

8. Vaccination Certificates

Health Requirements: Check if there are any specific vaccination requirements or health declarations needed for entry into France.

9. Driver's License

International Driving Permit (IDP): If you plan to drive in France, carry an IDP along with your home country driver's license.

10. Proof of Financial Means

Bank Statements: Some countries may require proof that you have sufficient funds for your stay. Carry recent bank statements or proof of financial means if needed.

11. Additional Documents

Student ID: If you are a student, a student ID card might provide access to discounts or special offers.

Business Documents: If traveling for business, carry relevant documentation such as invitation letters or meeting schedules.

12. Contact Information

Local Emergency Numbers: Keep a list of local emergency contact numbers (e.g., police, ambulance) in your travel documents.

2. Clothing

Packing the right clothing for your trip to Lyon ensures you stay comfortable and stylish throughout your visit. Here's a guide to help you pack appropriately for different seasons and activities:

1. General Guidelines

Comfort: Choose comfortable, versatile clothing suitable for walking and exploring.

Layers: Layers are essential for adjusting to changing temperatures throughout the day.

Fashion: Lyon is known for its stylish locals, so consider packing a mix of casual and smart attire.

2. Essential Clothing Items

Comfortable Walking Shoes: Opt for well-fitting, comfortable shoes suitable for long walks and sightseeing. Sneakers or walking shoes are ideal.

Casual Outfits:

T-Shirts and Blouses: Light and breathable for daytime wear.

Jeans or Trousers: Comfortable and versatile, suitable for various activities.

Casual Dresses or Skirts: For warmer weather or a relaxed look.

Smart Outfit:

Shirts and Blouses: Dressier options for dining out or special events.

Dress or Smart Trousers: A chic outfit for more formal settings.

Light Jacket or Sweater: Essential for cooler evenings or unexpected weather changes.

Rain Gear:

Lightweight Rain Jacket: Compact and waterproof, ideal for unexpected showers.

Compact Umbrella: For easy portability in case of rain.

Seasonal Clothing:

Spring/Summer:

Lightweight Fabrics: Cotton, linen, and other breathable materials.

Sunglasses and Hat: For sun protection.

Fall/Winter:

Warm Layers: Thermal tops, sweaters, and long-sleeve shirts.

Coat: A warm, waterproof coat for chilly or rainy weather.

Scarf, Gloves, and Hat: Essential for staying warm in colder temperatures.

Sleepwear: Comfortable pajamas or sleepwear for rest and relaxation.

Underwear and Socks: Pack enough for the duration of your stay, plus a few extra pairs.

3. Additional Considerations

Dress Code: Some restaurants or attractions may have dress codes, so pack accordingly if you plan to visit upscale venues.

Special Activities: If you plan specific activities such as hiking or swimming, pack appropriate gear (e.g., hiking boots, swimsuit).

Laundry: Consider packing a small amount of laundry detergent or locating a laundromat if you need to do laundry during your stay.

3. Accessories

Packing the right accessories can enhance your comfort and convenience while exploring Lyon. Here's a list of essential accessories to consider for your trip:

1. Daypack or Tote Bag

Purpose: Useful for carrying daily essentials like water, snacks, and a guidebook.

Features: Choose a lightweight, durable bag with secure closures and easy access.

2. Reusable Water Bottle

Purpose: Keeps you hydrated throughout the day and helps reduce plastic waste.

Features: Opt for a BPA-free, insulated bottle to keep drinks cool or hot.

3. Sunglasses

Purpose: Protects your eyes from the sun and adds a stylish touch.

Features: Choose sunglasses with UV protection to shield your eyes from harmful rays.

4. Hat or Cap

Purpose: Provides additional sun protection and keeps you cool.

Features: A wide-brimmed hat or a baseball cap can be useful for sunny days.

5. Travel Umbrella

Purpose: Offers protection against rain and can be easily carried around.

Features: Compact and lightweight for convenience.

6. Travel Wallet or Money Belt

Purpose: Keeps your money, cards, and travel documents secure and organized.

Features: Choose a wallet with RFID protection to prevent electronic theft.

7. Scarf or Pashmina

Purpose: Useful for warmth during cooler evenings or as a stylish accessory.

Features: Lightweight and versatile, can be used as a wrap or cover.

8. Portable Power Bank

Purpose: Ensures your devices stay charged during long days of exploring.

Features: Choose a power bank with enough capacity to charge your phone or other devices.

9. Camera or Smartphone Accessories

Purpose: Enhances your photography experience.

Features: Include items like a camera lens cleaning cloth, portable tripod, or extra memory cards.

10. Travel Adaptor

Purpose: Allows you to charge your electronic devices in France.

Features: Ensure it is compatible with Type C and E plugs used in France.

11. Binoculars

Purpose: Enhances your ability to enjoy scenic views or observe landmarks from a distance.

Features: Compact and lightweight for easy carrying.

12. Personal Safety Items

Purpose: Adds an extra layer of security.

Features: Include items like a whistle, small flashlight, or pepper spray if desired.

13. Travel Journal and Pen

Purpose: Useful for jotting down memories, notes, or travel tips.

Features: Compact and easy to carry.

4. Toiletries

Having a well-organized toiletry kit ensures you stay clean and comfortable throughout your trip to Lyon. Here's a list of essential toiletries to pack:

1. Basic Toiletries

Toothbrush and Toothpaste: Essential for maintaining oral hygiene. Consider travel-sized options for convenience.

Floss: For complete dental care.

Shampoo and Conditioner: Travel-sized bottles or refillable containers for easy packing.

Body Wash or Soap: Choose your preferred form, whether liquid or bar.

Deodorant: Travel-sized or your preferred brand to stay fresh throughout the day.

Hairbrush or Comb: For grooming and styling your hair.

Moisturizer: Facial and body moisturizer to keep your skin hydrated.

Sunscreen: Broad-spectrum SPF to protect your skin from UV rays.

Lip Balm: To prevent dry or chapped lips, especially in colder weather.

2. Skincare Essentials

Cleansers: Facial cleanser or wipes to remove dirt and makeup.

Serum or Treatment: Any specialized skincare products you use, like acne treatment or anti-aging serum.

Eye Cream: To address specific concerns like puffiness or dark circles.

Face Masks: Optional, for a relaxing skincare routine during your trip.

3. Personal Hygiene Items

Shaving Kit: Razor, shaving cream, and any other grooming essentials.

Menstrual Products: Tampons, pads, or menstrual cups, depending on your needs.

Cotton Swabs and Cotton Balls: For various personal care needs.

4. Medications

Personal Medications: Any prescription or over-the-counter medications you regularly take.

First Aid Supplies: Basic items like band-aids, antiseptic wipes, and pain relievers.

5. Miscellaneous Toiletries

Nail Clippers and Tweezers: For personal grooming.

Travel-Sized Detergent: For washing small items like underwear or delicate clothing.

Small Mirror: If needed, for makeup application or grooming.

6. Packing Tips

Travel Containers: Use leak-proof, travel-sized containers to comply with airport regulations and prevent spills.

Toiletry Bag: A waterproof or clear toiletry bag to keep all items organized and easily accessible.

Check Regulations: Be aware of liquid restrictions for carry-on luggage if flying, typically limited to containers of 100 ml (3.4 oz) or less.

5. Electronics

Bringing the right electronics can make your trip to Lyon more convenient and enjoyable. Here's a list of essential electronics and accessories to consider:

1. Smartphone and Charger

Smartphone: Essential for navigation, communication, and capturing photos.

Charger: Bring the charger specific to your phone, and consider a portable charger for on-the-go charging.

2. Camera

Purpose: To capture high-quality photos of your travels.

Accessories: Include extra memory cards and a lens cleaning cloth.

3. Laptop or Tablet

Laptop: Useful if you need to work or prefer a larger screen for browsing.

Tablet: More portable than a laptop, ideal for reading, streaming, or note-taking.

4. Power Bank

Purpose: To recharge your devices when you're away from an outlet.

Capacity: Choose a power bank with sufficient capacity to charge your phone or other electronics multiple times.

5. Travel Adaptor

Purpose: Allows you to plug your devices into French power outlets.

Compatibility: France uses Type C and E plugs. Make sure the adaptor is compatible with these types and supports the voltage in France (230V).

6. Headphones or Earbuds

Purpose: For enjoying music, podcasts, or movies while traveling.

Features: Consider noise-canceling options for a better listening experience in noisy environments.

7. E-Reader

Purpose: For reading books without carrying physical copies.

Features: Lightweight and portable, ideal for reading on the go.

8. USB Flash Drive or External Hard Drive

Purpose: For backing up important files or photos.

Capacity: Choose a drive with enough storage for your needs.

9. Travel Alarm Clock

Purpose: If you prefer not to rely on your phone for waking up.

Features: Choose a compact and reliable alarm clock.

10. Portable Speaker

Purpose: For playing music or sharing audio with others.

Features: Compact and Bluetooth-enabled for convenience.

11. Power Strip

Purpose: To charge multiple devices at once.

Features: Ensure it's compatible with the French power supply and has surge protection.

12. Electronic Travel Accessories

Cable Organizers: To keep your charging cables and small electronics organized.

Device Protection: Consider protective cases for your electronics to prevent damage.

Packing Tips

Check Voltage: Ensure all your electronics are compatible with the voltage in France or bring a voltage converter if necessary.

Protective Cases: Use cases or sleeves to protect your electronics from damage during transit.

Backup Power: Have a backup power source (like a power bank) in case of long travel days.

6. Money and Payment

Managing your finances effectively while traveling ensures a smooth and enjoyable experience in Lyon. Here's what you need to know about handling money and payments:

1. Currency

Euro (€): The official currency in Lyon and the rest of France. Familiarize yourself with the currency notes and coins (5, 10, 20, 50, 100, 200, and 500 euros for banknotes; 1, 2, 5, 10, 20, and 50 cents, and 1 and 2 euros for coins).

2. Cash

Bringing Cash: It's a good idea to have some euros on hand for small purchases, tips, or places that don't accept cards.

Currency Exchange:

Airports and Train Stations: Convenient but may have higher fees or less favorable exchange rates.

Banks: Offer currency exchange services, often with better rates.

Currency Exchange Offices: Found in tourist areas and shopping districts.

3. Credit and Debit Cards

Acceptance: Credit and debit cards are widely accepted in Lyon, including at hotels, restaurants, shops, and attractions.

Types: Visa and MasterCard are the most commonly accepted; American Express and other cards are also accepted at many locations.

Chip and PIN: France uses the chip and PIN system. Ensure your card has a chip and that you know your PIN.

Notification: Inform your bank of your travel plans to prevent your card from being flagged for suspicious activity.

4. ATMs

Availability: ATMs are widespread in Lyon, including at airports, train stations, and throughout the city.

Fees: Be aware of potential fees for international ATM withdrawals from your home bank and the local ATM provider.

Card Use: Most ATMs accept major credit and debit cards. Ensure your card is set up for international transactions.

5. Mobile Payments

Contactless Payments: Many places accept mobile payments through apps like Apple Pay, Google Pay, and Samsung Pay.

Setup: Make sure your mobile payment app is set up and linked to your bank account or credit card before you travel.

6. Banking Services

Opening a Bank Account: Generally unnecessary for short stays. For longer stays or if you're working in Lyon, consider opening a local bank account. This typically requires proof of residence and identification.

Banking Hours: Banks usually operate Monday to Friday, from 9 AM to 12:30 PM and 2 PM to 5 PM. Some branches may have extended hours or be open on Saturdays.

7. Safety and Security

Keep Cash Secure: Use a money belt or travel wallet to keep your cash and cards safe.

Notify Your Bank: Inform your bank of your travel plans to avoid any issues with your cards.

Emergency Contacts: Keep contact information for your bank or credit card issuer in case you need to report a lost or stolen card.

8. Budgeting Tips

Daily Budget: Set a daily budget for food, transportation, and activities to manage your spending.

Track Expenses: Use a budgeting app or keep receipts to track your expenses and stay within your budget.

Avoid High Fees: Withdraw larger amounts of cash at once to minimize transaction fees and use ATMs that are part of your bank's network if possible.

7. Health and Safety

Ensuring your health and safety while traveling to Lyon is essential for a smooth and enjoyable trip. Here's a guide to help you stay safe and healthy during your visit:

1. Health Precautions

Vaccinations:

Routine Vaccinations: Ensure you are up-to-date with routine vaccinations such as measles, mumps, rubella (MMR), and tetanus.

Travel Vaccinations: No specific vaccinations are required for France unless you're traveling from a country with a risk of yellow fever.

Travel Insurance:

Coverage: Obtain travel insurance that covers health issues, accidents, and emergencies.

Emergency Contact: Have your insurance details and emergency contact numbers handy.

Medication:

Prescription Medications: Bring sufficient supplies of any prescribed medications, along with a copy of your prescription.

Over-the-Counter Medications: Carry basic medications such as pain relievers, antihistamines, and motion sickness tablets.

Medication Regulations: Check if any of your medications are restricted or need special documentation.

Healthcare Services:

Emergency Services: Dial 112 for emergencies, including medical emergencies.

Pharmacies: Pharmacies (pharmacies) are widespread in Lyon and can provide over-the-counter medicines and advice.

Hospitals and Clinics: Know the location of nearby hospitals or clinics in case you need medical attention.

2. Safety Precautions

Personal Safety:

Stay Alert: Be aware of your surroundings, especially in crowded areas or tourist hotspots.

Secure Belongings: Keep valuables such as passports, money, and electronics secure. Use a money belt or anti-theft bag.

Avoid Risky Areas: Avoid walking alone at night in poorly lit or unfamiliar areas.

Transportation Safety:

Public Transport: Lyon's public transport system is generally safe. Keep an eye on your belongings and be cautious of pickpockets.

Taxi Services: Use official taxis or ride-sharing apps. Avoid accepting rides from unsolicited offers.

Emergency Numbers:

Police: 17

Ambulance: 15

Fire Brigade: 18

European Emergency Number: 112

3. Food and Water Safety

Eating Out:

Restaurants and Cafés: Lyon is renowned for its cuisine. Eat at reputable places and check reviews if unsure.

Street Food: Be cautious with street food. Ensure it is prepared in a clean environment.

Water:

Tap Water: Safe to drink in Lyon. If you prefer bottled water, it's widely available.

4. Travel Health Tips

Hydration: Drink plenty of water to stay hydrated, especially if you are walking a lot or visiting during hot weather.

Sun Protection: Use sunscreen with high SPF, wear a hat, and sunglasses to protect yourself from the sun.

Rest: Ensure you get enough rest to stay healthy and energetic during your trip.

5. COVID-19 Considerations

Travel Restrictions: Check for any travel restrictions or requirements related to COVID-19, such as testing, vaccination, or quarantine rules.

Masks and Hygiene: Follow local guidelines regarding mask-wearing and hygiene practices.

Health Apps: Download health-related apps if required for tracking COVID-19 exposure or updates.

6. Emergency Contacts and Resources

Local Embassy or Consulate: Contact information for your country's embassy or consulate in Lyon for assistance in case of emergencies or legal issues.

Local Health Authorities: Contact local health services if you have specific health concerns or need medical advice.

Packing Tips and Weather Considerations

Packing smartly and understanding the weather conditions in Lyon will help you make the most of your trip. Here's how to prepare:

Packing Tips

Check the Weather Forecast: Before packing, check the weather forecast for Lyon to anticipate the conditions during your stay. This will help you pack accordingly and avoid surprises.

Pack Light and Smart:

Layering: Use layers to adapt to varying temperatures. Include lightweight, breathable layers for warm weather and warmer layers for cooler conditions.

Versatile Items: Choose clothing items that can be mixed and matched, allowing you to create different outfits with fewer pieces.

Neutral Colors: Neutral-colored clothing can be easily combined and is less likely to show dirt.

Travel-Friendly Fabrics:

Wrinkle-Resistant: Pack clothes made from wrinkle-resistant fabrics to minimize the need for ironing.

Quick-Dry: Opt for quick-drying fabrics if you anticipate rain or plan to wash clothes during your trip.

Packing Cubes: Use packing cubes to organize your clothing and maximize space in your luggage. They help keep items compact and easily accessible.

Roll, Don't Fold: Rolling clothes instead of folding can save space and reduce wrinkles.

Keep Essentials Accessible: Pack important items like travel documents, medications, and electronics in your carry-on or in easily accessible compartments.

Footwear: Bring comfortable walking shoes for exploring and a pair of dressier shoes if you plan to dine out or attend formal events. Waterproof shoes or boots may be necessary for rainy weather.

Laundry Supplies: Include a small amount of laundry detergent or a laundry bag if you plan to wash clothes during your trip.

Weather Considerations

Spring (March to May):

Temperature: Mild temperatures ranging from 10°C to 20°C (50°F to 68°F).

Clothing: Light layers, a light jacket, and a mix of long-sleeve and short-sleeve shirts. A light raincoat or umbrella for occasional showers.

Summer (June to August):

Temperature: Warm temperatures ranging from 20°C to 30°C (68°F to 86°F), sometimes higher.

Clothing: Light, breathable clothing such as shorts, T-shirts, and dresses. Don't forget sun protection like a hat and sunglasses. A lightweight jacket or sweater for cooler evenings.

Fall (September to November):

Temperature: Cooling temperatures ranging from 10°C to 20°C (50°F to 68°F).

Clothing: Layers including long-sleeve shirts, sweaters, and a medium-weight jacket. Bring a raincoat or umbrella for rainy days.

Winter (December to February):

Temperature: Cooler temperatures ranging from 0°C to 10°C (32°F to 50°F), with occasional frost.

Clothing: Warm layers including thermal tops, sweaters, and a warm coat. Pack gloves, a hat, and a scarf to stay comfortable.

Rain and Snow:

Rain: Lyon can experience rain throughout the year, so a waterproof jacket or raincoat and a compact umbrella are essential.

Snow: Snow is less common but possible in winter. If visiting during this time, pack waterproof boots and consider thermal wear.

Sun Protection:

Sunscreen: Apply sunscreen daily, even in cooler months, to protect your skin from UV rays.

Sunglasses: Protect your eyes from glare and UV rays with quality sunglasses.

Local Climate: Lyon has a continental climate with mild winters and warm summers. Be prepared for occasional weather fluctuations and pack accordingly.

By considering these packing tips and weather considerations, you'll be well-prepared for your trip to Lyon and can focus on enjoying your travels.

Budgeting and Costs

Effective budgeting ensures a smooth and enjoyable trip to Lyon without overspending. Here's a guide to help you understand and manage your travel costs:

Accommodation:

Luxury Hotels: €150 - €300+ per night

Mid-Range Hotels: €80 - €150 per night

Budget Hotels and Hostels: €20 - €80 per night

Vacation Rentals: €60 - €200 per night, depending on size and location

Food and Drink:

Budget: €10 - €15 per meal at a casual restaurant or café

Mid-Range: €20 - €40 per meal at a standard restaurant

High-End: €50+ per meal at a fine dining restaurant

Street Food and Snacks: €5 - €10

Transportation:

Public Transport: €1.90 for a single metro or tram ticket; €14.50 for a 10-ride pass

Taxi: Starting fare around €5, with additional charges based on distance

Car Rental: €30 - €70 per day, depending on the type of car

Bike Rental: €10 - €20 per day

Attractions:

Museums: €5 - €15 per entry

Historic Sites: €5 - €10 per entry

Guided Tours: €20 - €60 depending on the length and type

Miscellaneous:

Souvenirs: €5 - €30 depending on the item

Tips: Not mandatory but appreciated; typically 5-10% of the bill at restaurants

Daily Budget: Estimate a daily budget based on your accommodation, food, transportation, and activity costs. Aim to set aside some extra for unexpected expenses.

Track Expenses: Use budgeting apps or keep a record of your expenses to stay within your budget and avoid overspending.

Dining:

Mix Meals: Combine dining at inexpensive cafés and street food with occasional meals at nicer restaurants to balance your budget.

Local Markets: Purchase snacks and drinks from local markets for a budget-friendly option.

Accommodation:

Book in Advance: Secure accommodations early to get the best rates and avoid last-minute price hikes.

Consider Alternatives: Look for vacation rentals or budget-friendly options if you're traveling with a group or family.

Transportation:

Public Transport Passes: Purchase multi-ride passes or travel cards if you plan to use public transportation frequently.

Walk or Bike: Explore central Lyon by walking or biking to save on transport costs and experience the city more intimately.

Attractions:

City Passes: Consider purchasing a city pass if available, which often provides discounts on multiple attractions.

Free Attractions: Take advantage of free attractions such as parks, markets, and some historic sites.

Currency Exchange and Payment

Currency Exchange: Exchange some money in advance for initial expenses. Use ATMs or currency exchange offices for additional cash as needed.

Credit and Debit Cards: Widely accepted in Lyon. Use cards to avoid carrying large amounts of cash and to benefit from better exchange rates.

Avoiding Fees: Use ATMs within your bank's network to avoid high withdrawal fees. Notify your bank of your travel plans to prevent card issues.

Emergency Fund

Contingency: Set aside a small amount of extra money for emergencies or unexpected costs.

By understanding and planning for these budgeting aspects, you'll be able to manage your finances effectively and enjoy your trip to Lyon without unnecessary stress.

Budget Travel Tips

Traveling on a budget doesn't mean sacrificing quality or experiences. Here are some practical tips to help you enjoy Lyon without breaking the bank:

Plan Ahead

Book Early: Secure flights, accommodations, and major attractions in advance to benefit from lower prices and avoid last-minute expenses.

Research Discounts: Look for deals and discounts on attractions, tours, and accommodations. Websites like Groupon or local tourist sites often have special offers.

Accommodation

Stay in Budget-Friendly Places: Consider hostels, budget hotels, or vacation rentals for more affordable lodging options.

Use Booking Sites: Compare prices on booking platforms like Booking.com, Airbnb, or Hostelworld to find the best deals.

Look for Deals: Many hotels offer discounts for longer stays or advanced bookings. Check for any special promotions or packages.

Dining

Eat Like a Local: Enjoy meals at local bistros or cafés instead of touristy restaurants. Lyon is famous for its food, and local eateries often offer delicious and affordable options.

Street Food and Markets: Visit markets like Les Halles de Lyon-Paul Bocuse for fresh produce and street food. This can be a cheaper and authentic way to experience Lyon's cuisine.

Picnic: Buy food from local markets or grocery stores and have a picnic in one of Lyon's many parks, such as Parc de la Tête d'Or.

Transportation

Use Public Transport: Lyon's public transport system is efficient and affordable. Consider purchasing a multi-ride pass or travel card if you plan to use public transport frequently.

Walk or Bike: Explore the city on foot or rent a bike. Lyon's central areas are pedestrian-friendly, and cycling is a great way to see the sights and save on transportation costs.

Avoid Taxis: Use taxis only when necessary, as they can be more expensive. Opt for public transport or walking whenever possible.

Attractions and Activities

Free Attractions: Take advantage of free attractions like Parc de la Tête d'Or, Vieux Lyon (Old Lyon), and many historic streets and neighborhoods.

City Passes: Look into city passes that offer discounted access to multiple attractions and public transport.

Student and Senior Discounts: Check if you're eligible for any discounts on tickets to museums and attractions.

Shopping

Avoid Tourist Traps: Shop at local markets or smaller shops for souvenirs instead of high-priced tourist stores.

Flea Markets: Visit flea markets for unique and affordable souvenirs. Lyon has several markets where you can find interesting items at lower prices.

Money Management

Use a Travel Card: Consider using a prepaid travel card or credit card with no foreign transaction fees to avoid high exchange rates and transaction costs.

ATM Withdrawals: Use ATMs that are part of your bank's network to avoid excessive fees. Withdraw larger amounts to reduce the frequency of withdrawals.

Track Your Spending: Use budgeting apps to monitor your expenses and stay within your budget.

Connectivity

Free Wi-Fi: Take advantage of free Wi-Fi available in cafes, restaurants, and public areas. This can help you avoid data roaming charges.

Local SIM Card: If you need internet access on the go, consider purchasing a local SIM card with data to save on international roaming fees.

Miscellaneous Tips

Pack Smart: Avoid paying for excess baggage fees by packing efficiently. Use packing cubes to organize and maximize space.

Travel During Off-Peak Times: Traveling during shoulder seasons or off-peak times can result in lower prices for flights, accommodations, and attractions.

By implementing these budget travel tips, you can make the most of your trip to Lyon, experiencing the city's rich culture and attractions while keeping expenses in check.

Chapter 3: Getting to Lyon

By Air

Traveling to Lyon by air is a convenient and efficient way to reach this vibrant French city. Lyon, being a major urban center, is well-connected by international and domestic flights. Here's an extensive look at everything you need to know about flying into Lyon for your vacation.

Major Airports Serving Lyon

Lyon-Saint Exupéry Airport (LYS)

Lyon-Saint Exupéry Airport is the primary gateway to Lyon. Named after the famous French writer and aviator Antoine de Saint-Exupéry, this airport is located about 25 kilometers (16 miles) east of Lyon's city center. As the main international airport serving Lyon, it offers a range of amenities and services designed to make your arrival as smooth as possible.

Other Nearby Airports

While Lyon-Saint Exupéry is the main airport, you might also consider other nearby airports depending on your travel plans:

Geneva Airport (GVA): Located about 150 kilometers (93 miles) from Lyon, Geneva Airport is a major international hub with flights from various global destinations. It is well-connected to Lyon via train and bus services.

Paris Airports (CDG and ORY): If you're already in Paris, you might fly into Charles de Gaulle (CDG) or Orly Airport (ORY) and then take a high-speed train (TGV) to Lyon. This option is often used for those traveling from long-haul international destinations.

Airlines and Routes

Airlines

Numerous airlines operate flights to Lyon from major cities around the world. Here are some prominent airlines you might consider:

Air France: Offers numerous daily flights to Lyon from various international hubs.

EasyJet: Provides budget-friendly options for travelers coming from various European cities.

Lufthansa: Connects Lyon with major German cities such as Frankfurt and Munich.

British Airways: Offers flights from London to Lyon.

KLM: Provides connections from Amsterdam to Lyon.

Routes

Direct flights to Lyon are available from many European cities, including London, Amsterdam, Barcelona, and Rome. For travelers from outside Europe, you might need to connect through major European hubs like Paris, Frankfurt, or Amsterdam before reaching Lyon.

Choosing Flights to Lyon

When choosing flights to Lyon, consider the following factors:

Flight Duration: Direct flights are typically the quickest way to reach Lyon. For those traveling from distant locations, check the duration of layovers if opting for connecting flights.

Airline Preferences: Choose airlines based on your preferences for amenities, in-flight services, and baggage policies. Some airlines offer more comfort and additional services, which can enhance your travel experience.

Budget: Compare prices across different airlines and booking platforms. Budget airlines like EasyJet might offer lower fares but check their baggage policies to avoid extra costs.

Travel Dates: Prices can fluctuate based on the season and demand. Booking well in advance often provides better rates and availability.

Arriving at Lyon-Saint Exupéry Airport

Customs and Immigration

Upon arrival, you'll go through customs and immigration checks. If you're traveling from a non-Schengen country, ensure you have your passport and any necessary visas ready. Schengen travelers will need to show a valid ID or passport but no visa is required for stays up to 90 days.

Baggage Claim

After clearing customs, head to the baggage claim area to collect your luggage. Lyon-Saint Exupéry Airport has clear signage and staff available to assist you if needed.

Airport Facilities

Lyon-Saint Exupéry offers various facilities to enhance your travel experience:

Dining and Shopping: A range of dining options and shops are available both before and after security.

Lounges: For added comfort, consider using one of the airport lounges if you have access.

Information Desks: Located throughout the airport, these can help you with any inquiries or assistance.

Airport to City Center Transportation Options

Once you've arrived, you'll need to get from Lyon-Saint Exupéry Airport to the city center. Here are the main transportation options:

1. Train

Rhonexpress: The Rhonexpress tram connects the airport with Lyon's city center (Part-Dieu train station) in about 30 minutes. It's a direct and efficient option with frequent departures.

2. Taxi

Taxi Services: Taxis are readily available outside the terminal. A taxi ride to the city center takes approximately 30-40 minutes, depending on traffic. Taxis are a convenient option if you have heavy luggage or prefer a direct route.

3. Car Rental

Car Rental Agencies: Several car rental agencies operate at the airport. Renting a car gives you flexibility and convenience, especially if you plan to explore the surrounding regions of Lyon.

4. Shuttle Services

Airport Shuttles: Private shuttle services are available and can be booked in advance. These can be a comfortable and hassle-free option if traveling with a group or family.

5. Public Bus

Local Buses: Public buses also connect the airport to various parts of Lyon. Though less direct and frequent compared to other options, they offer an economical choice.

Traveling to Lyon by air is a straightforward process with multiple options to suit different preferences and budgets. Whether you're flying directly to Lyon or connecting through another city, the journey is well-supported by efficient transportation and amenities, ensuring a pleasant start to your French adventure.

By Train

Traveling to Lyon by train is a fantastic option for many travelers, particularly those coming from within Europe. With its well-connected rail network, Lyon is easily accessible from major cities across France and neighboring countries. Here's a detailed guide to help you navigate your train journey to Lyon.

Major Train Stations Serving Lyon

Lyon Part-Dieu

Lyon Part-Dieu is the city's primary train station and the main hub for high-speed and regional trains. It's centrally located in Lyon, making it a convenient arrival point for travelers. The station is well-equipped with amenities including shops, restaurants, and connections to public transportation.

Lyon Perrache

Lyon Perrache is another major train station located in the southern part of the city. It serves regional and local trains and is a key stop for travelers coming from the southern regions of France. Although not as busy as Part-Dieu, it's well-connected and offers various services.

Lyon Vaise

Lyon Vaise is a smaller station located in the northwest part of the city. It mainly handles local trains and commuter services. It's less central than Part-Dieu or Perrache but can be a useful arrival point depending on your travel plans.

Major Train Routes to Lyon

High-Speed TGV Trains

From Paris: The TGV (Train à Grande Vitesse) connects Paris to Lyon with frequent departures from Gare de Lyon. The journey takes about 2 hours, making it a quick and comfortable option.

From Marseille: TGV trains also connect Lyon with Marseille, with a travel time of approximately 1.5 hours.

From Lille: TGV services link Lyon with Lille, typically involving a transfer in Paris. The total journey time is around 4.5 hours.

International Trains

From Geneva: The TGV Lyria connects Lyon with Geneva in about 2 hours. It's a convenient option for travelers from Switzerland.

From Milan: The Trenitalia and TGV trains offer connections between Milan and Lyon, with a travel time of around 7 hours.

Regional and Intercity Trains

From Grenoble: Regional trains link Grenoble with Lyon, with a journey time of approximately 1.5 hours.

From Clermont-Ferrand: Intercity trains connect Clermont-Ferrand with Lyon in about 2 hours.

Choosing Trains to Lyon

When choosing trains to Lyon, consider the following:

Direct vs. Connecting Trains: Direct trains are more convenient and time-efficient, but if you're traveling from a location not directly connected to Lyon, you might need to transfer. Check schedules for transfer options and total journey time.

Booking in Advance: Booking your train tickets in advance can save you money and guarantee a seat, especially for popular routes and high-speed trains.

Comfort and Class: High-speed trains like the TGV offer various classes of service, from standard to first class. Consider your comfort preferences and budget when selecting your ticket.

Discounts and Passes: Look for discounts and rail passes if you're traveling frequently or in a group. The Eurail Pass and Interrail Pass can offer cost savings for international travelers.

Arriving at Lyon Train Stations

At Lyon Part-Dieu

Facilities: Lyon Part-Dieu offers a range of facilities including baggage storage, information desks, and various dining and shopping options.

Local Transportation: The station is well-connected to the city via tram, metro, and bus services. It's easy to access various parts of Lyon from here.

At Lyon Perrache

Facilities: Lyon Perrache has essential facilities such as ticket counters and waiting areas. It's smaller compared to Part-Dieu but still well-equipped.

Local Transportation: The station is connected to Lyon's public transportation network, including trams and buses.

At Lyon Vaise

Facilities: Lyon Vaise is a smaller station with basic facilities. It's suitable for local and regional travelers.

Local Transportation: Local buses and metro lines connect the station to different parts of the city.

Transportation from Train Stations to City Center

From Lyon Part-Dieu

Metro: The Metro Line B connects Part-Dieu with the city center, providing a quick and direct route.

Tram: The tram lines T1 and T3 connect the station with various city areas.

Bus: Numerous bus lines operate from Part-Dieu, offering connections to different parts of Lyon.

Taxi: Taxis are readily available outside the station for a convenient and direct transfer to your destination.

From Lyon Perrache

Metro: Metro Line A connects Perrache with central Lyon.

Tram: Tram Line T1 serves the Perrache area, linking it with other parts of the city.

Bus: Several bus lines operate from Perrache.

Taxi: Taxis are available for direct transfers.

From Lyon Vaise

Metro: Metro Line D connects Vaise with the city center.

Bus: Local buses serve the Vaise area, offering connections to various city locations.

Taxi: Taxis are available for more personalized transportation.

Traveling to Lyon by train is a comfortable and efficient option, with well-connected stations and a variety of services to cater to your needs. Whether you're arriving from within France or traveling from neighboring countries, Lyon's rail network ensures a smooth and enjoyable journey to this dynamic French city.

By Bus

Traveling to Lyon by bus can be a cost-effective and convenient way to reach the city, especially for budget-conscious travelers or those coming from nearby regions. Lyon's bus connections are well-integrated, making it easy to arrive in the city from various domestic and international locations. Here's a detailed guide on how to travel to Lyon by bus.

Major Bus Terminals Serving Lyon

Gare routière de Lyon-Perrache

The primary bus terminal in Lyon is located at Gare routière de Lyon-Perrache, adjacent to the Lyon Perrache train station. This terminal handles both domestic and international bus services and offers convenient connections to Lyon's public transportation network.

Gare routière de Lyon-Part-Dieu

While not as central as Perrache, the Gare routière de Lyon-Part-Dieu is another key bus terminal serving the city. Located near the Lyon Part-Dieu train station, it handles various regional and intercity bus services.

Major Bus Routes to Lyon

Domestic Routes

From Paris: Several bus companies operate services between Paris and Lyon. The journey typically takes around 8-10 hours. Companies like FlixBus and BlaBlaBus offer direct routes with various amenities.

From Marseille: Buses from Marseille to Lyon usually take around 4-5 hours. FlixBus and BlaBlaBus provide frequent services.

From Grenoble: The bus journey from Grenoble to Lyon is approximately 1.5-2 hours. There are several regional bus services that cater to this route.

International Routes

From Geneva: Buses connect Geneva with Lyon in about 3-4 hours. Companies like FlixBus and Ouibus offer these services.

From Milan: Buses from Milan to Lyon typically take 7-8 hours. FlixBus and MarinoBus are common providers for this route.

From Barcelona: The journey from Barcelona to Lyon by bus is around 12-14 hours. FlixBus operates this route with several departures daily.

Choosing Bus Services to Lyon

When selecting a bus service to Lyon, consider the following factors:

Comfort and Amenities: Different bus companies offer varying levels of comfort and amenities. FlixBus, for example, provides options like Wi-Fi, power outlets, and extra legroom on many routes.

Duration and Frequency: Bus travel times can vary. Look for routes that best fit your schedule and preferences. Some companies offer overnight buses for longer journeys.

Pricing: Prices can vary depending on the company, route, and time of booking. Booking in advance often secures better rates.

Ticket Options: Most bus companies offer flexible ticket options, including refundable or exchangeable tickets. Check the company's policies when booking.

Arriving at Lyon Bus Terminals

At Gare routière de Lyon-Perrache

Facilities: The Perrache terminal is equipped with various facilities including ticket counters, waiting areas, and access to nearby shops and restaurants. It also offers easy access to Lyon's public transportation network.

Local Transportation: From Perrache, you can easily connect to the city center via Metro Line A, Tram Line T1, and several bus lines. Taxis are also available outside the terminal.

At Gare routière de Lyon-Part-Dieu

Facilities: The Part-Dieu terminal has basic amenities, including ticket counters and waiting areas. It's located near the Lyon Part-Dieu train station, providing additional facilities and services.

Local Transportation: The Part-Dieu terminal is well-connected to the city via Metro Line B and Tram Lines T1 and T3. Buses and taxis are also available for local travel.

Transportation from Bus Terminals to City Center

From Gare routière de Lyon-Perrache

Metro: Metro Line A provides a direct link from Perrache to central Lyon.

Tram: Tram Line T1 connects the terminal with various parts of the city.

Bus: Several local bus lines operate from the terminal, offering connections to different city areas.

Taxi: Taxis are readily available for direct transfers to your destination.

From Gare routière de Lyon-Part-Dieu

Metro: Metro Line B connects Part-Dieu with the city center, providing a quick route.

Tram: Tram Line T1 serves the Part-Dieu area, linking it with various city locations.

Bus: Local buses offer connections to different parts of Lyon.

Taxi: Taxis are available outside the terminal for convenient transfers.

Traveling to Lyon by bus is a practical option for many travelers, offering a balance of affordability and convenience. With multiple routes and frequent services, you can easily find a bus that fits your schedule and budget. Whether you're arriving from within France or from an international destination, Lyon's bus terminals provide excellent connections to the city's public transportation network, ensuring a smooth arrival and transition to your final destination.

By Car

Traveling to Lyon by car offers flexibility, convenience, and the opportunity to enjoy scenic drives through France and neighboring regions. Whether you're coming from a nearby city or embarking on a longer journey, driving to Lyon can be an enjoyable experience. Here's an extensive guide to help you plan your road trip to Lyon.

Major Routes to Lyon

From Paris to Lyon

Route: The most direct route from Paris to Lyon is via the A6 autoroute (motorway), also known as the "Autoroute du Soleil."

Distance: Approximately 470 kilometers (290 miles).

Driving Time: Around 4.5 to 5 hours, depending on traffic and driving speed.

Highlights: The drive takes you through scenic Burgundy, with opportunities to stop in charming towns and vineyards.

From Marseille to Lyon

Route: The A7 autoroute connects Marseille to Lyon.

Distance: About 315 kilometers (195 miles).

Driving Time: Approximately 3 to 4 hours.

Highlights: This route offers views of the Rhône Valley and the picturesque landscapes of southern France.

From Geneva to Lyon

Route: Travel via the A40 and A42 autoroutes.

Distance: Around 150 kilometers (93 miles).

Driving Time: Approximately 1.5 to 2 hours.

Highlights: Enjoy the scenic drive through the French Jura Mountains.

From Milan to Lyon

Route: The A40 autoroute connects to the A42 leading to Lyon.

Distance: Approximately 450 kilometers (280 miles).

Driving Time: Around 5 to 6 hours, depending on traffic and border crossing times.

Highlights: The route passes through the stunning landscapes of the Alps.

Preparing for Your Drive to Lyon

Vehicle Requirements

Rental Car: If you're renting a car, ensure you're familiar with the rental company's terms and conditions. Check that the vehicle is in good condition and equipped with necessary documents.

Insurance: Make sure you have adequate insurance coverage for your rental car or personal vehicle. Verify that it covers international travel if you're driving from another country.

Documents: Bring your driver's license, vehicle registration, and proof of insurance. For international travel, an International Driving Permit (IDP) may be required.

Road Rules and Regulations

Speed Limits: In France, speed limits are generally 130 km/h (81 mph) on highways, 90 km/h (56 mph) on main roads, and 50 km/h (31 mph) in urban areas. Always adhere to posted speed limits.

Toll Roads: Many major routes, including the A6 and A7, are toll roads. Be prepared for toll charges and consider using a toll tag for convenience.

Parking: Lyon has several parking options, including on-street parking and parking garages. Be aware of parking regulations and fees to avoid fines.

Navigation

GPS: Use a GPS device or smartphone navigation app to help with directions. Ensure you have updated maps and traffic information.

Road Signs: Familiarize yourself with French road signs and symbols to navigate safely.

Arriving in Lyon by Car

Entering the City

Traffic: Lyon is a bustling city with busy streets. Plan your arrival time to avoid peak traffic hours.

Parking: Consider parking your car in one of Lyon's parking facilities. Popular areas like Vieux Lyon and the Presqu'île have multiple parking options. Look for parking signs and follow local regulations.

Parking Options

Public Parking Garages: Lyon has several public parking garages, such as Parking Part-Dieu, Parking Bellecour, and Parking Vieux Lyon. These facilities are well-located for easy access to major attractions.

Street Parking: On-street parking is available in some areas, but be sure to check parking meters and signs for regulations. Parking fees apply in many zones.

Driving in Lyon

City Traffic: Lyon's city center can be congested, especially during rush hours. Plan your routes in advance and use parking facilities when exploring the city.

Low Emission Zones: Lyon has low-emission zones (Zones de Circulation Restreinte) where access is restricted for certain vehicles. Ensure your car complies with local environmental regulations or use public transport within these areas.

Scenic Drives and Day Trips

Exploring the Surroundings

Beaujolais Wine Region: A short drive north of Lyon, Beaujolais is famous for its wine and picturesque landscapes. It's a great area for wine tasting and exploring charming villages.

Pérouges: About 35 kilometers (22 miles) from Lyon, Pérouges is a beautifully preserved medieval village worth a visit.

Dombes Region: Known for its lakes and birdwatching opportunities, the Dombes region is a tranquil getaway just a short drive from Lyon.

Traveling to Lyon by car provides the flexibility to explore not just the city but also its beautiful surroundings. Whether you're driving from within France or from neighboring countries, proper planning and preparation will ensure a smooth and enjoyable journey. With scenic routes, convenient parking options, and the freedom to explore at your own pace, driving to Lyon is a rewarding experience for any traveler.

Chapter 4: Getting Around Lyon

Metro

Lyon's Metro system is a highly efficient and convenient way to explore the city. With four lines that cover major districts and landmarks, the Metro makes traveling around Lyon easy and straightforward. Here's an extensive guide to help tourists navigate Lyon's Metro system during their visit.

Overview of Lyon's Metro System

Metro Lines

Lyon's Metro system consists of four lines, each identified by a letter:

Line A (Red Line): Runs from Perrache in the south to Vaulx-en-Velin La Soie in the northeast. It passes through key areas such as Bellecour, Cordeliers, and Hôtel de Ville.

Line B (Blue Line): Connects Charpennes-Chêne Pointu in the north to Gare d'Oullins in the south. It serves important stops like Part-Dieu, Saxe-Gambetta, and Jean Macé.

Line C (Green Line): Runs from Cuire in the north to Croix-Rousse and connects to the downtown area. It is particularly useful for reaching the Croix-Rousse district and Fourvière.

Line D (Yellow Line): Connects Gare de Vaise in the west to Gare de Perrache in the south. It covers areas like Bellecour, and it's a good choice for traveling between the city center and the southern districts.

Operating Hours

Weekdays: Generally from 5:00 AM to 12:00 AM.

Weekends: Service is usually extended until around 1:00 AM.

Frequency: Trains run every 2-5 minutes during peak hours and every 5-10 minutes during off-peak times.

Ticketing

Single Ticket: Valid for a single journey within the Metro network and includes transfers to buses and trams.

Day Pass: Offers unlimited travel for one day and is a cost-effective option for tourists planning multiple Metro rides.

Multi-ride Cards: Available for 10 rides and provide a discount compared to single tickets.

Tourist Pass: The Lyon City Card includes unlimited travel on public transportation, along with discounts on various attractions.

How to Use the Metro in Lyon

Purchasing Tickets

Ticket Vending Machines: Available at all Metro stations, these machines offer a range of ticket options and accept cash or card payments.

Ticket Counters: At major stations like Part-Dieu and Perrache, you can purchase tickets and get information from the ticket counters.

Navigating the Stations

Station Signage: Stations are well-signposted in both French and English. Follow the signs for platforms, exits, and transfers.

Maps and Timetables: Maps and timetables are displayed throughout stations. You can also find detailed maps and route information online or via mobile apps.

Boarding the Train

Train Information: Each train displays its destination and intermediate stops. Listen for announcements and watch the digital displays inside the train for real-time updates.

Platform: Ensure you're on the correct platform for your intended direction. Metro lines are color-coded, making it easier to navigate.

During Your Journey

Stations: Metro stations are equipped with clear signage and announcements to help you understand your current location and upcoming stops.

Transfers: If you need to transfer between lines, follow the signs in the station for connections. Most major stations, like Bellecour and Part-Dieu, offer easy transfers between lines.

Key Metro Stations and Their Surroundings

Bellecour

Description: One of the busiest and most central Metro stations, serving both Line A and Line D.

Nearby Attractions: Place Bellecour, Hôtel de Ville, and numerous shopping and dining options.

Part-Dieu

Description: A major transport hub connecting Line B and Line D.

Nearby Attractions: The Part-Dieu shopping center, Lyon's business district, and the Lyon Museum of Contemporary Art.

Hôtel de Ville

Description: Located in the heart of Lyon, serving Line A.

Nearby Attractions: Lyon City Hall, Opera House, and the beautiful Place des Terreaux.

Vieux Lyon

Description: The station for Line D, close to Lyon's Old Town.

Nearby Attractions: The historic district of Vieux Lyon, Lyon Cathedral, and numerous Renaissance-era buildings.

Croix-Rousse

Description: The station on Line C, serving the distinctive Croix-Rousse district.

Nearby Attractions: The Croix-Rousse neighborhood known for its bohemian atmosphere, markets, and traboules (hidden passageways).

Tips for Navigating the Metro

Download the App: The TCL (Transports en Commun Lyonnais) app provides real-time information, route planning, and ticket purchasing options.

Watch for Pickpockets: As with any busy transit system, be mindful of your belongings and be cautious in crowded areas.

Plan Your Routes: Use online route planners or maps to plan your journeys and transfers in advance.

Respect the Rules: Follow the Metro etiquette, such as giving up seats for elderly passengers and keeping noise levels down.

Accessibility

Elevators and Escalators: Major stations are equipped with elevators and escalators to assist those with mobility challenges. Check station maps for their locations.

Assistance: If you need assistance, contact station staff or use the information counters available at major stations.

Tram

Lyon's tram network is a vital part of the city's public transportation system, offering a comfortable and scenic way to explore various neighborhoods and attractions. With its modern trams and efficient routes, the tram system complements Lyon's Metro and bus services. Here's an extensive guide to help you navigate Lyon's trams during your visit.

Overview of Lyon's Tram System

Tram Lines

Lyon's tram system includes several lines, each serving different parts of the city and surrounding areas:

Tram Line T1: Connects the Perrache area to the La Doua Gaston Berger university campus. It runs through the city center, passing by major attractions like the Hôtel de Ville and the Bellecour district.

Tram Line T2: Runs from Perrache to the La Soie district in Vaulx-en-Velin. It connects key areas such as the Part-Dieu shopping center and the Montrochet district.

Tram Line T3: Extends from Part-Dieu to the Meyzieu-Zola area. It serves the central business district and offers connections to the Lyon Part-Dieu train station.

Tram Line T4: Connects the La Doua campus to the Perrache area, passing through the Cité Internationale and other central locations.

Operating Hours

Weekdays: Trams typically operate from around 5:00 AM to midnight.

Weekends: Service usually extends until about 1:00 AM.

Frequency: Trams run every 7-10 minutes during peak hours and every 10-15 minutes during off-peak times.

Ticketing

Single Ticket: Valid for a single tram journey and includes transfers to buses and the Metro.

Day Pass: Offers unlimited travel for one day, ideal for tourists planning multiple tram rides.

Multi-ride Cards: Available for 10 rides and provide a discount compared to purchasing single tickets.

Tourist Pass: The Lyon City Card includes unlimited travel on public transportation, along with discounts on various attractions.

How to Use the Tram in Lyon

Purchasing Tickets

Ticket Vending Machines: Available at all tram stations. These machines accept cash and card payments and offer various ticket options.

Ticket Counters: At major stations like Part-Dieu and Perrache, you can purchase tickets and get information from ticket counters.

Navigating the Stations

Station Signage: Tram stations are well-signposted in both French and English. Look for signs indicating platforms, exits, and connections.

Maps and Timetables: Maps and timetables are displayed at stations and inside trams. You can also access detailed route information online or via mobile apps.

Boarding the Tram

Tram Information: Each tram displays its route number and destination. Check the displays and listen for announcements for information about stops and routes.

Platform: Ensure you're at the correct platform for your tram line. Tram lines are clearly marked, making it easy to find the right one.

During Your Journey

Stations: Tram stations are equipped with clear signage and announcements to help you understand your current location and upcoming stops.

Transfers: If you need to transfer to another tram, Metro, or bus, follow the signs in the station for connections. Major stations like Bellecour and Part-Dieu offer easy transfers.

Key Tram Stations and Their Surroundings

Bellecour

Description: A central tram stop serving Tram Line T1. It's a key interchange point with connections to Metro and bus services.

Nearby Attractions: Place Bellecour, Hôtel de Ville, and the shopping and dining areas of the Presqu'île district.

Part-Dieu

Description: Serves Tram Lines T1 and T3, and is a major transport hub connecting to the Lyon Part-Dieu train station.

Nearby Attractions: The Part-Dieu shopping center, Lyon's business district, and the Lyon Museum of Contemporary Art.

Perrache

Description: A central hub for Tram Lines T1, T2, and T4. It's connected to Lyon's main train station and offers easy access to various city areas.

Nearby Attractions: The Confluence district, Musée des Confluences, and the shopping areas around Perrache.

Cité Internationale

Description: Served by Tram Line T4, this station provides access to the Cité Internationale complex, which includes the Palais des Congrès and various hotels.

Nearby Attractions: Cité Internationale, Parc de la Tête d'Or, and the Lyon Convention Center.

Tips for Navigating the Tram System

Download the App: The TCL (Transports en Commun Lyonnais) app offers real-time information, route planning, and ticket purchasing options.

Watch for Pickpockets: As with any busy transit system, be mindful of your belongings and be cautious in crowded areas.

Plan Your Routes: Use online route planners or maps to plan your journeys and transfers in advance.

Respect the Rules: Follow tram etiquette, such as giving up seats for elderly passengers and keeping noise levels down.

Accessibility

Elevators and Ramps: Major tram stations are equipped with elevators and ramps for accessibility. Check station maps for their locations.

Assistance: If you need assistance, contact tram staff or use the information counters available at major stations.

Bus

Lyon's bus network is an essential part of the city's public transportation system, offering extensive coverage to areas that may not be directly served by the Metro or tram lines. With numerous routes connecting various neighborhoods, attractions, and suburbs, buses provide a convenient and economical way to explore Lyon. Here's a detailed guide on using Lyon's buses to navigate the city during your visit.

Overview of Lyon's Bus System

Bus Lines

Lyon's bus network consists of several types of routes:

Regular Bus Lines: Cover most areas of the city and suburbs. They are identified by a number and run frequently throughout the day.

Express Bus Lines (Lignes Express): Connect Lyon with surrounding cities and regions. They are designed for longer distances and often offer limited stops.

Night Buses (Lignes Nocturnes): Operate during the nighttime hours when other public transport services are less frequent. They provide connections between key areas and transport hubs.

Operating Hours

Regular Buses: Typically run from around 5:00 AM to 11:30 PM. Some routes may extend their service hours, especially during weekends.

Night Buses: Operate from approximately midnight to 5:00 AM, providing service during the early hours when other transport options are limited.

Ticketing

Single Ticket: Valid for a single journey on the bus and includes transfers to the Metro and tram within a certain time frame.

Day Pass: Offers unlimited travel on buses, trams, and the Metro for one day, ideal for tourists planning multiple rides.

Multi-ride Cards: Available for 10 rides and provide a discount compared to purchasing single tickets.

Tourist Pass: The Lyon City Card includes unlimited travel on all forms of public transportation, plus discounts on various attractions.

How to Use the Bus in Lyon

Purchasing Tickets

Ticket Vending Machines: Located at most major bus stops and transport hubs. These machines accept cash and card payments and offer various ticket options.

Ticket Counters: Available at major transport stations like Part-Dieu and Perrache, where you can purchase tickets and get information.

Navigating Bus Stops

Bus Stop Signage: Each bus stop is clearly marked with route numbers and schedules. Look for the bus stop signs indicating which routes serve that location.

Timetables: Bus stops display timetables showing departure times and route information. Real-time updates may also be available at some stops.

Boarding the Bus

Bus Information: Buses display their route number and destination on the front and side panels. Check the displays to ensure you are boarding the correct bus.

Fare Payment: Pay your fare upon boarding or use a pre-purchased ticket. Some buses may have contactless payment options.

During Your Journey

Stops: Listen for announcements and watch the digital displays inside the bus for information about upcoming stops.

Transfers: If you need to transfer to another bus, tram, or Metro line, follow the signs at major stations or check your route planner for details.

Key Bus Routes and Their Surroundings

Bus Route 1

Description: Connects the Lyon Part-Dieu area with the Gerland district, passing through major locations such as the university campus and the Lyon Confluence district.

Nearby Attractions: Part-Dieu shopping center, Musée des Confluences, and the Gerland Olympic Stadium.

Bus Route 28

Description: Serves the route from the La Part-Dieu train station to the Vaulx-en-Velin area, covering key areas including the Confluence district and the Montrochet area.

Nearby Attractions: Confluence district, the Parc de la Tête d'Or, and local shopping areas.

Bus Route C3

Description: A key route connecting the city center with the eastern suburbs, including stops at important locations such as the Croix-Rousse district and the Part-Dieu shopping center.

Nearby Attractions: Croix-Rousse neighborhood, Hôtel de Ville, and the Presqu'île district.

Bus Route 70

Description: Provides a connection between the central Part-Dieu area and the suburbs of Lyon, including stops in areas like Monplaisir and La Doua.

Nearby Attractions: Part-Dieu district, Monplaisir neighborhood, and local parks.

Tips for Navigating the Bus System

Download the App: The TCL (Transports en Commun Lyonnais) app provides real-time information, route planning, and ticket purchasing options.

Watch for Pickpockets: As with any busy transit system, be mindful of your belongings and stay alert, especially in crowded areas.

Plan Your Routes: Use online route planners or maps to determine the best bus routes for your destinations and transfers.

Respect the Rules: Follow bus etiquette, such as giving up seats for elderly passengers and keeping noise levels down.

Accessibility

Low-Floor Buses: Many buses are equipped with low floors and ramps to accommodate passengers with mobility challenges. Check for accessibility features at bus stops and on buses.

Assistance: If you require assistance, contact bus staff or use the information counters at major transport hubs.

Bicycle

Exploring Lyon by bicycle is a delightful and eco-friendly way to experience the city's scenic beauty and vibrant neighborhoods. With its extensive network of bike lanes, dedicated bike paths, and bike-sharing programs, Lyon offers excellent opportunities for cyclists. Here's a detailed guide on how to navigate Lyon by bicycle during your visit.

Overview of Cycling in Lyon

Bike-Friendly Infrastructure

Lyon has invested significantly in creating a cyclist-friendly environment. Key features of the city's infrastructure include:

Dedicated Bike Lanes: Many major roads and streets in Lyon have dedicated bike lanes, ensuring safer and more comfortable rides for cyclists.

Bike Paths: Alongside the Rhône and Saône rivers, you'll find scenic bike paths that offer a pleasant way to explore the city's waterfront and parks.

Bike Parking: Numerous bike racks and secure parking areas are available throughout the city, particularly near popular destinations and transport hubs.

Bike Sharing Programs

Lyon's bike-sharing system, known as **Vélo'v**, is a convenient option for both short-term and long-term rentals. Key features include:

Vélo'v Stations: Over 300 Vélo'v stations are scattered throughout the city, making it easy to pick up and drop off bikes at various locations.

Rental Options: You can rent bikes for a single ride, for a day, or for longer periods. Daily and monthly passes are available, offering flexibility depending on your needs.

Pricing: Rental rates are generally affordable. There are often free first 30 minutes included, and charges apply for additional time.

How to Use the Vélo'v System

Finding a Vélo'v Station

Station Locations: Vélo'v stations are well-distributed across Lyon, including key areas such as the city center, universities, and tourist attractions. Use the Vélo'v website or app to locate the nearest station.

Maps and Apps: The Vélo'v app provides real-time information on bike availability and station locations. It's a useful tool for planning your bike routes and finding available bikes.

Renting a Bike

At the Station: Use the Vélo'v kiosk to select your rental option. You can pay by credit card or use a subscription card if you have one.

Using the App: The Vélo'v app allows you to unlock and return bikes electronically, making the process quicker and more convenient.

Returning a Bike

Drop-off Locations: Return the bike to any Vélo'v station. Ensure the bike is securely locked at a station with available docking points to avoid additional charges.

Confirmation: Use the Vélo'v app or kiosk to confirm that the bike has been properly returned and docked.

Cycling Routes and Recommendations

Exploring the City Center

Presqu'île: Cycle through the Presqu'île district, where you can enjoy the architecture of Place Bellecour and explore shopping and dining options.

Vieux Lyon: Ride through the historic Vieux Lyon area, known for its Renaissance buildings, narrow streets, and lively atmosphere.

Along the Rhône and Saône Rivers

Rhône River Path: The bike path along the Rhône River offers beautiful views and connects various parks and attractions, including Parc de la Tête d'Or.

Saône River Path: This path provides scenic views of the Saône River and passes through charming neighborhoods and historic sites.

Exploring Parks and Green Spaces

Parc de la Tête d'Or: A large urban park with dedicated bike paths, ideal for a leisurely ride or a picnic. It's also home to a lake, botanical gardens, and a zoo.

Parc des Hauteurs: Located on the Croix-Rousse hill, this park offers panoramic views of Lyon and is accessible via bike paths.

Cycling to Outlying Areas

Confluence District: Ride to the modern Confluence district, known for its innovative architecture and cultural attractions like the Musée des Confluences.

Croix-Rousse: Explore the bohemian Croix-Rousse neighborhood, famous for its artistic vibe, market, and traboules (hidden passageways).

Safety and Tips for Cyclists

Safety Guidelines

Helmet: While not mandatory, wearing a helmet is highly recommended for safety.

Bike Lights: Use front and rear lights, especially when riding at night or in low-light conditions.

Traffic Rules: Follow traffic rules and be aware of your surroundings. Use hand signals to indicate turns and stops.

Navigating the City

Bike Maps: Obtain a bike map from the tourist information center or download one online to familiarize yourself with bike lanes and paths.

Weather: Check the weather forecast before heading out. Lyon experiences various weather conditions, so be prepared for rain or sun as needed.

Bike Maintenance

Check the Bike: Before setting off, ensure the bike is in good condition, with properly inflated tires and functioning brakes.

Repairs: Vélo'v stations have basic repair tools available. For more serious issues, contact the Vélo'v service center.

Accessibility

Bike Accessibility

Low-Step Bikes: Vélo'v offers bikes with low steps to accommodate cyclists of varying heights and mobility.

Child Seats: Some bike-sharing systems may provide options for child seats. Check availability and reserve in advance if needed.

Walking

Walking is a fantastic way to experience Lyon's charm and discover its hidden gems at a leisurely pace. The city's compact layout, historic neighborhoods, and pedestrian-friendly streets make it ideal for exploring on foot. Here's a detailed guide on how to navigate Lyon and make the most of your walking experience during your visit.

Why Walking is Ideal for Exploring Lyon

Compact City Center

Proximity: Many of Lyon's main attractions, historic sites, and neighborhoods are located close to each other, making walking a practical and enjoyable way to get around.

Pedestrian Zones: Certain areas, especially in the city center and historic districts, are designed to be pedestrian-friendly, enhancing the walking experience.

Scenic Routes

Architectural Beauty: Walking allows you to fully appreciate Lyon's diverse architecture, from Renaissance buildings in Vieux Lyon to modern structures in the Confluence district.

Hidden Gems: Strolling through Lyon's streets helps you discover charming courtyards, hidden passageways (traboules), and local shops that you might miss when using other forms of transportation.

Key Walking Routes and Neighborhoods

Presqu'île

Description: The Presqu'île district, located between the Rhône and Saône rivers, is the heart of Lyon. It's a vibrant area known for its shopping streets, dining options, and historical landmarks.

Highlights: Place Bellecour, Hôtel de Ville, and Rue de la République. Stroll along Rue des Marronniers for a selection of cafes and boutiques.

Vieux Lyon

Description: The Old Lyon (Vieux Lyon) area is a UNESCO World Heritage site known for its well-preserved Renaissance architecture and narrow cobblestone streets.

Highlights: Lyon Cathedral (Cathédrale Saint-Jean-Baptiste), traboules, and the Musée Gadagne. Wander through the traboules to discover hidden passages connecting courtyards and streets.

La Croix-Rousse

Description: Known for its bohemian atmosphere and historic silk-weaving heritage, the Croix-Rousse district offers steep streets and panoramic views of the city.

Highlights: La Maison des Canuts (silk-weaving museum), the Croix-Rousse market, and Parc des Hauteurs. Enjoy the artistic vibe and local markets.

Confluence

Description: The Confluence district is a modern area where the Rhône and Saône rivers meet. It features contemporary architecture and new cultural attractions.

Highlights: Musée des Confluences, the Confluence shopping center, and the urban park. Walk along the riverbanks for beautiful views and modern architecture.

Parc de la Tête d'Or

Description: A large urban park that offers a peaceful escape from the city's hustle and bustle.

Highlights: Botanical gardens, a large lake with boat rentals, and a zoo. Enjoy a leisurely walk or a picnic in this expansive green space.

Tips for Walking in Lyon

Planning Your Route

Maps: Obtain a city map from the tourist information center or use a navigation app to plan your walking routes and explore various neighborhoods.

Itineraries: Consider following self-guided walking tours available online or in travel guides to make sure you don't miss key attractions and hidden spots.

Comfort and Safety

Footwear: Wear comfortable walking shoes, as many of Lyon's streets are cobblestoned, and you may be walking for extended periods.

Weather: Check the weather forecast and dress appropriately for the conditions. Lyon can be warm in summer and chilly in winter, so layering is often a good option.

Navigating Lyon

Pedestrian Zones: Follow signs for pedestrian zones and be aware of traffic rules in mixed-use areas. Some streets are closed to vehicles, making them ideal for walking.

Crosswalks: Use crosswalks and be cautious at intersections. Traffic in Lyon can be busy, so ensure you're crossing safely.

Local Etiquette

Respect Local Customs: When walking in residential areas or smaller neighborhoods, be mindful of local residents and avoid making excessive noise.

Interactions: If you need directions or recommendations, don't hesitate to ask locals—they're often friendly and happy to help.

Accessibility

Walking Routes

Flat Terrain: Some areas, like the Presqu'île and Vieux Lyon, are relatively flat and easy to navigate. However, the Croix-Rousse district has steep hills that may be challenging for some visitors.

Assistance: If you have mobility issues, consider using public transport or bike rentals in combination with walking to navigate steeper areas.

Mobility Aids

Accessible Routes: Check for accessible walking routes and paths if you require a wheelchair or mobility aid. Lyon's main attractions and public spaces are generally accommodating.

Taxi and Ride-Sharing

Using taxis and ride-sharing services in Lyon offers a convenient and flexible way to get around the city, especially when you need a door-to-door service or are traveling with luggage. Here's a detailed guide on how to make the most of these options during your visit.

Taxis in Lyon

Overview of Taxi Services

Lyon's taxi system is well-regulated and provides a reliable means of transportation. Key points about taxis in Lyon include:

Availability: Taxis are widely available throughout the city, especially in busy areas, transport hubs, and popular districts.

Taxi Stands: Designated taxi stands are located at major transport terminals, including Lyon Part-Dieu train station, Perrache train station, and Lyon-Saint Exupéry Airport.

Hailing a Taxi: You can hail a taxi on the street, but it's often easier to use a taxi stand or call for a taxi.

Taxi Companies

G7 Taxis: One of Lyon's largest taxi operators, known for its reliability and wide coverage. You can book a taxi by phone, via their app, or at designated taxi stands.

Taxis Lyonnais: Another major provider offering similar services to G7. They can be booked through their website or app.

Taxi Rates

Initial Fare: There is usually a base fare for starting the ride.

Metered Charges: Taxis charge based on distance traveled and time spent in the vehicle. Rates may vary slightly based on the time of day and day of the week.

Airport and Station Surcharges: Additional surcharges may apply for trips to and from Lyon's airports and major train stations.

Booking a Taxi

Phone Booking: Call a taxi company directly to arrange a pickup.

Mobile Apps: Use taxi service apps like G7 or other local apps to book and track your ride.

In-Person: Visit a taxi stand to catch a taxi or arrange a pickup from a nearby hotel or public place.

Payment

Cash and Cards: Most taxis accept both cash and credit/debit cards. Confirm payment options with the driver before starting your journey.

Receipts: Request a receipt if needed for business or personal records.

Ride-Sharing Services

Overview of Ride-Sharing

Ride-sharing services like Uber and Bolt provide a modern alternative to traditional taxis, often with competitive pricing and user-friendly apps. Here's what you need to know:

Availability: Ride-sharing services are widely available in Lyon, with multiple options operating throughout the city.

Booking: Use the respective mobile app to book a ride. You'll receive details about the driver, vehicle, and estimated arrival time.

Popular Ride-Sharing Apps

Uber: A major global player offering a range of vehicle options, including standard, premium, and shared rides. Uber is well-integrated into Lyon's transportation network.

Bolt: Another popular option with competitive pricing and similar service offerings to Uber. Bolt is known for its efficiency and affordability.

Ride-Sharing Rates

Dynamic Pricing: Rates may fluctuate based on demand, time of day, and traffic conditions. Prices are usually calculated based on distance and time.

Estimates: The app provides fare estimates before you confirm the ride, so you know what to expect.

Booking a Ride

Using the App: Open the app, enter your pickup location and destination, and choose the type of ride you want. Confirm the booking, and the app will connect you with a nearby driver.

Track Your Ride: The app allows you to track your driver's arrival and view real-time updates.

Payment

App Payment: Payment is processed through the app, typically using a credit or debit card linked to your account. Cash payments are usually not accepted.

Receipts: Digital receipts are sent via email or available in the app for review.

Safety and Etiquette

Driver Identification: Always verify the driver's name and vehicle details before getting into the car.

Ratings and Feedback: Both taxis and ride-sharing services often include a rating and feedback system to ensure quality service. Provide feedback based on your experience to help improve the service.

Accessibility

Taxis

Wheelchair-Accessible Taxis: Some taxis are equipped to accommodate passengers with mobility challenges. You may need to request this service in advance.

Assistance: Taxi drivers can assist with luggage and other needs, but it's a good idea to confirm any special requirements when booking.

Ride-Sharing

Accessible Vehicles: Some ride-sharing services offer vehicles equipped for accessibility. Check the app for availability or contact customer support for assistance.

Special Requests: Include any special requests or needs in the app when booking your ride.

Tips for Using Taxis and Ride-Sharing Services in Lyon

Language: While many drivers speak basic English, it's helpful to know a few French phrases or have your destination written down to facilitate communication.

Local Knowledge: Drivers are usually familiar with local landmarks and can provide advice on routes and destinations.

Travel Time: Be aware of peak traffic hours and plan your journey accordingly to avoid delays.

Car Rental

Renting a car in Lyon can offer flexibility and convenience, especially if you plan to explore the city's surroundings or prefer a more private mode of transportation. Here's a detailed guide on how to rent a car in Lyon, including key considerations, rental agencies, and driving tips.

Why Rent a Car in Lyon?

Flexibility and Convenience

Explore Beyond the City: Renting a car is ideal for day trips to nearby regions such as the Beaujolais wine country, Pérouges, or the Alps. It allows you to travel at your own pace and explore off-the-beaten-path destinations.

Convenient Travel: A car provides flexibility for managing your schedule, transporting luggage, and navigating areas that may be less accessible by public transport.

Parking

Parking Availability: Lyon has several parking options, including street parking, public parking garages, and hotel parking facilities. Be aware of parking regulations to avoid fines.

Major Car Rental Agencies in Lyon

International Agencies

Hertz: Known for a wide range of vehicle options and global service standards. Located at Lyon-Saint Exupéry Airport and various city locations.

Avis: Offers a variety of rental cars with options for different budgets. Available at Lyon-Saint Exupéry Airport and city branches.

Europcar: Provides a selection of vehicles and flexible rental terms. Located at the airport and various city centers.

Enterprise: Offers competitive rates and a broad selection of vehicles. Available at the airport and in the city.

Local Agencies

Ada: A French rental company with several locations in Lyon, offering personalized service and competitive rates.

Rent A Car: Another local option with a range of vehicles and convenient city locations.

Booking a Car

Online Booking

Compare Prices: Use online platforms like Kayak, Rentalcars, or Auto Europe to compare prices and find the best deals from various rental agencies.

Reserve in Advance: Booking in advance can secure better rates and ensure availability, especially during peak travel seasons.

On-Site Booking

Airport and City Locations: If you prefer to book in person, visit rental desks at Lyon-Saint Exupéry Airport or city branches. This option may be useful for last-minute rentals or modifications.

Rental Requirements

Driver's License: A valid driver's license from your home country is required. An International Driving Permit (IDP) is recommended for non-European drivers.

Credit Card: A major credit card is typically required for security deposits and rental charges. Ensure it has sufficient credit available.

Age Restrictions: Most rental agencies require drivers to be at least 21 years old, with some imposing additional fees for drivers under 25.

Picking Up and Returning the Car

Picking Up the Car

Documentation: Bring your driver's license, credit card, and rental confirmation when picking up the car.

Inspection: Inspect the vehicle for any existing damage and confirm it with the rental agency before driving off. Take note of fuel levels and return policies.

Returning the Car

Return Location: Return the car to the agreed location, whether it's the same branch where you picked it up or a different drop-off point.

Condition: Return the car in the same condition as received, with a full tank of fuel unless otherwise specified.

Inspection: Conduct a final inspection with the rental agency to confirm there is no new damage and finalize the return process.

Driving in Lyon

Road Rules and Regulations

Traffic Rules: Follow French traffic laws, including speed limits, seat belt usage, and drink-driving regulations. Speed limits are typically 50 km/h in urban areas, 90 km/h on rural roads, and 130 km/h on highways.

Parking Regulations: Adhere to parking regulations and pay attention to signs indicating parking zones and restrictions. Unauthorized parking can result in fines or towing.

Navigation

GPS and Maps: Use a GPS device or smartphone app for navigation. Offline maps can be useful in areas with poor mobile signal.

City Roads: Lyon's city center can be challenging to navigate due to narrow streets and one-way systems. Familiarize yourself with key routes and landmarks.

Fuel

Fuel Stations: Fuel stations are available throughout Lyon. Note the fuel type required for your rental vehicle and plan refueling stops accordingly.

Traffic and Parking Tips

Traffic Congestion: Be aware of peak traffic times, particularly during rush hours (morning and evening). Plan your travel times to avoid heavy traffic.

Parking: Use public parking garages or designated parking areas to avoid fines. Many hotels and attractions offer parking facilities for guests.

Accessibility and Special Considerations

Accessibility

Accessible Vehicles: Some rental agencies offer vehicles with accessibility features. Request these options in advance if needed.

Special Requests: Notify the rental agency of any special requirements, such as child seats or additional driver needs, when booking.

Insurance

Rental Insurance: Consider purchasing rental insurance to cover potential damages or theft. Check if your personal car insurance or credit card provides coverage for rental vehicles.

Language

Communication: Rental agency staff in Lyon often speak English, but knowing some basic French phrases can be helpful and appreciated.

Renting a car in Lyon can offer flexibility and convenience, especially if you plan to explore the city's surroundings or prefer a more private mode of transportation. Here's a detailed guide on how to rent a car in Lyon, including key considerations, rental agencies, and driving tips.

Why Rent a Car in Lyon?

Flexibility and Convenience

Explore Beyond the City: Renting a car is ideal for day trips to nearby regions such as the Beaujolais wine country, Pérouges, or the Alps. It allows you to travel at your own pace and explore off-the-beaten-path destinations.

Convenient Travel: A car provides flexibility for managing your schedule, transporting luggage, and navigating areas that may be less accessible by public transport.

Parking

Parking Availability: Lyon has several parking options, including street parking, public parking garages, and hotel parking facilities. Be aware of parking regulations to avoid fines.

Major Car Rental Agencies in Lyon

International Agencies

Hertz: Known for a wide range of vehicle options and global service standards. Located at Lyon-Saint Exupéry Airport and various city locations.

Avis: Offers a variety of rental cars with options for different budgets. Available at Lyon-Saint Exupéry Airport and city branches.

Europcar: Provides a selection of vehicles and flexible rental terms. Located at the airport and various city centers.

Enterprise: Offers competitive rates and a broad selection of vehicles. Available at the airport and in the city.

Local Agencies

Ada: A French rental company with several locations in Lyon, offering personalized service and competitive rates.

Rent A Car: Another local option with a range of vehicles and convenient city locations.

Booking a Car

Online Booking

Compare Prices: Use online platforms like Kayak, Rentalcars, or Auto Europe to compare prices and find the best deals from various rental agencies.

Reserve in Advance: Booking in advance can secure better rates and ensure availability, especially during peak travel seasons.

On-Site Booking

Airport and City Locations: If you prefer to book in person, visit rental desks at Lyon-Saint Exupéry Airport or city branches. This option may be useful for last-minute rentals or modifications.

Rental Requirements

Driver's License: A valid driver's license from your home country is required. An International Driving Permit (IDP) is recommended for non-European drivers.

Credit Card: A major credit card is typically required for security deposits and rental charges. Ensure it has sufficient credit available.

Age Restrictions: Most rental agencies require drivers to be at least 21 years old, with some imposing additional fees for drivers under 25.

Picking Up and Returning the Car

Picking Up the Car

Documentation: Bring your driver's license, credit card, and rental confirmation when picking up the car.

Inspection: Inspect the vehicle for any existing damage and confirm it with the rental agency before driving off. Take note of fuel levels and return policies.

Returning the Car

Return Location: Return the car to the agreed location, whether it's the same branch where you picked it up or a different drop-off point.

Condition: Return the car in the same condition as received, with a full tank of fuel unless otherwise specified.

Inspection: Conduct a final inspection with the rental agency to confirm there is no new damage and finalize the return process.

Driving in Lyon

Road Rules and Regulations

Traffic Rules: Follow French traffic laws, including speed limits, seat belt usage, and drink-driving regulations. Speed limits are typically 50 km/h in urban areas, 90 km/h on rural roads, and 130 km/h on highways.

Parking Regulations: Adhere to parking regulations and pay attention to signs indicating parking zones and restrictions. Unauthorized parking can result in fines or towing.

Navigation

GPS and Maps: Use a GPS device or smartphone app for navigation. Offline maps can be useful in areas with poor mobile signal.

City Roads: Lyon's city center can be challenging to navigate due to narrow streets and one-way systems. Familiarize yourself with key routes and landmarks.

Fuel

Fuel Stations: Fuel stations are available throughout Lyon. Note the fuel type required for your rental vehicle and plan refueling stops accordingly.

Traffic and Parking Tips

Traffic Congestion: Be aware of peak traffic times, particularly during rush hours (morning and evening). Plan your travel times to avoid heavy traffic.

Parking: Use public parking garages or designated parking areas to avoid fines. Many hotels and attractions offer parking facilities for guests.

Accessibility and Special Considerations

Accessibility

Accessible Vehicles: Some rental agencies offer vehicles with accessibility features. Request these options in advance if needed.

Special Requests: Notify the rental agency of any special requirements, such as child seats or additional driver needs, when booking.

Insurance

Rental Insurance: Consider purchasing rental insurance to cover potential damages or theft. Check if your personal car insurance or credit card provides coverage for rental vehicles.

Language

Communication: Rental agency staff in Lyon often speak English, but knowing some basic French phrases can be helpful and appreciated.

Chapter 5: Top Attractions in Lyon

Basilica of Notre-Dame de Fourvière

The Basilica of Notre-Dame de Fourvière is one of Lyon's most iconic landmarks, offering visitors a captivating blend of history, culture, and breathtaking architecture. Perched atop Fourvière Hill, this basilica is a must-visit destination for anyone exploring Lyon. Here's an in-depth guide to help you make the most of your visit.

Overview

Location

Address: 8 Place de Fourvière, 69005 Lyon, France.

Perched: On Fourvière Hill, offering panoramic views of Lyon.

Significance

Religious Importance: Dedicated to the Virgin Mary, this basilica is a symbol of Lyon's deep Catholic heritage and has been a place of pilgrimage since its construction.

Cultural Icon: Known for its stunning architecture and as a prominent landmark visible from various parts of the city.

Historical and Cultural Significance

Historical Background

Construction: The basilica was built between 1872 and 1884, designed by architect Pierre Bossan. It was commissioned to celebrate the end of the Franco-Prussian War and to thank the Virgin Mary for protecting the city.

Historical Events: During the World Wars, the basilica played a role in offering spiritual support and solace to the people of Lyon.

Cultural Impact

Symbol of Faith: It represents the strong Catholic tradition in Lyon, a city known for its religious and historical significance in France.

Cultural Events: The basilica hosts various religious ceremonies, including annual processions and celebrations related to Lyon's Catholic traditions.

Opening Hours and Admission

Opening Hours

Daily Access: The basilica is generally open to visitors daily from 8:00 AM to 6:00 PM. The opening hours may vary slightly depending on the season and special events.

Mass Times: Regular Mass services are held in the basilica. Times for services can vary, so it's a good idea to check the schedule if you wish to attend a service.

Admission

Entry: Admission to the basilica is free. However, donations are encouraged to support its maintenance and preservation.

Special Visits: Certain parts of the basilica, such as the Treasury or the Crypt, may have specific visiting conditions or may require a guided tour.

Architectural Features

Exterior Design

Style: The basilica showcases a blend of Romanesque and Byzantine architectural styles. Its façade is adorned with intricate mosaics, sculptures, and decorative elements.

Towering Presence: The basilica is characterized by its two prominent towers and a grand dome, making it a striking feature on the Lyon skyline.

Interior Design

Nave and Sanctuary: The interior is richly decorated with colorful mosaics, marble columns, and gold leaf. The main altar and sanctuary are particularly ornate.

Chapels: The basilica houses several chapels dedicated to various saints and aspects of the Virgin Mary's life.

Notable Features

Panoramic Views: The basilica's location on Fourvière Hill provides breathtaking views of Lyon and its surroundings. Visitors can enjoy a panoramic vista from the forecourt.

Mosaic Artwork: The basilica's walls and ceilings are adorned with elaborate mosaics depicting religious themes and scenes from the life of the Virgin Mary.

Top Things to Do

Explore the Interior

Admire the Mosaics: Take time to appreciate the intricate mosaic artwork that adorns the walls and ceilings of the basilica.

Visit the Chapels: Explore the various chapels within the basilica, each with its own unique features and religious significance.

Enjoy the Views

Panoramic Terrace: Head to the forecourt or surrounding areas to enjoy stunning views of Lyon. The elevated position of the basilica offers one of the best vantage points in the city.

Attend a Service

Experience a Mass: If your visit coincides with a Mass or special religious event, attending a service can provide a deeper understanding of the basilica's role in the local community.

Guided Tours and Services

Guided Tours

Availability: Guided tours of the basilica are available and can be arranged through local tour operators or the basilica's visitor information desk.

Languages: Tours may be offered in multiple languages, including English, French, and others. Check availability and language options in advance.

Visitor Services

Information Desk: An information desk is available to provide assistance, maps, and details about the basilica's history and architecture.

Shop and Donations: A small shop sells religious items and souvenirs. Donations can be made to support the basilica's maintenance.

Tips for Visiting

Plan Your Visit

Best Time to Visit: Early morning or late afternoon are ideal times to visit to avoid peak tourist crowds. The basilica is also less crowded during weekdays.

Weather Considerations: Lyon's weather can vary, so dress appropriately and check the weather forecast before heading to the basilica.

Respect the Sacred Space

Dress Code: Dress modestly as the basilica is a place of worship. Avoid wearing shorts, sleeveless tops, or other casual attire.

Photography: Be respectful of signs regarding photography. Some areas may restrict photography to preserve the sacred environment.

Accessibility

Getting There: The basilica is accessible by public transportation, including buses and the funicular railway from the city center. The funicular provides a scenic and convenient way to reach the basilica.

Mobility: The basilica is accessible to visitors with limited mobility, but some areas may have stairs. Check with the visitor information desk for specific accessibility details.

Combine with Other Attractions

Fourvière Hill: Explore other attractions on Fourvière Hill, including the Roman theaters and the Musée Gallo-Romain. The area offers rich historical and cultural experiences.

Vieux Lyon (Old Lyon)

Vieux Lyon, or Old Lyon, is a captivating district that offers a glimpse into Lyon's rich history and medieval charm. As one of the city's most historic and picturesque areas, Vieux Lyon is a must-visit for anyone exploring the city. This guide provides an in-depth look at what makes Vieux Lyon so special, including its history, key attractions, and tips for visitors.

Overview

Location

Area: Vieux Lyon is situated on the west bank of the Saône River, nestled between the river and Fourvière Hill.

Boundaries: The district is bordered by the Saône River to the east, Place du Change to the south, and Rue du Boeuf to the west.

Significance

Historical Importance: Vieux Lyon is a UNESCO World Heritage site recognized for its well-preserved Renaissance architecture and historical significance.

Cultural Hub: The area is known for its vibrant cultural life, with a mix of historic buildings, charming streets, and local eateries.

Historical and Cultural Significance

Historical Background

Renaissance Era: Vieux Lyon's architectural style predominantly dates back to the Renaissance period (15th to 17th centuries). The district showcases Lyon's historical prosperity and importance as a major trading center.

Silk Weaving: The area was historically known for its silk weaving industry, which played a crucial role in Lyon's economic development.

Cultural Heritage

UNESCO Status: Recognized for its historical value, the district preserves the essence of medieval Lyon, including its narrow streets, traboules (hidden passageways), and ancient buildings.

Cultural Events: Vieux Lyon hosts various cultural events and festivals throughout the year, celebrating its rich heritage and traditions.

Key Attractions

Place du Change

Description: A historic square that was once the center of Lyon's commercial activities. It's surrounded by beautiful Renaissance buildings and features a charming fountain.

Notable Features: The square's architecture and lively atmosphere make it a focal point for visitors.

Lyon Cathedral (Cathédrale Saint-Jean-Baptiste)

Description: A stunning Gothic cathedral located in the heart of Vieux Lyon. It features impressive stained glass windows and an astronomical clock.

Highlights: The cathedral's architecture and historical significance make it a must-see attraction.

Musée Gadagne

Description: A museum housed in a Renaissance mansion, offering exhibits on the history of Lyon and the city's cultural heritage.

Collections: The museum includes displays on Lyon's history, puppet theatre, and art.

Traboules

Description: Hidden passageways that connect buildings and courtyards. These historical features were used by silk workers and offer a unique glimpse into Lyon's past.

Exploration: Guided tours are available to explore and learn about these secretive passages.

Maison du Chamarier

Description: An historic building that showcases the architectural style of the Renaissance period. It's known for its distinctive façade and historical significance.

Visit: View the building's façade and learn about its history through local guides or informational plaques.

Top Things to Do

Explore the Historic Streets

Stroll Through Vieux Lyon: Wander through the narrow, winding streets of Vieux Lyon. The area's medieval charm is best appreciated on foot.

Shop and Dine: Explore local shops, boutiques, and restaurants. Vieux Lyon is known for its traditional bouchons (restaurants serving Lyonnaise cuisine).

Visit Local Markets

Place du Change Market: Check out local markets and stalls in Place du Change. It's a great place to find souvenirs and sample local produce.

Experience Lyon's Gastronomy

Traditional Bouchons: Enjoy a meal at one of Vieux Lyon's traditional bouchons. These restaurants serve classic Lyonnaise dishes in a cozy, historic setting.

Local Delicacies: Sample local specialties such as quenelles, andouillette, and other regional dishes.

Discover the Traboules

Guided Tours: Join a guided tour to explore the traboules and learn about their historical significance. Tours provide insights into the hidden passages and their role in Lyon's history.

Attend Cultural Events

Festivals and Events: Check the local calendar for cultural events and festivals taking place in Vieux Lyon. These events celebrate the district's rich heritage and offer unique experiences.

Tips for Visiting

Best Time to Visit

Spring and Fall: The best times to visit are during the spring (April to June) and fall (September to October) when the weather is pleasant and the crowds are smaller.

Summer: Summer (July to August) is popular, but be prepared for more tourists and higher temperatures.

Getting There

Public Transport: Vieux Lyon is accessible by metro (Line D, Vieux Lyon station) and bus. The funicular railway also connects the area to Fourvière Hill.

Walking: The district is best explored on foot, allowing you to fully appreciate its narrow streets and hidden corners.

Navigating the Streets

Footwear: Wear comfortable walking shoes, as the streets are cobblestoned and uneven in places.

Maps and Guides: Use a map or guide to navigate the district and locate key attractions. Free maps are available at tourist information centers.

Respect Local Customs

Dress Modestly: When visiting religious sites, dress modestly and follow any guidelines provided.

Local Etiquette: Be respectful of local residents and businesses. Vieux Lyon is a vibrant, lived-in area, and courtesy is appreciated.

Accessibility

Mobility: Vieux Lyon's narrow streets and cobblestones may pose challenges for those with mobility issues. Consider using public transport or taxis for easier access.

Language

Basic French: While many people speak English, knowing a few basic French phrases can enhance your experience and interactions.

Musée des Beaux-Arts de Lyon

The Musée des Beaux-Arts de Lyon is one of France's premier fine arts museums, offering an extensive and diverse collection of art spanning centuries. Located in the heart of Lyon, this museum is a cultural gem that attracts art enthusiasts and casual visitors alike. Here's an in-depth guide to help you make the most of your visit.

Overview

Location

Address: 20 Place des Terreaux, 69001 Lyon, France.

Setting: The museum is situated in the vibrant Place des Terreaux, a historic square in Lyon's Presqu'île district.

Significance

Artistic Importance: Known for its rich collection of paintings, sculptures, and decorative arts, the Musée des Beaux-Arts de Lyon is one of the largest fine arts museums in France.

Cultural Landmark: Housed in a former Benedictine convent, the museum itself is an architectural masterpiece and a historical landmark.

Historical and Cultural Significance

Historical Background

Founding: Established in 1803, the museum was originally intended to house the art collections of the Lyon Museum of Fine Arts, which dates back to the 18th century.

Architecture: The museum is located in a grand 17th-century building that was once a convent of the Order of Saint-Benedict. The architecture reflects the rich history and grandeur of the building.

Cultural Heritage

Diverse Collections: The museum's collections span ancient Egypt to contemporary art, showcasing works by renowned artists and offering insights into various art movements and historical periods.

Educational Role: The museum plays a key role in promoting art education and appreciation, hosting exhibitions, workshops, and educational programs.

Key Attractions

Permanent Collections

Painting: The museum's painting collection includes works by masters such as Caravaggio, Rembrandt, Monet, and Van Gogh. It features a wide range of styles, from Renaissance to Impressionism.

Sculpture: The sculpture collection showcases works from ancient Greece to modern times, including pieces by Rodin and other notable sculptors.

Decorative Arts: The museum's decorative arts section includes furniture, ceramics, and textiles from various historical periods, reflecting the evolution of design and craftsmanship.

Temporary Exhibitions

Varied Themes: The museum regularly hosts temporary exhibitions that explore different themes, artists, and art movements. These exhibitions provide opportunities to see works not permanently on display and to engage with current trends in the art world.

Historical Rooms

Architectural Features: Explore the museum's historical rooms, which include beautifully preserved spaces from the original convent, such as the cloisters and refectory.

Opening Hours and Admission

Opening Hours

General Hours: The museum is typically open from 10:00 AM to 6:00 PM, Tuesday through Sunday. It is closed on Mondays.

Extended Hours: Check for any extended hours or special openings during peak tourist seasons or for special events.

Admission

General Ticket: Admission fees vary, with discounts available for students, seniors, and groups. A general ticket usually covers access to both permanent and temporary exhibitions.

Free Entry: Admission is often free for visitors under 18, and on the first Sunday of each month, the museum may offer free entry for all visitors.

Special Offers

Combined Tickets: Consider purchasing combined tickets if available, which may include access to other local attractions or museums.

Architectural Features

Building Design

Exterior: The museum is housed in a grand building with Baroque and Renaissance architectural elements. The façade features intricate details and is a striking example of 17th-century design.

Interior: Inside, the museum combines historic architecture with modern gallery spaces. Highlights include the grand staircase, impressive hallways, and beautifully restored convent rooms.

Notable Rooms

Cloisters: The tranquil cloisters, with their arches and courtyards, provide a serene backdrop to the museum's art collections.

Refectory: The former dining hall, or refectory, is a notable architectural feature with its vaulted ceilings and historic ambiance.

Top Things to Do

Explore the Collections

Must-See Works: Focus on masterpieces from different periods, such as Caravaggio's "The Death of the Virgin," Monet's "The Japanese Bridge," and Rodin's sculptures.

Interactive Displays: Engage with interactive displays and multimedia presentations that provide deeper insights into the artworks and their contexts.

Attend Special Events

Exhibitions and Talks: Participate in special exhibitions, artist talks, and workshops. Check the museum's schedule for upcoming events and educational programs.

Enjoy the Museum's Architecture

Architectural Tour: Take time to appreciate the museum's architectural features, including its historical rooms and beautifully restored convent spaces.

Visit the Museum Shop

Souvenirs and Books: Browse the museum shop for art-related books, prints, and unique souvenirs. It's a great place to find gifts and mementos from your visit.

Relax in the Surrounding Area

Place des Terreaux: After your visit, explore the vibrant Place des Terreaux, where you can enjoy local cafés, shops, and the famous Bartholdi Fountain.

Guided Tours and Services

Guided Tours

Availability: The museum offers guided tours in various languages, providing detailed insights into the collections and exhibitions.

Booking: Book tours in advance, especially during peak seasons, to ensure availability and to tailor the tour to your interests.

Visitor Services

Information Desk: The museum has an information desk to assist with inquiries, provide maps, and offer guidance on exhibitions and events.

Accessibility: The museum is accessible to visitors with disabilities. Facilities include ramps, elevators, and accessible restrooms.

Educational Programs

Workshops and Lectures: The museum hosts educational programs, including workshops for children and lectures on art history. Check the museum's website for schedules and details.

Tips for Visiting

Plan Your Visit

Check the Calendar: Review the museum's schedule for special exhibitions and events to enhance your visit.

Avoid Crowds: Visit during weekdays or early in the day to avoid the busiest times.

Dress Comfortably

Comfortable Footwear: Wear comfortable shoes, as you'll be walking and standing for extended periods.

Weather Considerations: Dress appropriately for the weather, especially if you plan to explore the surrounding area.

Respect Museum Etiquette

Photography: Follow museum guidelines on photography. Some areas may restrict photography to protect the artworks.

Quiet Environment: Maintain a respectful and quiet atmosphere to enhance the experience for all visitors.

Use Public Transportation

Convenient Access: The museum is easily accessible by public transportation, including metro and bus. The nearest metro station is Hôtel de Ville – Louis Pradel (Line A and C).

Combine with Other Attractions

Nearby Sites: Explore other attractions in Lyon's Presqu'île district, including the Hôtel de Ville and the Lyon Opera House.

Parc de la Tête d'Or

Parc de la Tête d'Or is Lyon's largest and most beloved public park, offering a vast array of recreational and leisure activities in a picturesque setting. Covering 117 hectares, it is a green oasis in the heart of the city and a perfect destination for nature lovers, families, and anyone seeking relaxation. Here's a detailed guide to help you make the most of your visit to this iconic park.

Overview

Location

Address: Quai Charles de Gaulle, 69006 Lyon, France.

Setting: Located in the 6th arrondissement, the park is easily accessible from central Lyon and lies along the Rhône River.

Significance

Historical Importance: The park was created in 1857 and has since become a central feature of Lyon's urban landscape, offering a blend of natural beauty and recreational facilities.

Cultural Hub: It serves as a popular spot for local events, outdoor activities, and cultural gatherings.

Historical and Cultural Significance

Historical Background

Establishment: Designed by landscape architect Denis Bühler, the park was inspired by English landscape gardens and was originally intended to provide a green space for the growing city of Lyon.

Evolution: Over the years, the park has evolved to include a variety of features such as a botanical garden, a zoo, and numerous sports facilities.

Cultural Impact

Community Space: The park is a vital community space where locals and visitors come together for leisure activities, cultural events, and family outings.

Cultural Events: It hosts various events throughout the year, including open-air concerts, festivals, and seasonal activities.

Key Attractions

Botanical Garden

Description: The park features an extensive botanical garden with a diverse collection of plants, including exotic species, medicinal herbs, and beautiful floral displays.

Highlights: Explore themed gardens such as the rose garden and the Mediterranean garden, and enjoy the seasonal bloom of various flowers.

Zoo

Description: The park is home to a free-entry zoo that houses a variety of animals, including deer, monkeys, and exotic birds.

Highlights: The zoo offers educational displays and is a favorite attraction for families with children.

Lake

Description: A large artificial lake at the center of the park, offering opportunities for boating and leisurely walks along the water's edge.

Activities: Rent a rowboat or paddleboat to enjoy a relaxing time on the lake, or simply stroll around and enjoy the scenic views.

Rose Garden

Description: A beautifully landscaped area dedicated to roses, featuring over 30,000 rose bushes of various types and colors.

Highlights: Visit during the blooming season (late spring to early summer) to see the rose garden in full bloom.

Sports Facilities

Description: The park offers a range of sports facilities, including tennis courts, basketball courts, and cycling paths.

Activities: Engage in recreational sports, join a local game, or take advantage of the park's jogging paths for exercise.

Playgrounds

Description: Several well-equipped playgrounds are scattered throughout the park, providing safe and fun spaces for children.

Features: Play structures, swings, and climbing equipment are available for various age groups.

Opening Hours and Admission

Opening Hours

Daily Access: The park is open daily from early morning until dusk. Specific opening times may vary depending on the season.

Botanical Garden: The botanical garden typically opens around 10:00 AM and closes in the late afternoon or early evening.

Admission

General Access: Entrance to the park is free. Some attractions within the park, such as special exhibitions or guided tours, may have a fee.

Zoo: Admission to the zoo is free, making it a popular family-friendly attraction.

Special Offers

Events: Check the park's schedule for special events, workshops, and seasonal activities that may require pre-registration or a fee.

Architectural and Natural Features

Design

Landscape Architecture: The park's design reflects the English landscape garden style, featuring winding paths, naturalistic plantings, and open green spaces.

Historic Buildings: The park includes several historic buildings and monuments, such as the old greenhouse and the park's original gates.

Natural Beauty

Green Spaces: The park is known for its lush lawns, wooded areas, and beautifully maintained gardens.

Wildlife: In addition to the zoo animals, the park is home to various bird species and local wildlife.

Top Things to Do

Relax by the Lake

Boating: Rent a rowboat or paddleboat for a peaceful time on the lake.

Picnicking: Bring a picnic and enjoy a meal by the lake, taking in the serene surroundings.

Explore the Gardens

Botanical Wonders: Wander through the botanical garden and enjoy the diverse plant collections.

Rose Viewing: Visit the rose garden during the blooming season for a visual treat of colorful roses.

Engage in Outdoor Activities

Sports and Recreation: Participate in sports activities or join a local game on the park's facilities.

Cycling and Jogging: Use the park's paths for cycling or jogging and enjoy the scenic beauty while exercising.

Family Fun

Zoo Visit: Explore the zoo and learn about the animals, making it a fun and educational experience for children.

Playgrounds: Let children enjoy the various playgrounds and play areas.

Attend Events

Concerts and Festivals: Check for any events, concerts, or festivals taking place in the park during your visit.

Tips for Visiting

Best Time to Visit

Spring and Summer: The best times to visit are during spring (April to June) and summer (June to August) when the gardens are in full bloom and the weather is pleasant.

Avoid Peak Hours: Early mornings or late afternoons are ideal times to visit to avoid crowds.

Getting There

Public Transport: The park is accessible by metro (Line A, Masséna station) and bus. There are also bike-sharing services available.

Parking: Limited parking is available near the park. Consider using public transport or cycling to reduce parking stress.

Dress Comfortably

Footwear: Wear comfortable walking shoes, as the park is expansive and you'll likely be walking a lot.

Weather: Dress appropriately for the weather and bring sun protection or a raincoat as needed.

Accessibility

Facilities: The park is accessible to visitors with disabilities. Facilities include ramps, accessible restrooms, and well-maintained paths.

Respect the Environment

Clean Up: Use designated bins for trash and recyclables to help keep the park clean.

Respect Wildlife: Avoid feeding or disturbing the animals in the zoo and respect all park rules.

Combine with Nearby Attractions

Cultural Sites: After visiting the park, explore nearby attractions such as the Musée des Beaux-Arts de Lyon and the historic center of Lyon.

Musée des Confluences

The Musée des Confluences is one of Lyon's most striking and innovative museums, dedicated to the exploration of science, society, and the environment. Its futuristic design and diverse exhibitions make it a must-visit destination for anyone interested in the intersections of culture, science, and history. Here's an extensive guide to help you make the most of your visit to this iconic museum.

Overview

Location

Address: 86 Quai Perrache, 69002 Lyon, France.

Setting: Situated at the confluence of the Rhône and Saône rivers, the museum enjoys a prominent location in the Confluence district, known for its modern architecture and revitalization projects.

Significance

Architectural Marvel: The museum is renowned for its striking architecture, designed by the architectural firm Coop Himmelb(l)au, which combines futuristic design with sustainability.

Cultural Impact: It serves as a center for learning and cultural exchange, showcasing exhibitions that blend scientific inquiry with artistic expression.

Historical and Cultural Significance

Historical Background

Establishment: Opened in December 2014, the Musée des Confluences was built on the site of an old freight yard. The museum's creation was part of a larger urban redevelopment project aimed at revitalizing the Confluence area.

Mission: The museum's mission is to explore the intersections of science, culture, and society through its diverse and dynamic exhibitions.

Cultural Role

Educational Hub: The museum offers educational programs, workshops, and lectures that encourage visitors to engage with its exhibits and themes.

Innovative Exhibitions: The museum is known for its innovative exhibitions that explore contemporary issues and scientific advancements through engaging displays.

Key Attractions

Permanent Exhibitions

"Origins": This exhibition delves into the origins of humanity and the universe, exploring themes such as evolution, anthropology, and cosmology. It features interactive displays, fossils, and artifacts.

"Eternities": Focused on the concept of eternity, this exhibition examines cultural and scientific perspectives on time, memory, and the quest for immortality. It includes a range of artifacts, multimedia installations, and conceptual artworks.

Temporary Exhibitions

Varied Themes: The museum hosts a rotating schedule of temporary exhibitions that cover a wide range of topics, from contemporary art and technology to historical artifacts and environmental issues.

Special Events: Temporary exhibitions often include special events such as lectures, workshops, and guided tours that provide deeper insights into the exhibition themes.

The Crystal Pavilion

Design: The museum's iconic Crystal Pavilion is a striking architectural feature with a futuristic design, symbolizing transparency and openness. It's an excellent example of contemporary architectural innovation.

Functions: The pavilion houses the museum's main entrance, ticketing area, and temporary exhibition spaces. Its unique structure provides a dramatic and immersive experience for visitors.

The Garden of the Confluence

Description: Located around the museum, this green space offers a relaxing environment for visitors to unwind and enjoy views of the Rhône and Saône rivers.

Features: The garden includes walking paths, seating areas, and landscaped spaces that complement the museum's modern design.

Opening Hours and Admission

Opening Hours

General Hours: The museum is open from 10:00 AM to 6:30 PM, Tuesday through Sunday. It is closed on Mondays.

Extended Hours: During peak seasons or for special events, the museum may have extended hours. Check the museum's website for the latest information.

Admission

General Ticket: Admission fees vary. A general ticket typically includes access to both permanent and temporary exhibitions.

Discounts: Reduced rates are available for students, seniors, and groups. Some days or periods may offer free entry or special promotions.

Special Offers

Combined Tickets: Look for combined tickets or passes that may offer access to other local attractions or museums.

Free Days: The museum may offer free entry on certain days or for specific groups (e.g., children under 18).

Architectural Features

Design

Architectural Firm: Designed by Coop Himmelb(l)au, the museum features a bold and futuristic design characterized by its glass and metal façade.

Key Elements: The museum's design includes the Crystal Pavilion, organic-shaped structures, and extensive use of glass to create a sense of transparency and fluidity.

Sustainability

Eco-Friendly Design: The museum incorporates sustainable design principles, including energy-efficient systems and environmentally friendly materials.

Integration with Nature: The design integrates the building with its natural surroundings, enhancing the connection between the museum and the riverside environment.

Top Things to Do

Explore Permanent Exhibitions

Interactive Displays: Engage with the museum's interactive exhibits to learn about scientific concepts and cultural themes in an immersive way.

Key Artifacts: Pay special attention to significant artifacts and multimedia installations that offer insights into the museum's themes.

Visit Temporary Exhibitions

Check the Schedule: Review the museum's schedule of temporary exhibitions before your visit to plan which exhibits to see.

Special Events: Participate in special events, workshops, and lectures related to the temporary exhibitions.

Admire the Architecture

Photography: Take time to photograph the museum's striking architecture and the surrounding Confluence district.

Architectural Tours: Consider joining a guided tour or using an audio guide to learn more about the museum's design and its architectural significance.

Relax in the Garden

Stroll the Gardens: Enjoy a leisurely walk in the Garden of the Confluence and take in the views of the Rhône and Saône rivers.

Picnic: Bring a picnic and relax in the green space, enjoying the peaceful surroundings.

Visit the Museum Shop

Souvenirs: Browse the museum shop for unique souvenirs, books, and gifts related to the museum's exhibitions and themes.

Art and Design: Find art and design items inspired by the museum's collections and architecture.

Guided Tours and Services

Guided Tours

Availability: The museum offers guided tours in various languages, providing in-depth information about the exhibitions and the museum's architecture.

Booking: Book tours in advance to ensure availability and to customize the tour to your interests.

Visitor Services

Information Desk: The information desk provides assistance with tickets, maps, and general inquiries.

Accessibility: The museum is accessible to visitors with disabilities, with facilities including ramps, elevators, and accessible restrooms.

Educational Programs

Workshops and Lectures: The museum hosts educational programs for all ages, including workshops, lectures, and interactive sessions.

School Programs: Special programs are available for school groups, focusing on topics related to the museum's exhibitions and themes.

Tips for Visiting

Plan Your Visit

Check Exhibition Schedule: Review the museum's schedule and exhibition list before your visit to make the most of your time.

Allow Enough Time: Allocate several hours to explore both the permanent and temporary exhibitions thoroughly.

Dress Comfortably

Footwear: Wear comfortable shoes, as you'll be walking and standing for extended periods.

Weather: Dress appropriately for the weather if you plan to explore the surrounding garden or riverside area.

Respect Museum Etiquette

Photography: Follow the museum's guidelines on photography. Some exhibits may have restrictions.

Quiet Environment: Maintain a quiet and respectful atmosphere to enhance the experience for all visitors.

Use Public Transportation

Convenient Access: The museum is easily accessible by public transport, including tram and bus. The nearest tram station is Musée des Confluences (Line T1).

Combine with Nearby Attractions

Explore Confluence: After visiting the museum, explore the Confluence district, including its modern architecture, shopping centers, and waterfront areas.

Lyon Cathedral (Cathédrale Saint-Jean-Baptiste)

Lyon Cathedral, also known as Cathédrale Saint-Jean-Baptiste, is one of the city's most significant and historic landmarks. Situated in the heart of Vieux Lyon (Old Lyon), this Gothic masterpiece offers visitors a rich blend of history, architecture, and religious significance. Here's a detailed guide to help you make the most of your visit to this iconic cathedral.

Overview

Location

Address: Place Saint-Jean, 69005 Lyon, France.

Setting: Located in the historic district of Vieux Lyon, the cathedral stands prominently in the city's medieval quarter, surrounded by charming narrow streets and Renaissance architecture.

Significance

Historical Landmark: Lyon Cathedral is an important historical and architectural landmark, reflecting Lyon's rich religious and cultural heritage.

Religious Center: The cathedral serves as the seat of the Archdiocese of Lyon and has been a center of religious activity and ceremonial functions for centuries.

Historical and Cultural Significance

Historical Background

Construction: Construction of the cathedral began in 1180 and continued over several centuries, with significant additions and modifications made through the 13th to 15th centuries.

Architectural Evolution: The cathedral exhibits a blend of Romanesque and Gothic architectural styles due to its long period of construction and subsequent modifications.

Cultural Impact

Religious Role: As the main cathedral of Lyon, it plays a central role in the religious life of the city, hosting numerous liturgical ceremonies and special events.

Cultural Heritage: The cathedral's rich history and architectural beauty contribute to its status as a cultural and historical treasure of Lyon.

Architectural Features

Exterior

Facade: The cathedral features an intricate Gothic facade adorned with detailed sculptures, including biblical scenes and figures of saints. The façade is known for its striking rose window and elaborate doorways.

Towers: The cathedral has two asymmetric towers, with the northern tower being slightly higher than the southern one. The towers are adorned with decorative pinnacles and statues.

Interior

Nave: The interior boasts a spacious nave with high vaulted ceilings, supported by slender Gothic columns that create a sense of grandeur and verticality.

Stained Glass Windows: The cathedral's stained glass windows are a highlight, showcasing vibrant colors and intricate designs that illuminate the interior with natural light.

Astronomical Clock: One of the cathedral's notable features is its astronomical clock, which dates back to the 14th century. The clock is renowned for its mechanical complexity and the display of astronomical and religious information.

Key Artifacts

Altarpiece: The cathedral's altarpiece is a significant religious work, featuring detailed carvings and paintings that depict important biblical scenes.

Relics: The cathedral houses various relics and religious artifacts, which are preserved and displayed in the cathedral's treasury.

Opening Hours and Admission

Opening Hours

General Hours: The cathedral is typically open to visitors from 8:00 AM to 7:00 PM daily. During religious services, access may be restricted.

Special Services: The cathedral's opening hours may vary during special liturgical events or ceremonies.

Admission

General Access: Entrance to the cathedral is generally free. Donations are encouraged to support the maintenance and preservation of the site.

Guided Tours: Guided tours are available for a fee and provide deeper insights into the cathedral's history, architecture, and significance.

Special Offers

Audio Guides: Audio guides are available for rent, offering informative commentary on the cathedral's history and key features.

Group Tours: Special arrangements can be made for group tours, which may include additional services and personalized guidance.

Top Things to Do

Explore the Interior

Admire the Stained Glass: Take time to appreciate the intricate designs and vibrant colors of the cathedral's stained glass windows.

Observe the Astronomical Clock: Examine the details of the medieval astronomical clock, noting its mechanical intricacies and historical significance.

Attend a Service

Participate in a Mass: If your visit coincides with a service, consider attending to experience the cathedral's religious ambiance and traditional liturgical practices.

Special Events: Check the cathedral's schedule for special events, concerts, or religious ceremonies that may coincide with your visit.

Visit the Treasury

Religious Artifacts: Explore the cathedral's treasury to view important religious artifacts, relics, and historical items.

Photography

Exterior Shots: Capture the cathedral's façade, towers, and surrounding area. The gothic architecture and historical surroundings provide excellent photo opportunities.

Interior Shots: Respect the cathedral's guidelines on photography, particularly during services or if flash photography is restricted.

Guided Tours and Services

Guided Tours

Availability: Guided tours are available in various languages and offer detailed explanations of the cathedral's history, architecture, and religious significance.

Booking: It's advisable to book tours in advance, especially for larger groups or during peak tourist seasons.

Visitor Services

Information Desk: The cathedral provides information desks for visitor assistance, including maps, brochures, and general inquiries.

Accessibility: The cathedral is accessible to visitors with disabilities, with facilities including ramps and accessible restrooms.

Educational Programs

Workshops and Lectures: The cathedral occasionally offers educational programs, workshops, and lectures focused on its history and architecture.

School Programs: Special programs for school groups are available, providing educational experiences related to the cathedral's religious and historical context.

Tips for Visiting

Plan Ahead

Check Service Times: Verify the cathedral's service times and special events before your visit to ensure access and avoid disruptions.

Allocate Time: Set aside sufficient time to explore both the exterior and interior of the cathedral, as well as to participate in any guided tours or events.

Respect the Setting

Dress Code: Dress modestly and respectfully, as the cathedral is an active place of worship.

Quiet Environment: Maintain a quiet demeanor to respect the solemnity of the space and the experience of other visitors.

Combine with Nearby Attractions

Explore Vieux Lyon: After visiting the cathedral, explore the charming streets of Vieux Lyon, including its Renaissance buildings, cafes, and shops.

Other Landmarks: Visit nearby attractions such as the Basilica of Notre-Dame de Fourvière and the Musée Gadagne to complete your historical exploration of Lyon.

Place Bellecour

Place Bellecour is one of Lyon's most iconic and bustling public squares, known for its impressive size, historical significance, and central location. As a key landmark in the heart of the city, it offers a blend of history, culture, and vibrant city life. Here's an extensive guide to help you make the most of your visit to this famous square.

Overview

Location

Address: Place Bellecour, 69002 Lyon, France.

Setting: Situated in the Presqu'île district of Lyon, Place Bellecour is centrally located between the Rhône and Saône rivers, making it a prominent focal point in the city.

Significance

Central Hub: Place Bellecour is a major transportation and social hub, known for its open spaces, historical monuments, and lively atmosphere.

Cultural Landmark: The square hosts various public events, festivals, and markets, reflecting its role as a central gathering place in Lyon.

Historical and Cultural Significance

Historical Background

Origins: The square's origins date back to the late 17th century when it was redesigned by the architect Simon Maupin. It was created to serve as a grand public space and has since become one of the largest squares in Europe.

Historical Events: Place Bellecour has been the site of numerous historical events, including public celebrations, military parades, and political demonstrations.

Cultural Impact

Public Events: The square is a popular venue for festivals, concerts, and open-air performances. It often hosts seasonal markets, including Christmas markets and fairs.

Iconic Status: As one of Lyon's most recognizable landmarks, Place Bellecour plays a key role in the city's cultural and social life.

Architectural Features

Statue of Louis XIV

Description: At the center of Place Bellecour stands a prominent equestrian statue of King Louis XIV, created by sculptor Louis-Simon Boizot in 1825.

Design: The statue depicts the king on horseback, symbolizing his role in shaping the city's history. It is a focal point of the square and a popular spot for photographs.

Surrounding Architecture

Historic Buildings: The square is bordered by a mix of historical and modern buildings, including traditional Lyonnais architecture and contemporary structures.

Shops and Cafés: The surrounding area features numerous shops, cafés, and restaurants, making it a vibrant place for shopping and dining.

Top Things to Do

Explore the Square

Statue Viewing: Take time to admire and photograph the statue of Louis XIV, which is a key feature of the square.

People-Watching: Relax on one of the benches or enjoy a coffee at a nearby café while watching the bustling activity of the square.

Visit Nearby Attractions

Lyon Cathedral: Just a short walk from Place Bellecour, Lyon Cathedral (Cathédrale Saint-Jean-Baptiste) offers a glimpse into the city's rich religious history and Gothic architecture.

Musée des Beaux-Arts: Located nearby, the Musée des Beaux-Arts de Lyon showcases an extensive collection of fine arts and historical artifacts.

Attend Events

Festivals and Markets: Check the local calendar for any events, festivals, or markets taking place in Place Bellecour during your visit. Seasonal markets and public celebrations are common.

Shopping and Dining

Explore Shops: Wander around the square and explore the variety of shops and boutiques in the surrounding area.

Dining Options: Enjoy a meal or a drink at one of the many cafés and restaurants around Place Bellecour, offering a range of culinary experiences.

Guided Tours and Services

Guided Tours

Availability: Guided tours of Place Bellecour and the surrounding area can provide historical and cultural insights into the square's significance and architecture.

Booking: Consider booking a guided tour in advance, especially during peak tourist seasons.

Visitor Services

Information Centers: Visitor information centers in the area can provide maps, brochures, and details about local attractions and events.

Accessibility: The square is accessible to visitors with disabilities, with paved paths and accessible facilities.

Tips for Visiting

Plan Your Visit

Check for Events: Look up any special events, markets, or festivals taking place at Place Bellecour during your visit to enhance your experience.

Allocate Time: Set aside some time to fully explore the square, enjoy its atmosphere, and visit nearby attractions.

Respect the Space

Public Etiquette: Be mindful of the square's role as a public space and respect local customs and guidelines.

Keep It Clean: Help keep the area clean by disposing of litter properly and respecting the environment.

Combine with Other Attractions

Explore the Presqu'île: The Presqu'île district offers a wealth of attractions, including shopping, dining, and historical sites, all within walking distance from Place Bellecour.

Walk Along the Rhône: Enjoy a leisurely stroll along the Rhône riverbanks, which are easily accessible from the square.

The Traboules of Lyon are a network of secret passageways that run through buildings and courtyards, connecting streets and neighborhoods. These unique architectural features are one of Lyon's most fascinating attractions, offering a glimpse into the city's rich history and urban development. Here's an extensive guide to help you explore and appreciate the traboules of Lyon.

Overview

Location

Districts: The traboules are primarily located in two districts of Lyon: Vieux Lyon (Old Lyon) and La Croix-Rousse.

Access Points: While many traboules are accessible to the public, some are private and can only be visited with a guided tour.

Significance

Historical Pathways: Originally built in the 4th century and expanded in later centuries, the traboules were used by silk workers, merchants, and residents for quick and sheltered passage.

Cultural Heritage: The traboules are a unique aspect of Lyon's urban heritage, reflecting the city's historical and social development.

Historical and Cultural Significance

Historical Background

Origins: The concept of traboules dates back to Roman times, but most of the existing passages were constructed in the 16th and 17th centuries.

Silk Industry: The traboules played a crucial role during the height of Lyon's silk industry, allowing silk workers to transport their goods efficiently and protected from the elements.

Cultural Impact

Resistance Movement: During World War II, the traboules were used by the French Resistance as secret routes to evade German occupiers.

Architectural Value: The design and construction of the traboules showcase various architectural styles, including Renaissance and Gothic influences.

Architectural Features

Design

Passageways: The traboules are narrow, often dimly lit corridors that cut through buildings, connecting one street to another.

Courtyards: Many traboules open into picturesque courtyards, featuring ornate staircases, arches, and decorative elements.

Notable Traboules

Maison du Chamarier: Located in Vieux Lyon, this traboule connects 37 Rue Saint-Jean to 6 Rue des Trois Maries and is known for its beautiful Renaissance courtyard.

Traboule de la Cour des Voraces: Situated in La Croix-Rousse, this famous traboule at 9 Place Colbert is notable for its impressive six-story staircase.

Top Things to Do

Self-Guided Exploration

Discover Public Traboules: Wander through the public traboules in Vieux Lyon and La Croix-Rousse. Look for small signs or plaques indicating their presence.

Admire Courtyards: Take time to explore and appreciate the architecture and historical charm of the courtyards hidden within the traboules.

Guided Tours

Expert Insights: Join a guided tour to gain deeper insights into the history, architecture, and stories behind the traboules. Tours often provide access to private traboules not open to the public.

Specialized Tours: Some tours focus on specific themes, such as the silk industry, World War II history, or architectural heritage.

Photography

Capture Unique Angles: The traboules offer unique photographic opportunities, from narrow passages and spiral staircases to ornate courtyards and historical details.

Respect Privacy: Be mindful of residents' privacy, especially in traboules that are part of private buildings.

Opening Hours and Admission

Public Access

Hours: Many traboules are open to the public during daylight hours. Specific opening times can vary, so it's best to visit during the day.

Free Entry: Most public traboules are free to access, though donations for their maintenance are appreciated.

Guided Tours

Availability: Guided tours are available year-round, with more frequent offerings during the tourist season.

Cost: Tour prices vary depending on the provider and the length of the tour. It's advisable to book in advance, especially during peak seasons.

Tips for Visiting

Plan Ahead

Research Locations: Look up maps and guides to locate the public traboules you want to visit. Some may be hard to find without prior knowledge.

Wear Comfortable Shoes: The passages can be uneven and involve stairs, so comfortable footwear is recommended.

Respect the Space

Quiet Exploration: Keep noise levels down as many traboules are in residential areas. Respect the privacy and tranquility of the space.

Follow Guidelines: Adhere to any posted signs or guidelines regarding access and photography.

Combine with Other Attractions

Vieux Lyon: While exploring the traboules, take time to visit other attractions in Vieux Lyon, such as Lyon Cathedral and the Basilica of Notre-Dame de Fourvière.

La Croix-Rousse: Pair your visit to the traboules with a walk through the vibrant La Croix-Rousse district, known for its markets, cafés, and artistic atmosphere.

The Palais des Congrès de Lyon, also known as the Lyon Convention Center, is a premier destination for conferences, events, and cultural activities. Located in the modern Cité Internationale complex, it offers state-of-the-art facilities and a vibrant environment for both business and leisure visitors. Here's an extensive guide to help you make the most of your visit to the Palais des Congrès.

Overview

Location

Address: 50 Quai Charles de Gaulle, 69006 Lyon, France.

Setting: Situated in the Cité Internationale district, the Palais des Congrès is nestled between the Rhône River and the Parc de la Tête d'Or, Lyon's largest urban park.

Significance

Event Hub: The Palais des Congrès hosts a wide range of events, including international conferences, trade shows, concerts, and exhibitions.

Architectural Landmark: Designed by the renowned architect Renzo Piano, the complex is noted for its modern and innovative architecture.

Historical and Cultural Significance

Historical Background

Construction: The Palais des Congrès was inaugurated in 1996 as part of the larger Cité Internationale project, which aimed to create a modern business and cultural district in Lyon.

Development: The project was a collaborative effort between the city of Lyon and various international partners, reflecting Lyon's status as a global city.

Cultural Impact

Cultural Venue: Beyond business events, the Palais des Congrès serves as a cultural venue, hosting concerts, theater productions, and other artistic performances.

Community Engagement: The center plays a significant role in the local community, providing a space for public events, educational programs, and social gatherings.

Architectural Features

Exterior

Modern Design: The building's exterior features sleek lines, large glass facades, and a harmonious blend of materials that create a contemporary aesthetic.

Integration with Nature: The design includes green spaces and open areas that connect seamlessly with the adjacent Parc de la Tête d'Or.

Interior

Spacious Halls: The interior includes several large conference halls and auditoriums equipped with the latest technology to accommodate a variety of events.

Versatile Spaces: The center offers a range of versatile spaces, from small meeting rooms to large exhibition halls, allowing for flexible event setups.

Key Areas

Amphitheater 3000: One of the main highlights, this amphitheater can seat up to 3,000 people and is used for major conferences and performances.

Exhibition Halls: Multiple exhibition halls provide ample space for trade shows and large-scale exhibitions.

Meeting Rooms: Numerous meeting rooms and breakout spaces cater to smaller gatherings and business meetings.

Top Things to Do

Attend an Event

Conferences and Trade Shows: Check the schedule for upcoming conferences, trade shows, and business events that might align with your interests.

Cultural Performances: Look for concerts, theater productions, and other cultural events that take place at the Palais des Congrès.

Explore the Cité Internationale

Museum of Contemporary Art: Visit the nearby Museum of Contemporary Art to explore its diverse collection of modern artworks.

Cinemas and Restaurants: Enjoy a movie at the multiplex cinema or dine at one of the many restaurants and cafes in the Cité Internationale complex.

Visit the Parc de la Tête d'Or

Botanical Gardens: Explore the botanical gardens and the vast green spaces of Parc de la Tête d'Or, located just a short walk from the Palais des Congrès.

Boating and Zoo: Engage in recreational activities such as boating on the lake or visiting the park's zoo.

Guided Tours and Services

Guided Tours

Architectural Tours: Some guided tours focus on the architectural aspects of the Palais des Congrès and the Cité Internationale, providing insights into their design and construction.

Event-Specific Tours: During major events, guided tours may be available to help attendees navigate the complex and learn more about the event's highlights.

Visitor Services

Information Desks: Information desks are available to provide assistance, maps, and brochures about the Palais des Congrès and its events.

Accessibility: The center is fully accessible to visitors with disabilities, offering ramps, elevators, and accessible restrooms.

Business Services

Wi-Fi and Tech Support: Free Wi-Fi and technical support services are available throughout the complex to assist business visitors.

Conference Services: Event organizers can access a range of services, including catering, audiovisual equipment rental, and logistical support.

Tips for Visiting

Plan Ahead

Check the Schedule: Visit the Palais des Congrès website or contact the information desk to check the schedule of events and plan your visit accordingly.

Register Early: For conferences and major events, register in advance to secure your spot and benefit from early bird discounts.

Explore the Surroundings

Combine Visits: Plan to visit the nearby Parc de la Tête d'Or or the Museum of Contemporary Art to make the most of your time in the area.

Stay Nearby: Consider booking accommodation in the Cité Internationale district for convenient access to the Palais des Congrès and its surrounding attractions.

Transportation

Public Transport: The Palais des Congrès is easily accessible by public transport, including buses and trams. Check local transit options for the most convenient routes.

Parking: If you are driving, ample parking facilities are available in the Cité Internationale complex.

The Musée Lumière, located in the Monplaisir district of Lyon, is a must-visit destination for anyone interested in the history of cinema and photography. This museum is dedicated to the Lumière brothers, pioneers of early filmmaking, and offers a fascinating insight into their contributions to the art and science of motion pictures. Here's an extensive guide to help you explore the Musée Lumière.

Overview

Location

Address: 25 Rue du Premier Film, 69008 Lyon, France.

Setting: The museum is housed in the Villa Lumière, the former home of the Lumière family, and is situated in a beautiful park in the Monplaisir district.

Significance

Cinema History: The Musée Lumière celebrates the groundbreaking work of Auguste and Louis Lumière, who are credited with creating some of the first motion pictures.

Cultural Landmark: The museum not only preserves the legacy of the Lumière brothers but also serves as a center for the study and appreciation of cinema.

Historical and Cultural Significance

Historical Background

The Lumière Brothers: Auguste and Louis Lumière were among the earliest filmmakers in history. They invented the Cinématographe, a device that could record, develop, and project motion pictures, and held the first public screening of films in 1895.

Villa Lumière: The family mansion, built in the early 20th century, is an architectural gem and has been preserved to showcase the life and work of the Lumière family.

Cultural Impact

Birthplace of Cinema: Lyon is recognized as the birthplace of cinema due to the Lumière brothers' pioneering work. The museum highlights this cultural heritage and the global influence of their inventions.

Film Preservation: The museum plays a vital role in the preservation and promotion of early films, including the Lumière brothers' extensive catalog of short films.

Architectural Features

Exterior

Villa Design: The Villa Lumière is a stunning example of early 20th-century architecture, featuring elegant facades, intricate details, and beautifully landscaped gardens.

Park Setting: The museum is surrounded by a peaceful park, offering a pleasant environment for visitors to stroll and relax.

Interior

Historic Rooms: The interior of the villa has been meticulously preserved, with rooms furnished in the style of the period to reflect the Lumière family's lifestyle.

Exhibition Spaces: The museum includes several exhibition rooms that display artifacts, photographs, and film equipment related to the Lumière brothers' work.

Top Things to Do

Explore the Exhibitions

Early Films: Watch some of the Lumière brothers' earliest films, including the famous "Workers Leaving the Lumière Factory" and "Arrival of a Train at La Ciotat."

Film Equipment: View original film cameras, projectors, and other pioneering equipment used by the Lumière brothers.

Photography: Explore exhibits on the Lumière brothers' contributions to photography, including their advancements in color photography.

Visit the Cinematograph Room

Cinématographe Display: See the original Cinématographe device and learn about its invention and impact on the film industry.

Interactive Displays: Engage with interactive exhibits that explain the science and mechanics behind early filmmaking.

Stroll the Gardens

Relaxation: Enjoy a leisurely walk through the villa's gardens, which provide a tranquil setting and a glimpse into the lifestyle of the Lumière family.

Photography: The picturesque surroundings offer excellent photo opportunities.

Guided Tours and Services

Guided Tours

Availability: Guided tours are available and provide detailed insights into the Lumière brothers' lives, their inventions, and the history of the villa.

Booking: It is advisable to book guided tours in advance, especially during peak tourist seasons.

Visitor Services

Information Desk: An information desk is available to assist visitors with questions, provide maps, and offer additional resources about the museum and its exhibits.

Accessibility: The museum is accessible to visitors with disabilities, with ramps and elevators available for easy navigation.

Educational Programs

Workshops: The museum offers workshops and educational programs for children and adults, focusing on the history of cinema and filmmaking techniques.

Lectures: Special lectures and events are often held, featuring experts in film history and technology.

Opening Hours and Admission

Opening Hours

General Hours: The museum is typically open from Tuesday to Sunday, 10:00 AM to 6:30 PM. It is closed on Mondays and some public holidays.

Special Events: Hours may vary during special events or exhibitions, so it's best to check the museum's website for the latest information.

Admission

General Admission: There is an admission fee for entry to the museum. Discounts are available for students, seniors, and groups.

Special Offers: The museum occasionally offers special deals, such as combined tickets for multiple attractions or discounted rates during certain times of the year.

Tips for Visiting

Plan Your Visit

Check the Schedule: Visit the museum's website to check for any temporary exhibitions, special events, or changes in opening hours before planning your visit.

Allocate Time: Set aside a few hours to fully explore the museum, watch the films, and enjoy the gardens.

Combine with Nearby Attractions

Lumière Institute: The nearby Lumière Institute offers additional resources, screenings, and exhibitions related to the history of cinema.

Explore Monplaisir: Take time to explore the Monplaisir district, which has charming streets, local shops, and cafes.

Photography and Conduct

Respect the Exhibits: Be mindful of the museum's rules regarding photography, particularly with flash, and respect the exhibits and other visitors.

Quiet Environment: Maintain a quiet demeanor, especially in film viewing areas, to ensure an enjoyable experience for everyone.

Les Halles de Lyon-Paul Bocuse

Les Halles de Lyon-Paul Bocuse is a renowned indoor food market in Lyon, named after the legendary chef Paul Bocuse. This culinary hub is a must-visit destination for food lovers, offering a wide variety of gourmet foods, fresh produce, and artisanal products. Here's an extensive guide to help you explore and enjoy Les Halles de Lyon-Paul Bocuse.

Overview

Location

Address: 102 Cours Lafayette, 69003 Lyon, France.

Setting: Situated in the Part-Dieu district, Les Halles de Lyon-Paul Bocuse is easily accessible and close to major transportation hubs.

Significance

Culinary Landmark: Known as the "stomach of Lyon," Les Halles is a symbol of the city's rich gastronomic heritage and a tribute to Paul Bocuse, one of the most influential chefs in French culinary history.

Gourmet Destination: The market attracts both locals and tourists who seek high-quality foods and culinary experiences.

Historical and Cultural Significance

Historical Background

Origins: Les Halles was originally established in 1859. The current building, named after Paul Bocuse, was opened in 1971 and has since undergone several renovations to maintain its modern appeal.

Paul Bocuse: The market was renamed in honor of Paul Bocuse in 2006, celebrating his contributions to French cuisine and his strong ties to Lyon.

Cultural Impact

Gastronomy: Les Halles de Lyon-Paul Bocuse represents Lyon's status as the gastronomic capital of France. It embodies the city's culinary traditions and innovation.

Community Hub: The market serves as a meeting point for chefs, food enthusiasts, and local residents, fostering a sense of community through food.

Architectural Features

Exterior

Modern Design: The building features a sleek, modern design with large glass windows that provide a glimpse into the bustling market inside.

Signage: Prominent signage bearing Paul Bocuse's name and image welcomes visitors, emphasizing the market's connection to the famous chef.

Interior

Spacious Layout: Inside, the market is organized into wide aisles lined with stalls and shops, creating a lively and vibrant atmosphere.

Stalls and Shops: Over 50 stalls and shops offer a diverse range of products, including fresh produce, meats, seafood, cheeses, baked goods, and specialty items.

Top Things to Do

Explore the Market

Gourmet Foods: Sample gourmet foods, from freshly baked bread and pastries to fine chocolates and confectioneries.

Cheese Tasting: Try a variety of cheeses, including local specialties like Saint-Marcellin and Beaufort, from expert cheesemongers.

Charcuterie: Discover an array of cured meats, sausages, and pates from skilled charcutiers.

Dine at the Restaurants

On-Site Dining: Enjoy a meal at one of the market's many restaurants and bistros, which offer traditional Lyonnaise cuisine, fresh seafood, and other culinary delights.

Wine Tasting: Pair your meal with a selection of wines from the market's wine shops, featuring both local and international varieties.

Attend Culinary Events

Cooking Demonstrations: Participate in cooking demonstrations and workshops led by professional chefs, often showcasing seasonal ingredients and traditional recipes.

Food Festivals: Check for special events and food festivals that highlight different aspects of Lyon's culinary culture.

Guided Tours and Services

Guided Tours

Availability: Guided tours of Les Halles are available and offer an in-depth look at the market's history, vendors, and culinary offerings.

Booking: It's recommended to book guided tours in advance, especially during peak tourist seasons.

Visitor Services

Information Desk: An information desk is available to assist visitors with questions, provide maps, and offer recommendations for exploring the market.

Accessibility: The market is accessible to visitors with disabilities, with wide aisles and facilities designed for easy navigation.

Shopping Services

Packaging: Many vendors offer vacuum-sealing and packaging services for items purchased, making it easy for travelers to take their culinary treasures home.

Delivery: Some stalls provide delivery services for larger orders or fragile items.

Opening Hours and Admission

Opening Hours

General Hours: Les Halles de Lyon-Paul Bocuse is typically open from Tuesday to Saturday, 7:00 AM to 7:00 PM, and on Sundays from 7:00 AM to 1:00 PM. The market is closed on Mondays.

Special Hours: Hours may vary during holidays and special events, so it's advisable to check the market's website or contact the information desk for the latest information.

Admission

Free Entry: There is no admission fee to enter Les Halles. Visitors can freely explore the market and purchase items as they wish.

Event Fees: Some special events, workshops, or cooking classes may have associated fees.

Tips for Visiting

Plan Your Visit

Timing: Visit early in the day to avoid crowds and have the best selection of fresh produce and other goods.

Explore Thoroughly: Take your time to explore all the stalls and shops, as there are many hidden gems and unique products to discover.

Sampling and Purchasing

Ask for Samples: Don't hesitate to ask vendors for samples before making a purchase, especially for cheeses, charcuterie, and other specialty foods.

Buy Local Specialties: Look for local Lyonnaise specialties such as quenelles, praline tarts, and bouchons lyonnais (traditional sausages).

Dining

Try Local Cuisine: Make sure to try traditional Lyonnaise dishes at the on-site restaurants, such as coq au vin, andouillette, and pike quenelles.

Reserve a Table: If you plan to dine at one of the market's more popular restaurants, consider making a reservation in advance.

Combine with Other Attractions

Nearby Sites: Combine your visit to Les Halles with nearby attractions such as the Part-Dieu shopping center or the Auditorium Maurice Ravel.

Public Transport: The market is well-served by public transport, making it easy to visit as part of a larger itinerary exploring Lyon.

The Basilica of Saint-Martin d'Ainay is one of Lyon's most treasured historical and religious sites. Located in the Presqu'île district, this basilica is renowned for its rich history, architectural beauty, and cultural significance. Here's an extensive guide to help you explore and appreciate the Basilica of Saint-Martin d'Ainay.

Overview

Location

Address: 11 Rue Bourgelat, 69002 Lyon, France.

Setting: Situated in the heart of the Presqu'île district, the basilica is easily accessible and surrounded by a charming neighborhood with shops, cafes, and other historical sites.

Significance

Religious Importance: The Basilica of Saint-Martin d'Ainay is an important place of worship and pilgrimage, reflecting Lyon's deep-rooted Christian heritage.

Architectural Landmark: It is one of the finest examples of Romanesque architecture in Lyon, showcasing intricate design and craftsmanship.

Historical and Cultural Significance

Historical Background

Origins: The basilica was originally part of a Benedictine abbey founded in the 4th century. The current structure dates back to the 11th century, making it one of Lyon's oldest churches.

Evolution: Over the centuries, the basilica has undergone various modifications and restorations, reflecting the architectural and cultural developments of each period.

Cultural Impact

Heritage Site: The Basilica of Saint-Martin d'Ainay is classified as a Monument Historique, recognizing its significance in France's cultural and religious history.

Community Hub: The basilica continues to serve as a center for religious activities, community events, and cultural programs.

Architectural Features

Exterior

Romanesque Style: The basilica's exterior features classic Romanesque elements, including thick stone walls, rounded arches, and small windows.

Bell Tower: The prominent bell tower is a notable feature, offering a glimpse into the basilica's medieval origins.

Interior

Nave and Aisles: The interior of the basilica is characterized by a spacious nave flanked by side aisles, creating a sense of grandeur and solemnity.

Apse and Choir: The apse and choir are adorned with beautiful frescoes and mosaics, showcasing religious art from different periods.

Capitals and Columns: Intricately carved capitals and columns depict biblical scenes, flora, and fauna, demonstrating the artistry of medieval craftsmen.

Key Areas

Main Altar: The main altar is a focal point, often decorated with liturgical objects and flowers, especially during religious ceremonies.

Chapels: Several side chapels dedicated to various saints provide quiet spaces for prayer and reflection.

Top Things to Do

Explore the Architecture

Admire the Details: Take time to appreciate the intricate details of the Romanesque architecture, from the stone carvings to the frescoes and mosaics.

Photograph the Interior: Capture the beauty of the basilica's interior, especially the stained glass windows and the detailed capitals of the columns.

Attend a Service

Mass: Participate in or observe a Mass service to experience the spiritual atmosphere and the basilica's role as a place of worship.

Special Ceremonies: Check the schedule for special religious ceremonies, concerts, or cultural events that may be taking place during your visit.

Learn the History

Guided Tours: Join a guided tour to gain deeper insights into the basilica's history, architectural features, and religious significance.

Informational Displays: Look for informational displays and plaques throughout the basilica that provide historical context and explanations of the art and architecture.

Guided Tours and Services

Guided Tours

Availability: Guided tours are available and offer a comprehensive overview of the basilica's history, architecture, and cultural importance.

Booking: It is advisable to book guided tours in advance, especially during peak tourist seasons.

Visitor Services

Information Desk: An information desk is available to assist visitors with questions, provide brochures, and offer additional resources about the basilica and its history.

Accessibility: The basilica is accessible to visitors with disabilities, with ramps and designated areas for easy navigation.

Religious Services

Mass Schedule: Regular Mass services are held, and visitors are welcome to attend. Check the basilica's website or information desk for the current schedule.

Confessions: Confession services are available for those who wish to participate in this sacrament.

Opening Hours and Admission

Opening Hours

General Hours: The Basilica of Saint-Martin d'Ainay is typically open to visitors from Tuesday to Sunday, 9:00 AM to 6:00 PM. It is closed on Mondays.

Special Hours: Hours may vary during religious holidays and special events, so it's best to check the basilica's website or contact the information desk for the latest information.

Admission

Free Entry: Entry to the basilica is free, but donations are appreciated to help maintain the building and support its activities.

Special Events: Some special events or concerts may have associated fees.

Tips for Visiting

Plan Your Visit

Check the Schedule: Visit the basilica's website to check for any special events, services, or changes in opening hours before planning your visit.

Quiet Times: For a more peaceful experience, consider visiting during weekdays or early in the morning.

Respect the Sacred Space

Dress Code: Modest dress is recommended out of respect for the religious nature of the site. Shoulders and knees should be covered.

Conduct: Maintain a respectful demeanor, speak quietly, and avoid using flash photography, especially during services.

Combine with Nearby Attractions

Explore Presqu'île: The basilica is located in the vibrant Presqu'île district, so take time to explore the nearby shops, cafes, and other historical sites.

Visit Other Churches: Lyon has many beautiful churches and basilicas, including the nearby Saint-Nizier Church and the Basilica of Notre-Dame de Fourvière.

Photography and Conduct

Respectful Photography: Photography is generally allowed, but be mindful of other visitors and avoid disrupting religious services.

No Flash: Avoid using flash photography to preserve the integrity of the art and the serene atmosphere.

La Croix-Rousse

La Croix-Rousse is one of Lyon's most vibrant and historically rich neighborhoods, known for its unique character, stunning views, and deep-rooted silk weaving heritage. This guide provides an in-depth look at what makes La Croix-Rousse a must-visit destination for tourists.

Overview

Location

Setting: La Croix-Rousse is situated on a hill in the 4th arrondissement of Lyon, offering panoramic views of the city. It is divided into two main areas: the plateau (the top of the hill) and the pentes (the slopes leading down to the city center).

Significance

Historical Importance: Historically known as the center of Lyon's silk industry, La Croix-Rousse is often referred to as "the hill that works," in contrast to Fourvière, "the hill that prays."

Cultural Hub: Today, it is a lively area filled with markets, cafes, and cultural sites, reflecting both its industrial past and its modern bohemian vibe.

Historical and Cultural Significance

Historical Background

Silk Weaving: In the 19th century, La Croix-Rousse was the heart of Lyon's silk industry. The neighborhood was populated by canuts (silk workers) who worked in the tall, narrow buildings designed to accommodate their large looms.

Revolts: The canuts were known for their uprisings in the 1830s, fighting for better working conditions, which played a significant role in the social history of Lyon.

Cultural Impact

Artistic Community: Today, La Croix-Rousse is known for its artistic and alternative scene, with many artists, musicians, and creatives living and working in the area.

Cultural Events: The neighborhood hosts various cultural events and festivals throughout the year, celebrating its rich history and vibrant community.

Architectural Features

Buildings and Streets

Traboules: The famous traboules (hidden passageways) are a key feature of La Croix-Rousse. Originally used by silk workers to transport goods, these passages are a fascinating architectural and historical element.

Silk Workshops: Many of the buildings still have their original silk workshops, with high ceilings and large windows designed to accommodate the canuts' looms.

Public Spaces

Mur des Canuts: This large mural is a striking feature of the neighborhood, depicting the history and life of the canuts. It's one of the most famous trompe-l'œil (optical illusion) paintings in Lyon.

Place de la Croix-Rousse: The main square is a bustling hub of activity, especially on market days, and offers a variety of cafes and shops.

Top Things to Do

Explore the Markets

Marché de la Croix-Rousse: Held on the main boulevard, this market is one of the largest in Lyon, offering fresh produce, local specialties, and artisan goods.

Antique Market: On weekends, the area also hosts an antique market where you can find unique treasures and vintage items.

Visit Historical Sites

Traboules Tour: Take a guided tour of the traboules to learn about their history and see some of the most interesting passages.

Maison des Canuts: This museum offers insights into the history of silk weaving in Lyon, with demonstrations of traditional looms.

Enjoy the View

Panoramic Views: The top of La Croix-Rousse hill offers stunning panoramic views of Lyon and the surrounding area, perfect for photography and relaxation.

Guided Tours and Services

Guided Tours

Availability: Various guided tours are available, focusing on different aspects of La Croix-Rousse's history, architecture, and culture.

Booking: Tours can be booked through local tourism offices or online platforms. It's advisable to book in advance, especially during peak tourist seasons.

Visitor Services

Information Points: There are several information points and kiosks throughout the neighborhood where you can get maps, brochures, and advice on what to see and do.

Accessibility: While the steep slopes of La Croix-Rousse can be challenging, there are accessible routes and public transport options to help visitors navigate the area.

Opening Hours and Admission

Opening Hours

General Access: La Croix-Rousse is an open neighborhood with no specific opening hours. Shops, cafes, and markets generally follow standard business hours.

Museums and Tours: Specific sites like the Maison des Canuts have their own opening hours, typically from 10:00 AM to 6:00 PM, but it's best to check ahead for exact times.

Admission

Free Access: Walking through the neighborhood and exploring the traboules is generally free, though some guided tours and museums may charge an admission fee.

Event Fees: Certain cultural events or special exhibitions may have associated fees.

Tips for Visiting

Plan Your Visit

Comfortable Footwear: The hilly terrain and cobblestone streets of La Croix-Rousse can be demanding, so wear comfortable shoes suitable for walking.

Weather Considerations: Check the weather forecast and dress appropriately, as the area is best explored on foot.

Respect the Community

Local Etiquette: Be respectful of local residents, especially in quieter residential areas and when exploring traboules, as some are located within private properties.

Photography: Feel free to take photos, but be mindful of privacy, especially in residential areas and during local events.

Combine with Other Attractions

Nearby Sites: Combine your visit with other attractions in Lyon, such as the nearby Presqu'île district, the Basilica of Notre-Dame de Fourvière, and the Old Town (Vieux Lyon).

Public Transport: Utilize Lyon's public transport system, including the metro and buses, to easily access La Croix-Rousse and other parts of the city.

Quais de Saône

The Quais de Saône, or the banks of the Saône River, is one of Lyon's most scenic and culturally significant areas. Stretching along the river, these quays offer a blend of historical landmarks, picturesque views, and vibrant local life. This guide will provide you with everything you need to know about visiting the Quais de Saône.

Overview

Location

Setting: The Quais de Saône extend along the Saône River, running through the heart of Lyon. They cover a significant area, from the northern part of the city to the southern confluence with the Rhône River.

Significance

Historical Importance: The banks of the Saône have been central to Lyon's history, serving as major trade routes and settlement areas since Roman times.

Cultural Hub: Today, they are a popular destination for both locals and tourists, known for their beautiful promenades, historic architecture, and cultural activities.

Historical and Cultural Significance

Historical Background

Roman Era: The Saône River has been a critical part of Lyon since its founding as Lugdunum by the Romans. The river facilitated trade and transportation, contributing to the city's growth.

Medieval to Modern Times: Throughout the centuries, the banks of the Saône have seen various developments, including the construction of bridges, buildings, and cultural sites.

Cultural Impact

Living Heritage: The Quais de Saône are lined with historical buildings, churches, and museums, reflecting the rich cultural tapestry of Lyon.

Community Space: The quays are popular for leisure activities, including walking, cycling, and boating, fostering a vibrant community atmosphere.

Architectural Features

Buildings and Landmarks

Old Town (Vieux Lyon): Adjacent to the Quais de Saône, Vieux Lyon features Renaissance architecture and narrow cobblestone streets, offering a glimpse into Lyon's past.

Historic Churches: Several notable churches, such as Saint-Georges and Saint-Paul, are located along the quays, showcasing stunning architectural styles.

Bridges: Iconic bridges like the Passerelle Saint-Vincent and Pont Bonaparte connect the quays to different parts of the city, each with its own historical and architectural significance.

Public Spaces

Promenades: The well-maintained promenades along the quays provide scenic walking and cycling paths, with benches and green spaces for relaxation.

Parc des Hauteurs: Located nearby, this park offers elevated views of the Saône River and the surrounding area.

Top Things to Do

Explore the Promenades

Walking Tours: Take a leisurely stroll along the quays to enjoy the river views, historic buildings, and vibrant street life.

Cycling: Rent a bike and explore the extensive cycling paths that run along the river.

Visit Historical Sites

Basilica of Notre-Dame de Fourvière: Located on the hill overlooking the Saône, this basilica offers panoramic views of the quays and the city.

Musée Gadagne: This museum complex in Vieux Lyon includes the Museum of Lyon History and the Museum of Puppetry, providing insights into the city's past.

Enjoy Local Cuisine

Quai Saint-Antoine Market: Visit this bustling market to sample local produce, cheeses, meats, and other specialties.

Riverside Cafes and Restaurants: Dine at one of the many cafes and restaurants along the quays, offering everything from casual snacks to gourmet meals.

Guided Tours and Services

Guided Tours

Boat Tours: Several companies offer boat tours along the Saône River, providing a unique perspective of the quays and historical landmarks.

Walking Tours: Guided walking tours are available, focusing on different aspects of the quays' history, architecture, and cultural significance.

Visitor Services

Information Centers: Visitor information centers are located nearby, providing maps, brochures, and advice on exploring the area.

Accessibility: The promenades and major sites along the quays are generally accessible, with ramps and paths suitable for visitors with disabilities.

Opening Hours and Admission

General Access

Public Spaces: The promenades and public areas along the Quais de Saône are open 24/7, allowing for leisurely exploration at any time.

Market Hours: The Quai Saint-Antoine Market is typically open in the mornings and early afternoons, but hours may vary, so it's best to check in advance.

Admission

Free Access: Walking along the quays and exploring public spaces is free of charge. Some museums and attractions may have admission fees.

Event Fees: Special events, boat tours, and guided tours may require tickets or admission fees.

Tips for Visiting

Plan Your Visit

Check the Weather: Lyon's weather can vary, so check the forecast and dress appropriately, especially if you plan to spend a lot of time outdoors.

Peak Times: The quays can be busy during weekends and holidays. For a quieter experience, visit during weekdays or early in the morning.

Respect the Environment

Cleanliness: Help keep the quays clean by disposing of litter properly and respecting the natural surroundings.

Wildlife: Be mindful of local wildlife, particularly birds along the riverbanks.

Combine with Nearby Attractions

Old Town (Vieux Lyon): Combine your visit to the quays with a tour of Vieux Lyon, including its traboules, museums, and historic sites.

Fourvière Hill: Take the funicular up to Fourvière Hill for stunning views and a visit to the Basilica of Notre-Dame de Fourvière.

Safety and Conduct

Stay Safe: While the Quais de Saône are generally safe, be mindful of your belongings, especially in crowded areas.

Respect Local Customs: Lyonnais are known for their hospitality, but it's important to respect local customs and traditions, especially in historical and religious sites.

Parc des Hauteurs

Parc des Hauteurs is a unique urban park in Lyon that offers stunning views, historical pathways, and a serene environment. This guide provides detailed information to help visitors make the most of their experience at Parc des Hauteurs.

Overview

Location

Setting: Parc des Hauteurs is located on Fourvière Hill, in the 5th arrondissement of Lyon. It stretches from the Basilica of Notre-Dame de Fourvière to the Loyasse Cemetery, providing a green corridor along the hill.

Significance

Historical Importance: The park is built along the former ramparts of Lyon, with pathways that follow historical routes, offering insights into the city's past.

Cultural Hub: It connects several significant cultural and historical sites, making it an important area for both locals and tourists.

Historical and Cultural Significance

Historical Background

Ancient Fortifications: The park traces the line of the ancient city fortifications, offering a walk through Lyon's military history.

Pilgrimage Route: It includes parts of the traditional pilgrimage route to the Basilica of Notre-Dame de Fourvière.

Cultural Impact

Symbolic Pathways: The pathways, such as the Jardins du Rosaire and the Quatre Vents, are symbolic routes that connect religious and historical landmarks.

Art Installations: The park features various art installations that reflect Lyon's cultural heritage.

Architectural Features

Structures and Landmarks

Metal Bridge: This bridge provides a unique architectural feature and offers spectacular views of the city.

Loyasse Cemetery: An old cemetery with historical tombs and mausoleums, providing a quiet and reflective space within the park.

Natural Features

Terraced Gardens: The park's terraced layout offers beautifully landscaped gardens with a variety of plants and flowers.

Panoramic Views: Elevated points within the park provide some of the best panoramic views of Lyon, including vistas of the Rhône and Saône rivers.

Top Things to Do

Explore the Pathways

Jardins du Rosaire: This path leads from the basilica down to the old town, offering a scenic and peaceful walk.

Quatre Vents: A pathway that winds through the park, providing various viewpoints and resting spots.

Visit Historical Sites

Basilica of Notre-Dame de Fourvière: Start or end your visit at this iconic basilica, which is one of Lyon's most famous landmarks.

Loyasse Cemetery: Explore the historical cemetery, which offers insights into the city's past and notable figures.

Enjoy the Views

Metal Bridge: Walk across this bridge for unobstructed views of Lyon.

Lookout Points: Take in the cityscape from various lookout points throughout the park.

Guided Tours and Services

Guided Tours

Availability: Several guided tours are available that cover the historical and cultural significance of the park.

Booking: Tours can be booked through local tourism offices or online, providing detailed insights into the park's features.

Visitor Services

Information Centers: Visitor information centers near the basilica and other entry points provide maps, brochures, and assistance.

Accessibility: The park's main pathways are generally accessible, though some parts may be steep or uneven.

Opening Hours and Admission

Opening Hours

General Access: The park is open 24/7, allowing visitors to enjoy it at any time. However, specific sites like the basilica may have their own opening hours.

Admission

Free Access: Entry to the park is free. Some guided tours or special events may charge a fee.

Event Fees: Occasional cultural or historical events in the park may have associated costs.

Tips for Visiting

Plan Your Visit

Comfortable Footwear: Wear comfortable shoes suitable for walking, as the park includes various paths and some uneven terrain.

Weather Considerations: Check the weather forecast and dress appropriately, as the park is primarily outdoors.

Respect the Environment

Cleanliness: Help maintain the park's beauty by disposing of litter properly and respecting the natural surroundings.

Quiet Zones: Be mindful of quiet zones, especially near the Loyasse Cemetery and other reflective areas.

Combine with Nearby Attractions

Old Town (Vieux Lyon): Combine your visit with a tour of Vieux Lyon, which is easily accessible from the park.

Fourvière Hill: Explore other attractions on Fourvière Hill, including the Roman theaters and museums.

Safety and Conduct

Stay Safe: While the park is generally safe, be mindful of your belongings, especially in more secluded areas.

Respect Local Customs: Lyonnais are known for their hospitality, but it's important to respect local customs and traditions, especially in historical and religious sites.

Architectural Features

Structures and Landmarks

Metal Bridge: This bridge provides a unique architectural feature and offers spectacular views of the city.

Loyasse Cemetery: An old cemetery with historical tombs and mausoleums, providing a quiet and reflective space within the park.

Natural Features

Terraced Gardens: The park's terraced layout offers beautifully landscaped gardens with a variety of plants and flowers.

Panoramic Views: Elevated points within the park provide some of the best panoramic views of Lyon, including vistas of the Rhône and Saône rivers.

Chapter 6: Neighborhood of Lyon

Vieux Lyon (Old Lyon)

Vieux Lyon (Old Lyon) is a captivating and historically rich neighborhood that is a must-visit for anyone traveling to Lyon, France. As one of the best-preserved Renaissance districts in Europe, it offers a window into the city's medieval and Renaissance past. Here's an extensive look at what makes Vieux Lyon a standout destination:

Historical Significance

Historical Background:

Origins: Vieux Lyon is the old town of Lyon, which dates back to the Roman period. The district is located on the left bank of the Saône River and is renowned for its well-preserved Renaissance architecture.

Renaissance Influence: During the 15th and 16th centuries, Lyon became a major center for trade and finance. This period saw the construction of many of the beautiful Renaissance buildings that still stand today.

UNESCO World Heritage Site:

In 1998, Vieux Lyon was designated a UNESCO World Heritage Site as part of Lyon's historic center. This recognition underscores the area's architectural and historical importance.

Architectural Marvels

Renaissance Architecture:

Stunning Facades: The neighborhood is characterized by its narrow streets, colorful facades, and intricate details. Many buildings feature decorative plasterwork and wrought iron balconies.

Bouchons: These traditional Lyonnaise eateries are housed in historic buildings and offer a glimpse into the city's culinary history.

Notable Buildings:

Saint-Jean Cathedral: A prominent Gothic cathedral with stunning stained glass windows and an impressive astronomical clock.

Saint-Georges Church: A beautiful church located in the Place Saint-Georges, showcasing Gothic and Renaissance elements.

Saint-Paul Church: Known for its impressive Gothic architecture and serene interior.

Unique Features

Traboules:

Hidden Passageways: One of the most distinctive features of Vieux Lyon is its traboules—hidden passageways that connect the streets and courtyards. These were historically used by silk merchants to transport their goods and are now a fascinating part of the city's heritage.

Lyonnaise Cuisine:

Traditional Bouchons: Vieux Lyon is famous for its traditional Lyonnaise restaurants known as bouchons. These establishments serve local specialties such as quenelles, andouillette, and gratin dauphinois.

Food Tours: Many guided food tours are available, offering a chance to sample local delicacies and learn about Lyon's culinary traditions.

Cultural Experiences

Museums:

Gadagne Museum: Located in the Hôtel des Gadagne, this museum offers insights into Lyon's history and culture, including exhibits on the city's past and its role in the silk trade.

Musée Miniature et Cinéma: This museum features a fascinating collection of miniature scenes and movie props, showcasing the art of film and model-making.

Festivals and Events:

Festival of Lights: Held annually in December, the Festival of Lights is a spectacular event where the city is illuminated with artful light displays, attracting visitors from around the world.

Practical Information

Getting Around:

Walking: Vieux Lyon is best explored on foot, as the narrow, winding streets are often too tight for vehicles.

Public Transport: Lyon's public transport system, including buses and trams, provides easy access to and from Vieux Lyon.

Best Time to Visit:

Spring and Fall: The best times to visit are in the spring (April to June) and fall (September to October) when the weather is mild, and the crowds are smaller.

Christmas Season: Visiting during the Christmas season allows you to experience the Festival of Lights and the charming holiday atmosphere.

Presqu'île

The Presqu'île (literally "peninsula" in French) is another must-visit area in Lyon, located between the Rhône and Saône rivers. This vibrant district is known for its rich history, impressive architecture, and lively atmosphere. Here's a detailed exploration of what makes the Presqu'île a standout destination:

Historical and Geographical Context

Geographical Location:

Peninsula: As its name suggests, the Presqu'île is a peninsula formed by the confluence of the Rhône and Saône rivers. It stretches between the two rivers and is central to Lyon's urban layout.

Historical Development:

Urban Growth: The area became an important hub during the 19th century with the development of Lyon as a major economic and cultural center. The Presqu'île was transformed with the construction of grand boulevards, public squares, and elegant buildings during this period.

Architectural Highlights

Historical Buildings:

Place Bellecour: One of the largest public squares in Europe, Place Bellecour is a focal point of the Presqu'île. It features a statue of Louis XIV on horseback and is surrounded by impressive buildings and shops.

Place des Terreaux: Another significant square, Place des Terreaux is known for its grand architecture, including the Hôtel de Ville (City Hall) and the Palais Saint-Pierre. The square also features a magnificent Bartholdi Fountain.

Imposing Structures:

Lyon's City Hall (Hôtel de Ville): This grand building is a fine example of French Renaissance architecture. It houses the city's administrative offices and is renowned for its ornate façade and opulent interior.

Opera House (Opéra Nouvel): An architectural gem combining historic and contemporary elements. The building's façade features a blend of old and new design, with a glass dome that contrasts with the classical architecture.

Cultural and Shopping Districts

Shopping and Dining:

Rue de la République: This major shopping street is lined with elegant boutiques, department stores, and cafes. It's a bustling thoroughfare that offers a mix of high-end and mainstream retail options.

Les Halles de Lyon-Paul Bocuse: Located a short walk from the Presqu'île, this renowned indoor market showcases Lyon's culinary excellence. It offers a wide range of gourmet foods, including cheeses, charcuterie, and pastries.

Cultural Experiences:

Musée des Beaux-Arts: Located on Place des Terreaux, this museum houses one of France's largest and most impressive art collections. It features works from ancient Egypt to contemporary art.

Museum of Fine Arts: Renowned for its extensive collection of paintings, sculptures, and artifacts, including works by masters like Rembrandt and Monet.

Activities and Attractions

Walks and Tours:

Walking Tours: Exploring the Presqu'île on foot is a delightful experience, with its grand boulevards, picturesque squares, and historic buildings offering endless visual interest.

River Cruises: Consider taking a boat tour along the Rhône and Saône rivers to see the city from a different perspective.

Entertainment and Nightlife:

Cinemas and Theaters: The area is home to several theaters and cinemas, offering a range of cultural performances and film screenings.

Bars and Clubs: The Presqu'île boasts a vibrant nightlife with a variety of bars, clubs, and live music venues.

Practical Information

Accessibility:

Public Transport: The Presqu'île is well-served by Lyon's public transport system, including metro lines, trams, and buses. The Hôtel de Ville-Louis Pradel metro station is a major interchange.

Walking and Cycling: The area is pedestrian-friendly, with many attractions easily accessible on foot or by bicycle.

Best Time to Visit:

Spring and Summer: The Presqu'île is particularly lively during the spring and summer months when outdoor cafes and markets are in full swing.

Events and Festivals: Visiting during Lyon's major events, such as the Festival of Lights (Fête des Lumières) in December, offers a chance to experience the city's vibrant cultural scene.

La Croix-Rousse

La Croix-Rousse is a distinctive and culturally rich district in Lyon, known for its bohemian atmosphere, historical significance, and unique character. Situated on a hill to the north of the city center, it offers a different perspective on Lyon compared to the more tourist-centric areas like Vieux Lyon and the Presqu'île. Here's an in-depth look at what makes La Croix-Rousse a must-visit neighborhood:

Historical and Cultural Background

Historical Significance:

Silk Weaving Hub: La Croix-Rousse has a deep connection to Lyon's silk industry. During the 19th century, it became the center of silk production, with many "canuts" (silk weavers) living and working in the area. This history is still evident in the district's architecture and culture.

Bohemian Heritage:

Artistic Community: In the 20th century, La Croix-Rousse evolved into a vibrant, bohemian neighborhood known for its artistic and creative community. This legacy continues today with numerous artists, musicians, and craftspeople calling the area home.

Architectural and Historical Highlights

Traboules:

Hidden Passages: Like Vieux Lyon, La Croix-Rousse is home to traboules—hidden passageways that once facilitated the transport of silk. These passageways are less frequented by tourists but offer an intriguing glimpse into the district's industrial past.

Theatres and Cultural Venues:

Théâtre de la Croix-Rousse: An important cultural venue in the area, this theater hosts a variety of performances, including plays, music, and dance.

Key Attractions

La Croix-Rousse Market:

Local Market: The Croix-Rousse Market, held on Place de la Croix-Rousse, is a bustling and lively market known for its fresh produce, local cheeses, and other regional specialties. It's a great place to experience local life and sample some of Lyon's famous cuisine.

Mur des Canuts:

Wall Murals: The Mur des Canuts is a massive fresco located on the side of a building. It's one of the largest trompe-l'œil murals in Europe and depicts scenes from daily life in the district, celebrating its history and culture.

Maison des Canuts:

Silk Museum: This museum provides an in-depth look at the history of Lyon's silk industry. It features demonstrations of traditional weaving techniques and exhibitions about the life of the canuts.

Cultural and Artistic Vibe

Artistic Scene:

Galleries and Studios: La Croix-Rousse is home to many art galleries, studios, and workshops. Visitors can explore local art, crafts, and design, often finding unique pieces that reflect the district's creative spirit.

Street Art:

Murals and Graffiti: The area is also known for its vibrant street art. Walking through the streets, you'll encounter various murals and graffiti that add to the district's dynamic and eclectic atmosphere.

Practical Information

Getting Around:

Public Transport: La Croix-Rousse is well-connected by Lyon's public transport system, including metro and bus lines. The metro line C runs through the area, providing easy access to the city center.

Walking and Cycling: The district's hilly terrain offers some great walking and cycling opportunities, though be prepared for steep inclines.

Best Time to Visit:

Spring and Summer: The best times to visit La Croix-Rousse are during the spring and summer months when the weather is pleasant and outdoor markets and cultural events are in full swing.

Local Events: Check out local events and festivals that often take place in La Croix-Rousse, adding to the vibrant and lively atmosphere of the neighborhood.

Fourvière

Fourvière is a historically and culturally significant district in Lyon, renowned for its stunning views, rich history, and architectural marvels. Perched on a hill to the west of the city center, it offers a unique perspective on Lyon's past and present. Here's an extensive look at what makes Fourvière a must-visit area:

Historical and Cultural Background

Historical Significance:

Roman Roots: Fourvière's history dates back to Roman times. The area was known as Lugdunum, the Roman capital of Gaul, and several ancient ruins can still be explored today.

Religious Importance:

Religious Center: The district is named after the Latin term "Forum Verri," meaning "Verrius' Forum," and has been a significant religious site since the early days of Christianity in Lyon.

Key Attractions

Basilica of Notre-Dame de Fourvière:

Architectural Masterpiece: The Basilica of Notre-Dame de Fourvière is one of Lyon's most iconic landmarks. Built in the late 19th century in a neo-Byzantine style, it features intricate mosaics, stunning stained glass windows, and an ornate interior.

Panoramic Views: The basilica is situated on a hill, providing breathtaking panoramic views of Lyon and the surrounding area. The observation decks offer some of the best vantage points in the city.

Fourvière Roman Theaters:

Ancient Ruins: The Roman theaters in Fourvière are well-preserved remnants from Lyon's time as Lugdunum. The Grand Theater and the Odeon were once major entertainment venues and are still used for performances today.

Archaeological Site: The site also includes the remains of ancient temples, a triumphal arch, and other significant structures, offering a fascinating glimpse into Lyon's Roman past.

Gallo-Roman Museum of Lyon-Fourvière:

Museum of Antiquities: Located near the Roman theaters, this museum houses a comprehensive collection of artifacts from the Roman period, including sculptures, mosaics, and everyday items. It provides context and background to the archaeological sites.

Cultural Experiences

Festival of Lights (Fête des Lumières):

Annual Event: Held in December, this major festival transforms Lyon into a city of light with spectacular light displays and installations. Fourvière is one of the key locations for viewing these displays, especially around the basilica.

Local Festivals:

Cultural Events: Throughout the year, Fourvière hosts various cultural and religious festivals, adding to the vibrant atmosphere of the district.

Scenic and Leisure Activities

Parks and Gardens:

Parc des Hauteurs: A beautiful park offering pleasant walks and further views of the city. It's a great spot for relaxation and taking in the natural beauty of the area.

Jardin des Curiosités: Located near the basilica, this garden provides a peaceful setting with panoramic views of Lyon.

Walking Tours:

Historical Walks: Exploring Fourvière on foot allows you to appreciate its historical significance and stunning architecture. Guided tours are available and provide deeper insights into the area's past.

Practical Information

Getting Around:

Funicular: The Fourvière funicular is a convenient way to reach the basilica and Roman theaters from the city center. It provides a scenic ride and avoids the steep climb up the hill.

Public Transport: Several bus lines also serve the area, providing easy access from other parts of Lyon.

Best Time to Visit:

Spring and Fall: The best times to visit Fourvière are during the spring (April to June) and fall (September to October) when the weather is mild, and the views are particularly clear.

Festival Season: If you're in Lyon during the Festival of Lights in December, Fourvière is a prime location to experience the festivities.

Part-Dieu

Part-Dieu is a major business and commercial district in Lyon, located to the east of the city center. It's a bustling area known for its modern architecture, shopping centers, and transportation hub. Here's a detailed overview of what makes Part-Dieu an interesting and important part of Lyon:

Historical and Geographical Context

Development:

Modern District: Part-Dieu began to develop significantly in the 1960s and 1970s as part of Lyon's urban expansion. It was designed to be a major business district, with modern high-rise buildings and infrastructure.

Economic Hub: Over the decades, it has become one of Lyon's key economic areas, housing numerous businesses, offices, and commercial spaces.

Location:

East of Lyon: Part-Dieu is situated to the east of the city center, between the Rhône and Saône rivers. Its strategic location makes it a central point for both business and travel.

Key Attractions and Features

La Part-Dieu Shopping Center:

Large Mall: This is one of the largest shopping centers in Lyon and France. It features a wide range of shops, from high-end fashion boutiques to electronics stores, as well as a variety of restaurants and cafes.

Entertainment: The shopping center also includes a cinema complex, offering the latest films in a modern setting.

Tour Part-Dieu:

Iconic Skyscraper: Often referred to as the "Crayon" (pencil) due to its unique cylindrical shape, Tour Part-Dieu is a prominent landmark in the district. It's one of the tallest buildings in Lyon and offers impressive views of the city from its upper floors.

Gare Part-Dieu:

Major Train Station: This is one of Lyon's main railway stations, connecting the city to other major French cities and international destinations. It's a crucial transportation hub, with frequent trains to Paris, Marseille, and beyond.

Transportation Hub: The station also links to Lyon's metro and tram networks, providing easy access to other parts of the city.

Cultural and Leisure Activities

Cultural Institutions:

Musée Lumière: Located a short distance from Part-Dieu, this museum is dedicated to the Lumière brothers, pioneers of cinema. It offers exhibits on the history of film and the contributions of the Lumière family to the industry.

Parks and Green Spaces:

Parc de la Tête d'Or: A large and popular urban park located to the north of Part-Dieu. It features a lake, botanical gardens, and a zoo, providing a pleasant escape from the city's bustle.

Business and Events:

Conference Centers: Part-Dieu hosts several business and conference centers, making it a key location for corporate events, meetings, and exhibitions.

Practical Information

Getting Around:

Public Transport: Part-Dieu is well-connected by Lyon's public transport system, including the metro (Line B), trams, and buses. The Gare Part-Dieu also provides regional and national train services.

Cycling and Walking: The area is pedestrian-friendly and has facilities for cycling, making it easy to explore on foot or by bike.

Best Time to Visit:

Year-Round: Part-Dieu is a vibrant district throughout the year, but it's especially lively during the sales seasons in winter and summer, when the shopping center attracts many visitors.

Business Events: If you're visiting for business purposes, check the schedules of local conferences and events that might be taking place.

Confluence

Confluence is one of Lyon's most modern and rapidly developing districts, located at the confluence of the Rhône and Saône rivers. It's known for its innovative urban planning, contemporary architecture, and vibrant cultural scene. Here's an extensive overview of what makes Confluence a noteworthy destination:

Historical and Geographical Context

Urban Renewal:

Development: The Confluence district has undergone significant redevelopment since the early 2000s. It was once an industrial area and has been transformed into a cutting-edge urban space with a focus on sustainable development and modern living.

Vision: The redevelopment plan aimed to create a dynamic and eco-friendly urban environment, integrating residential, commercial, and recreational spaces.

Location:

Confluence of Rivers: Situated at the point where the Rhône and Saône rivers meet, the district offers unique waterfront views and has been designed to enhance the relationship between the city and its rivers.

Key Attractions and Features

Confluence Shopping Center:

Modern Mall: This contemporary shopping center is a central feature of the district, offering a range of shops, from high-end fashion to everyday essentials, as well as restaurants, cafes, and entertainment options.

Architectural Design: The mall itself is an architectural marvel, with a sleek, futuristic design that complements the district's modern aesthetic.

Musée des Confluences:

Science and Anthropology Museum: This striking museum is one of Lyon's architectural landmarks. Designed by architects Coop Himmelb(l)au, it features a unique, futuristic design with a "crystal" structure.

Exhibitions: The museum hosts a diverse range of exhibits, focusing on natural history, anthropology, and the history of science. Its engaging displays and interactive exhibits make it a great place for visitors of all ages.

La Sucrière:

Cultural Venue: Once a sugar factory, La Sucrière has been converted into a cultural space that hosts exhibitions, art shows, and events. It's a hub for contemporary art and creative projects.

Cultural and Recreational Activities

Riverfront Promenade:

Scenic Walks: The riverfront areas in Confluence are designed for leisure and relaxation, with pleasant promenades along both the Rhône and Saône rivers. It's a great place for a stroll, bike ride, or simply enjoying the views.

Outdoor Activities: The area also features green spaces and recreational areas where visitors can enjoy outdoor activities and events.

Architectural Tours:

Modern Design: Confluence is notable for its innovative architecture, including residential complexes, office buildings, and public spaces. Architectural tours can provide insight into the district's design philosophy and urban planning.

Practical Information

Getting Around:

Public Transport: Confluence is well-connected by Lyon's public transport system, including tram lines, buses, and metro stations. The district is easily accessible from other parts of Lyon.

Cycling: The area is also bike-friendly, with dedicated lanes and bike rental options available.

Best Time to Visit:

Year-Round: Confluence is vibrant throughout the year, but spring and summer are particularly pleasant for enjoying outdoor activities along the riverfront and exploring the district's green spaces.

Events: Check local event schedules for exhibitions, cultural events, and festivals that might be taking place in Confluence.

La Guillotière

La Guillotière is a vibrant and diverse district in Lyon, situated to the south of the city center. Known for its multicultural atmosphere and eclectic mix of old and new, La Guillotière offers a unique slice of Lyonese life. Here's an in-depth look at what makes La Guillotière an interesting and important area to visit:

Historical and Cultural Context

Historical Background:

Industrial and Working-Class Roots: La Guillotière developed as an industrial and working-class neighborhood in the 19th century. It has historically been a melting pot of different communities and cultures, which is reflected in its contemporary character.

Cultural Diversity:

Multicultural Atmosphere: Over the years, La Guillotière has become one of the most culturally diverse districts in Lyon. It is home to a variety of ethnic communities, contributing to a vibrant and multicultural atmosphere.

Key Attractions and Features

Place Gabriel Péri:

Central Square: This square is a focal point of the district, surrounded by a mix of shops, cafes, and eateries. It often hosts local events and markets, adding to the district's lively ambiance.

Rue de la République and Rue du Président Édouard Herriot:

Shopping and Dining: These streets are lined with a variety of shops, restaurants, and international food markets. The area offers a diverse range of dining options, reflecting the multicultural nature of the district.

Marché de la Guillotière:

Local Market: The market is a vibrant hub where you can find fresh produce, international foods, and various goods. It's an excellent place to experience the local and international flavors of the district.

Cultural Experiences

Multicultural Community:

Cultural Diversity: The district is known for its mix of cultures, including a significant presence of North African, Asian, and other international communities. This diversity is evident in the variety of restaurants, shops, and cultural events available in the area.

Art and Performances:

Local Arts Scene: La Guillotière is home to various cultural and artistic venues, including small galleries and performance spaces. The district hosts local art exhibitions, music performances, and other cultural events.

Recreational and Leisure Activities

Parks and Green Spaces:

Parc de la Tête d'Or: Located a short distance from La Guillotière, this large urban park offers green spaces, a lake, botanical gardens, and a zoo. It's a popular spot for relaxation and outdoor activities.

Local Parks: Within the district, there are smaller parks and green areas where residents and visitors can enjoy a break from the urban environment.

Walking Tours:

Exploring the Neighborhood: Walking through La Guillotière provides a chance to experience its eclectic mix of old and new architecture, bustling streets, and diverse cultural influences.

Practical Information

Getting Around:

Public Transport: La Guillotière is well-served by Lyon's public transport system, including metro lines (Line D), trams, and buses. This makes it easy to access from other parts of the city.

Cycling and Walking: The district is accessible on foot and by bike, with several bike lanes and pedestrian-friendly areas.

Best Time to Visit:

Year-Round: La Guillotière is lively throughout the year, but visiting in spring and summer can be particularly pleasant for exploring outdoor markets and enjoying local events.

Local Events: Check for local festivals, markets, and cultural events that might be taking place during your visit to experience the district's vibrant community spirit.

Chapter 7: Accommodation Options in Lyon

Luxury Hotels

For travelers seeking an exceptional stay in Lyon, luxury hotels offer unparalleled comfort and elegance. These high-end accommodations provide top-notch amenities, including gourmet dining, spa services, and stylish rooms with stunning city views. Located in prime areas, luxury hotels ensure a refined and memorable experience, perfect for those looking to enjoy the best of Lyon in style.

Top 5 Luxury Hotels

1. Villa Florentine

Villa Florentine is a distinguished luxury hotel in Lyon, renowned for its elegance and historic charm. Housed in a 17th-century former convent, the hotel combines historical architecture with contemporary comforts, making it an exceptional choice for travelers seeking an upscale experience. The property is celebrated for its sophisticated ambiance, stunning views, and impeccable service.

Location:

Address: 25 Montée Saint-Barthélemy, 69005 Lyon, France.

Proximity: Situated in the heart of Lyon's old town (Vieux Lyon), the hotel offers panoramic views of the city and the Saône River. It's conveniently close to major attractions such as Lyon Cathedral, the Basilica of Notre-Dame de Fourvière, and various museums. The location also provides easy access to public transport, including the metro and bus services.

Highlights:

Historic Charm: The hotel's design reflects its origins as a convent, featuring a blend of classic French architecture with modern luxury.

Stunning Views: Guests enjoy breathtaking vistas of Lyon from many rooms and public areas.

Exquisite Dining: The on-site restaurant offers gourmet French cuisine, complementing the luxurious experience.

Spa and Wellness:

Spa Facilities: The hotel boasts a luxurious spa and wellness center that includes a range of treatments such as massages, facials, and body therapies.

Wellness Amenities: Guests can also enjoy a sauna, steam room, and a well-equipped fitness center. The serene environment enhances relaxation and rejuvenation.

Bars:

Hotel Bar: The Villa Florentine features an elegant bar area where guests can enjoy a selection of fine wines, cocktails, and premium spirits. The bar's sophisticated atmosphere is perfect for unwinding after a day of exploring the city.

Events and Conferences:

Meeting Facilities: The hotel offers well-appointed meeting rooms and event spaces suitable for conferences, seminars, and private events.

Event Services: Professional event planning and catering services are available to ensure the success of business meetings and social gatherings.

Basic Facilities and Amenities:

Accommodation: The hotel provides a range of luxurious rooms and suites, each with refined decor and modern amenities.

Dining: In addition to the bar, the hotel features a high-end restaurant serving gourmet meals.

Other Amenities: Complimentary Wi-Fi, 24-hour room service, valet parking, and a concierge service are standard offerings.

Opening and Closing Hours:

Reception: Open 24/7.

Restaurant: Typically open for breakfast, lunch, and dinner. Hours may vary, so it's advisable to check in advance.

Bar: Generally open in the evening; exact hours can be confirmed with the hotel.

Price:

Room rates at Villa Florentine generally start at around €300 per night for a standard room. Prices can vary significantly based on the season, room type, and special offers. Suites and premium rooms are priced higher.

Pros:

Historical Elegance: The unique setting in a former convent adds a distinctive charm.

Prime Location: Central location offers easy access to Lyon's cultural and historical sites.

Exceptional Service: High level of personalized service and attention to detail.

Luxury Amenities: High-quality spa, fitness center, and gourmet dining.

Cons:

Price: The luxury nature of the hotel means it is on the higher end of the price spectrum, which might not be suitable for all budgets.

Limited Accessibility: The historic building may have some limitations in terms of accessibility for guests with mobility issues.

Local Tips:

Explore Vieux Lyon: Take time to wander around the old town area, known for its Renaissance architecture and charming narrow streets.

Try Local Cuisine: Lyon is renowned for its culinary scene, so don't miss out on tasting traditional dishes in nearby bouchons (local eateries).

Public Transport: Use the Lyon City Card for convenient access to public transport and discounts at various attractions.

Advance Booking: Reserve your dining and spa treatments in advance to ensure availability, especially during peak tourist seasons.

2. InterContinental Lyon - Hotel Dieu

The InterContinental Lyon - Hotel Dieu is a luxurious 5-star hotel situated in a historic building that has been a significant landmark in Lyon since the 17th century. Originally a hospital, the building has been meticulously restored to offer a unique blend of historic grandeur and modern elegance. The hotel is renowned for its opulent interiors, exceptional service, and prime location.

Location:

Address: 20 Quai Jules Courmont, 69002 Lyon, France.

Proximity: The hotel is located along the Rhône River, close to the heart of Lyon's business and cultural districts. It's within walking distance to attractions such as Place Bellecour, the Lyon Opera House, and the Museum of Fine Arts. The hotel is also well-connected by public transport, with nearby metro stations and bus stops.

Highlights:

Historic Significance: The building's rich history as a former hospital is evident in its stunning architecture and grand interiors.

Elegant Design: The hotel's design features a blend of classical and contemporary styles, including beautifully restored facades and luxurious interiors.

Gourmet Dining: The hotel offers top-notch dining experiences with its Michelin-starred restaurant and chic bar.

Spa and Wellness:

Spa Facilities: The hotel features a state-of-the-art spa and wellness center, including a range of treatments such as massages, facials, and wellness therapies.

Fitness Center: A modern fitness center is available for guests looking to maintain their workout routines during their stay.

Relaxation Areas: The wellness center also includes relaxation areas and a sauna to enhance the overall guest experience.

Bars:

Hotel Bar: The hotel boasts a stylish bar offering a selection of fine wines, cocktails, and premium beverages. It's an ideal spot for a sophisticated drink in a refined setting.

Events and Conferences:

Event Spaces: The InterContinental Lyon - Hotel Dieu provides a variety of event spaces, including grand ballrooms and intimate meeting rooms, perfect for conferences, weddings, and other gatherings.

Event Services: The hotel offers comprehensive event planning and catering services to ensure successful events, with professional staff available to assist with all aspects of event management.

Basic Facilities and Amenities:

Accommodation: The hotel offers a range of luxurious rooms and suites, featuring elegant decor, modern amenities, and stunning views of the city or the river.

Dining: In addition to the Michelin-starred restaurant, the hotel has a gourmet dining option and a chic bar.

Other Amenities: The hotel provides complimentary Wi-Fi, 24-hour room service, valet parking, and a concierge service to assist with various guest needs.

Opening and Closing Hours:

Reception: Open 24/7.

Restaurant: Typically open for breakfast, lunch, and dinner; hours may vary, so checking in advance is recommended.

Bar: Usually open in the evening; exact hours can be confirmed with the hotel.

Price:

Room rates at the InterContinental Lyon - Hotel Dieu start around €350 per night for standard accommodations. Prices can vary based on the season, room type, and availability. Suites and premium rooms are available at higher rates.

Pros:

Historic Setting: The unique historical building adds a significant cultural and architectural value to the stay.

Prime Location: Conveniently located near key attractions and with scenic views of the Rhône River.

Luxury Experience: High standard of luxury with exceptional service, dining, and wellness facilities.

Event Facilities: Excellent facilities and services for hosting various types of events.

Cons:

Cost: The luxury level of the hotel means it is on the higher end of the pricing spectrum, which may not fit all budgets.

Busy Area: The central location might mean more foot traffic and noise compared to more secluded hotels.

Local Tips:

Explore the Presqu'île: Take time to wander around the Presqu'île district, known for its shopping, dining, and historical landmarks.

Visit Local Markets: Lyon is famous for its markets, such as the Les Halles de Lyon Paul Bocuse, which is a must-visit for food enthusiasts.

River Cruises: Consider taking a river cruise along the Rhône or Saône for a different perspective of the city.

Cultural Experiences: Don't miss out on visiting Lyon's numerous museums and galleries, as well as its vibrant cultural scene.

3. Cour des Loges

Cour des Loges is a prestigious 5-star hotel located in the heart of Lyon's Vieux Lyon (Old Lyon) district. Renowned for its unique blend of Renaissance architecture and modern luxury, this boutique hotel provides an opulent and intimate experience. It occupies a historic building with richly decorated interiors, offering guests a distinctive and charming stay.

Location:

Address: 6 Rue de l'Ancienne Préfecture, 69002 Lyon, France.

Proximity: Situated in the historic center of Lyon, the hotel is within walking distance of major attractions such as Lyon Cathedral, the Basilica of Notre-Dame de Fourvière, and the Museum of Fine Arts. The area is known for its picturesque streets and historic charm, providing guests with easy access to local restaurants, shops, and cultural sites. Public transport options, including metro and bus services, are nearby.

Highlights:

Architectural Beauty: The hotel's design features a stunning Renaissance facade and a beautifully restored interior with ornate decorations, including exposed wooden beams and stone walls.

Intimate Atmosphere: The boutique nature of the hotel offers a more personalized and cozy atmosphere compared to larger establishments.

Exceptional Dining: Cour des Loges boasts a renowned restaurant, which provides gourmet dining in an elegant setting.

Spa and Wellness:

Spa Facilities: The hotel features a luxurious spa offering a range of treatments, including massages, facials, and body treatments designed to rejuvenate and relax guests.

Wellness Amenities: A well-equipped fitness center is also available for guests who wish to maintain their exercise routines.

Relaxation Spaces: The spa includes relaxation areas such as a sauna and a steam room.

Bars:

Hotel Bar: Cour des Loges has a sophisticated bar where guests can enjoy a selection of fine wines, cocktails, and other beverages in a refined environment. It's an excellent place for unwinding after a day of exploring the city.

Events and Conferences:

Meeting Facilities: The hotel offers elegant meeting rooms and event spaces suitable for conferences, seminars, and private events.

Event Services: Professional event planning and catering services are available to ensure the smooth execution of various events, with a focus on personalized service and attention to detail.

Basic Facilities and Amenities:

Accommodation: The hotel offers a range of luxurious rooms and suites, each featuring a unique design and high-quality furnishings.

Dining: In addition to the bar, the hotel has a Michelin-starred restaurant known for its exquisite French cuisine.

Other Amenities: Complimentary Wi-Fi, 24-hour room service, concierge services, and valet parking are among the standard offerings.

Opening and Closing Hours:

Reception: Open 24/7.

Restaurant: Typically open for breakfast, lunch, and dinner; specific hours may vary, so checking with the hotel is advisable.

Bar: Usually open in the evening; exact hours can be confirmed with the hotel.

Price:

Room rates at Cour des Loges generally start around €250 to €350 per night for standard rooms. Prices can fluctuate based on the season, room type, and any special promotions. Suites and more luxurious rooms are priced higher.

Pros:

Historic Charm: The blend of Renaissance architecture and modern luxury creates a unique and charming atmosphere.

Prime Location: The central location in Vieux Lyon provides easy access to historic sites, dining, and shopping.

Personalized Service: The boutique nature of the hotel allows for a more personalized guest experience.

Exceptional Dining and Spa: High-quality dining and spa services enhance the overall luxury experience.

Cons:

Cost: The luxury level of the hotel places it in the higher price range, which might not suit all budgets.

Limited Accessibility: The historic nature of the building may present challenges for guests with mobility issues.

Local Tips:

Explore Vieux Lyon: Take time to explore the charming streets of Vieux Lyon, which are filled with historical architecture, quaint shops, and local eateries.

Try Local Bouchons: Experience Lyon's renowned culinary scene by dining at traditional bouchons, which offer local specialties.

Visit the Croix-Rousse: Explore the nearby Croix-Rousse district, known for its vibrant market and bohemian atmosphere.

Public Transport: Use the Lyon City Card for convenient access to public transportation and discounts at various attractions.

4. **Les Loges de Saint-Dominique**

Les Loges de Saint-Dominique is a charming boutique hotel nestled in the historic and picturesque district of Vieux Lyon. Known for its warm and welcoming atmosphere, this hotel provides a more intimate and personalized experience compared to larger establishments. It's perfect for travelers seeking a unique stay with a blend of modern amenities and historical charm.

Location:

Address: 1 Rue Saint-Dominique, 69005 Lyon, France.

Proximity: Located in the heart of Vieux Lyon, the hotel offers easy access to many of the city's historic and cultural attractions. Notable sites like Lyon Cathedral, the Basilica of Notre-Dame de Fourvière, and the Lyon Museum of Fine Arts are all within walking distance. The area is also known for its quaint shops, local eateries, and charming streets.

Highlights:

Historic Character: The hotel's building reflects the traditional architecture of Lyon's old town, with well-preserved details and a unique character.

Boutique Experience: The small size of the hotel allows for a more personalized and cozy atmosphere, with attentive service and attention to detail.

Comfortable Accommodations: Rooms are designed to provide a blend of modern comfort and historic charm, creating a relaxing retreat for guests.

Spa and Wellness:

Spa Facilities: While Les Loges de Saint-Dominique may not have a full-service spa, it offers a range of wellness amenities. Guests can often enjoy relaxing features such as a small wellness area or access to nearby spa facilities.

Fitness: The hotel may provide recommendations for nearby fitness centers or wellness options for guests looking to maintain their exercise routine.

Bars:

On-site Bar: The hotel may feature a small bar or lounge area where guests can enjoy a selection of beverages in a cozy setting. This is typically a more relaxed and intimate space compared to larger hotel bars.

Events and Conferences:

Meeting Facilities: Les Loges de Saint-Dominique is a boutique hotel with a focus on personal service rather than large-scale events. For business meetings or smaller gatherings, the hotel may offer a comfortable and intimate setting, though more extensive conference facilities may not be available.

Event Services: The hotel may assist with planning small events or provide recommendations for nearby venues suitable for larger gatherings.

Basic Facilities and Amenities:

Accommodation: The hotel offers a selection of well-appointed rooms that blend historic charm with modern amenities. Each room is designed to be comfortable and inviting.

Dining: The hotel may provide breakfast services, and there are numerous dining options nearby where guests can experience local cuisine.

Other Amenities: Basic amenities include complimentary Wi-Fi, 24-hour reception, and concierge services to assist with local recommendations and bookings.

Opening and Closing Hours:

Reception: Typically open throughout the day, but specific hours may vary, so it's best to confirm directly with the hotel.

Bar: Hours of operation for any on-site bar or lounge area can be confirmed with the hotel.

Price:

Room rates at Les Loges de Saint-Dominique generally start around €150 to €250 per night. Prices may vary depending on the season, room type, and availability. Special offers or packages may also be available.

Pros:

Charming Location: Located in the historic Vieux Lyon district, providing a picturesque and culturally rich environment.

Boutique Atmosphere: Offers a personalized and cozy experience, ideal for travelers seeking a more intimate stay.

Comfortable Rooms: Rooms are designed to combine historic charm with modern comforts.

Cons:

Limited Facilities: As a boutique hotel, it may lack some of the extensive facilities found in larger luxury hotels, such as a full-service spa or extensive event spaces.

Smaller Size: The small size of the hotel might mean fewer amenities and services compared to larger establishments.

Local Tips:

Explore the Old Town: Wander through the narrow streets of Vieux Lyon to discover hidden gems, including local shops, historic buildings, and charming cafes.

Try Local Specialties: Don't miss out on sampling Lyon's famous cuisine at nearby bouchons or other local restaurants.

Visit Key Attractions: Take time to explore nearby attractions such as the Basilica of Notre-Dame de Fourvière and the Lyon Cathedral.

Use Public Transport: Utilize public transport or the Lyon City Card for easy access to various attractions and discounts.

5. Maison Nô

Maison Nô is a chic boutique hotel located in Lyon, offering a blend of modern design and comfort. Known for its contemporary aesthetics and personalized service, Maison Nô provides a stylish retreat in the city center, making it ideal for both leisure and business travelers seeking a unique and sophisticated experience.

Location:

Address: 9 Rue d'Amboise, 69002 Lyon, France.

Proximity: Maison Nô is situated in the Presqu'île district, a central and vibrant area of Lyon. It is close to major attractions such as Place Bellecour, the Lyon Opera House, and the Museum of Fine Arts. The hotel's central location provides easy access to shopping, dining, and cultural experiences. Public transportation options, including metro and bus services, are readily available.

Highlights:

Modern Design: The hotel features a contemporary design with stylish decor, creating a trendy and comfortable environment for guests.

Central Location: Positioned in a prime area, Maison Nô offers easy access to Lyon's main attractions, shopping, and dining.

Personalized Service: Known for its attentive and friendly service, ensuring a memorable stay for each guest.

Spa and Wellness:

Spa Facilities: Maison Nô offers a small wellness area with basic relaxation amenities. For a more extensive spa experience, guests can seek out nearby spa facilities.

Fitness Center: The hotel may provide access to a fitness center or offer recommendations for nearby gyms to help guests maintain their fitness routines.

Bars:

Hotel Bar: The hotel features a stylish bar area where guests can enjoy a selection of cocktails, wines, and other beverages. The bar's modern design and relaxed atmosphere make it a great place to unwind.

Events and Conferences:

Meeting Facilities: Maison Nô is a boutique hotel with a focus on personal service and comfort. It may offer small meeting rooms or event spaces for business meetings or private gatherings. For larger events, the hotel may provide recommendations for nearby venues.

Event Services: The hotel staff can assist with planning and organizing small events, ensuring a tailored and successful experience.

Basic Facilities and Amenities:

Accommodation: The hotel offers a range of stylish and well-appointed rooms, featuring modern amenities and chic decor.

Dining: While the hotel may not have a full-service restaurant, it typically offers a breakfast service. There are numerous dining options in the surrounding area, providing guests with a variety of culinary choices.

Other Amenities: Standard amenities include complimentary Wi-Fi, 24-hour reception, and concierge services to assist with local recommendations and bookings.

Opening and Closing Hours:

Reception: Open 24/7.

Bar: Generally open in the evening; specific hours can be confirmed with the hotel.

Price:

Room rates at Maison Nô typically start around €150 to €200 per night. Prices may vary based on the season, room type, and availability. Special offers or packages might be available.

Pros:

Contemporary Design: Modern and stylish interiors create a trendy and comfortable atmosphere.

Central Location: Conveniently located in the heart of Lyon, offering easy access to attractions, dining, and shopping.

Personalized Service: Attentive and friendly service ensures a pleasant and memorable stay.

Chic Bar: The stylish bar provides a great space for relaxation and socializing.

Cons:

Limited Spa Facilities: The hotel's wellness options are more basic compared to larger hotels with extensive spa services.

Dining Options: Limited in-house dining options may require guests to explore the nearby area for meals.

Local Tips:

Explore the Presqu'île: Take advantage of the hotel's central location to explore the vibrant Presqu'île district, known for its shopping, dining, and cultural attractions.

Try Local Cuisine: Lyon is famous for its gastronomy, so be sure to visit local bouchons and restaurants to sample traditional dishes.

Visit Key Attractions: Make time to visit nearby landmarks such as Place Bellecour, the Lyon Opera House, and the Museum of Fine Arts.

Use the Lyon City Card for convenient access to public transportation and discounts on various attractions.

Mid-Range Hotels

Mid-range hotels in Lyon offer a perfect balance of comfort, quality, and affordability for tourists. These accommodations provide well-appointed rooms, convenient amenities, and a pleasant stay without the high costs of luxury options. Located throughout the city, they offer easy access to key attractions, dining, and public transport, making them an excellent choice for travelers seeking a comfortable and budget-friendly option during their visit to Lyon.

Top 5 Mid-Range Hotels

1. **Hôtel des Artistes**

Hôtel des Artistes provides a welcoming atmosphere with a focus on personalized service and stylish accommodations. The hotel's name reflects its commitment to celebrating the artistic heritage of Lyon, with decor and services designed to enhance guests' experience in this culturally rich city.

Location

Address: 8 Rue Gaspard André, 69002 Lyon, France

Proximity:

Place Bellecour: 10-minute walk – One of Lyon's most famous squares and a central hub for shopping and dining.

Vieux Lyon: 15-minute walk – The historic district with Renaissance architecture and cultural attractions.

Lyon Part-Dieu Train Station: 10-minute drive – Major transportation hub with connections to other French cities and international destinations.

Lyon-Saint Exupéry Airport: 30-minute drive – Convenient for international travelers arriving by air.

Highlights

Artistic Decor: The hotel features art-inspired decor that reflects Lyon's rich artistic heritage.

Comfortable Rooms: Rooms are well-furnished with modern amenities, providing a cozy and relaxing environment.

Central Location: Located in the heart of Lyon, the hotel offers easy access to major attractions, restaurants, and shopping areas.

Spa and Wellness

Spa Services: Hôtel des Artistes does not have an on-site spa, but guests can access nearby wellness facilities and spa services through partnerships with local establishments.

Fitness: The hotel does not have a fitness center, but nearby gyms and wellness centers are available for guest use.

Bars

On-Site Bar: The hotel features a stylish bar where guests can enjoy a range of beverages in a relaxed setting.

Nearby Options: The central location means guests have easy access to various bars and cafes in the vicinity, offering a diverse range of dining and drinking experiences.

Events and Conferences

Event Spaces: The hotel does not have dedicated conference or event spaces. However, it can accommodate small meetings or private gatherings upon request.

Nearby Venues: For larger events or conferences, there are several nearby venues and business centers that guests can utilize.

Basic Facilities and Amenities

Wi-Fi: Complimentary high-speed internet is available throughout the hotel.

Breakfast: A daily continental breakfast is offered, featuring a selection of pastries, fruits, and beverages.

Room Features: Rooms come equipped with air conditioning, flat-screen TVs, minibars, and in-room safes.

Reception: 24-hour front desk service ensures that guests' needs are met around the clock.

Laundry: Laundry and dry-cleaning services are available for an additional fee.

Opening and Closing Hours

Check-In: 2:00 PM

Check-Out: 11:00 AM

Bar Hours: Typically open from early morning until late evening, but hours may vary.

Price

Average Rate: Prices for a standard double room typically range from €120 to €180 per night, depending on the season and booking conditions. Rates may vary based on room type and booking channel.

Pros

Prime Location: Close to key attractions, dining options, and shopping areas.

Artistic Ambiance: Decor and atmosphere reflect Lyon's artistic heritage, enhancing the cultural experience.

Comfortable Rooms: Well-appointed rooms with modern amenities and a cozy environment.

Personalized Service: Friendly and attentive staff committed to providing a pleasant stay.

Cons

No On-Site Spa: Lack of a dedicated spa or wellness center may be a drawback for guests seeking relaxation and spa treatments.

Limited Event Facilities: The hotel does not offer extensive conference or event facilities, which may be a limitation for business travelers with larger needs.

Small Fitness Options: Absence of an on-site fitness center requires guests to seek alternative fitness options.

Local Tips

Explore Vieux Lyon: Take a leisurely stroll through the historic district of Vieux Lyon, known for its Renaissance architecture and charming traboules.

Visit Place Bellecour: Spend some time at Place Bellecour, where you can enjoy shopping, dining, and people-watching in one of Lyon's most iconic squares.

Try Local Cuisine: Don't miss out on dining at local bouchons to experience traditional Lyonnaise cuisine, including specialties like quenelles and coq au vin.

Public Transport: Utilize Lyon's efficient public transport system, including trams and buses, to explore the city beyond the immediate neighborhood.

2. Hôtel la Résidence

Hôtel la Résidence is known for its cozy atmosphere and practical amenities, making it a great choice for both short and extended stays. The hotel emphasizes a friendly service and strives to make guests feel at home while they explore Lyon.

Location

Address: 1 Avenue de la République, 69002 Lyon, France

Proximity:

Place Bellecour: Approximately a 10-minute walk – A major square and shopping hub in Lyon.

Vieux Lyon: Around a 15-minute walk – The historic district with medieval and Renaissance architecture.

Lyon Part-Dieu Train Station: About a 15-minute drive – Key transportation link for national and international travel.

Lyon-Saint Exupéry Airport: Roughly a 30-minute drive – Convenient for travelers arriving by air.

Highlights

Central Location: Positioned in a prime area, providing easy access to Lyon's major attractions, dining, and shopping.

Comfortable Rooms: Offers well-furnished rooms designed to ensure a restful stay.

Affordability: Provides mid-range pricing, offering good value for money in a central location.

Spa and Wellness

On-Site Spa: The hotel does not feature an on-site spa. Guests seeking wellness treatments can find nearby options.

Fitness: The hotel does not have a fitness center. Visitors can access local gyms or fitness facilities.

Bars

On-Site Bar: The hotel does not have a bar. However, the central location means there are numerous bars and cafes within walking distance where guests can enjoy drinks and socialize.

Events and Conferences

Event Spaces: Hôtel la Résidence does not have dedicated conference or event spaces. For business meetings or events, guests will need to use external venues or facilities in the vicinity.

Nearby Venues: There are several conference centers and meeting venues nearby that can accommodate larger events.

Basic Facilities and Amenities

Wi-Fi: Free high-speed internet is available throughout the hotel.

Breakfast: A continental breakfast is offered daily, featuring a selection of pastries, fruits, and beverages.

Room Features: Rooms are equipped with air conditioning, flat-screen TVs, work desks, and in-room safes.

Reception: The front desk operates 24/7 to assist with guest needs.

Laundry: Laundry and dry-cleaning services are available for an additional charge.

Opening and Closing Hours

Check-In: 3:00 PM

Check-Out: 11:00 AM

Breakfast: Typically served from 7:00 AM to 10:00 AM, but times may vary.

Price

Average Rate: Rates for a standard double room generally range from €80 to €120 per night, depending on the season and availability. Pricing can vary based on room type and booking method.

Pros

Central Location: Close to major attractions, shopping areas, and dining options.

Comfortable Accommodation: Provides a cozy and pleasant stay with essential amenities.

Affordable Rates: Offers good value for money in a prime location.

Friendly Service: Known for its welcoming and helpful staff.

Cons

No On-Site Bar or Restaurant: Lack of on-site dining options may be a drawback for guests looking for convenience.

No Spa or Fitness Center: Absence of wellness facilities means guests need to find alternatives nearby.

Basic Facilities: May not offer some of the more luxurious amenities found in higher-end hotels.

Local Tips

Explore Local Dining: Take advantage of the nearby dining options to sample Lyon's renowned cuisine.

Public Transport: Utilize the city's efficient public transport system to explore beyond the immediate neighborhood.

Visit Place Bellecour: Enjoy shopping and leisure activities in this central square, one of Lyon's major landmarks.

Discover Vieux Lyon: Explore the historic district of Vieux Lyon, with its Renaissance architecture and charming streets.

3. Hôtel Mercure Lyon Centre Beaux Arts

Hôtel Mercure Lyon Centre Beaux Arts is part of the global Mercure hotel chain and provides a blend of contemporary amenities with a touch of local character. The hotel's central location and well-appointed rooms make it a favored choice for both leisure and business travelers.

Location

Address: 73 Rue du Président Édouard Herriot, 69002 Lyon, France

Proximity:

Place Bellecour: About a 10-minute walk – One of Lyon's main squares, known for its shopping and dining options.

Vieux Lyon: Approximately a 15-minute walk – The historic district famous for its Renaissance architecture.

Lyon Part-Dieu Train Station: Roughly a 15-minute drive – Major transportation hub connecting to various destinations.

Lyon-Saint Exupéry Airport: Around a 30-minute drive – Convenient for international and domestic flights.

Highlights

Central Location: Positioned in Lyon's city center, providing easy access to key attractions, shopping, and restaurants.

Elegant Design: Combines modern amenities with classic decor, reflecting Lyon's sophisticated style.

Comfortable Rooms: Offers well-furnished rooms designed for relaxation and convenience.

Spa and Wellness

On-Site Spa: The hotel does not feature a dedicated spa. However, guests can access nearby wellness centers and spas for relaxation treatments.

Fitness Center: The hotel includes a small fitness center for guests looking to stay active during their stay.

Bars

On-Site Bar: The hotel features a stylish bar where guests can unwind with a variety of drinks in a relaxed atmosphere. It's a great place to enjoy a cocktail or a light snack.

Events and Conferences

Meeting Rooms: Hôtel Mercure Lyon Centre Beaux Arts provides several meeting rooms equipped with modern technology, making it suitable for business meetings and small conferences.

Event Services: The hotel's event spaces can be customized to fit different types of gatherings, from corporate meetings to social events.

Basic Facilities and Amenities

Wi-Fi: Complimentary high-speed internet is available throughout the hotel.

Breakfast: A generous buffet breakfast is served daily, including a selection of hot and cold dishes.

Room Features: Rooms come with air conditioning, flat-screen TVs, minibars, work desks, and in-room safes.

Reception: The 24-hour front desk offers assistance with check-in, check-out, and any guest needs.

Laundry: Laundry and dry-cleaning services are available for an additional charge.

Opening and Closing Hours

Check-In: 2:00 PM

Check-Out: 12:00 PM

Breakfast: Typically served from 6:30 AM to 10:00 AM on weekdays and until 10:30 AM on weekends.

Price

Average Rate: Standard rates for a double room generally range from €130 to €200 per night, depending on the season, booking conditions, and room type. Prices may vary based on promotions and availability.

Pros

Prime Location: Centrally located with easy access to major attractions, shopping, and dining.

Elegant Ambiance: Stylish and comfortable rooms with a blend of modern and classic decor.

Business-Friendly: Equipped with meeting rooms and business services.

Friendly Service: Professional and attentive staff dedicated to providing a pleasant stay.

Cons

No On-Site Spa: The absence of an on-site spa might be a drawback for guests seeking extensive wellness treatments.

Price: Rates may be on the higher end of mid-range pricing, especially during peak seasons.

Limited Fitness Facilities: The fitness center is small and may not offer extensive workout options.

Local Tips

Explore the City Center: Take advantage of the hotel's central location to explore nearby attractions, such as the historic district of Vieux Lyon and the lively Place Bellecour.

Dine Locally: Enjoy Lyon's renowned gastronomy by dining at local restaurants and bouchons in the area.

Public Transport: Utilize the nearby public transport options, including trams and buses, to further explore Lyon and its surroundings.

Cultural Visits: Visit local museums and landmarks, such as the Musée des Beaux-Arts de Lyon and the Basilica of Notre-Dame de Fourvière, to immerse yourself in Lyon's rich cultural heritage.

4. Ibis Lyon Part Dieu Les Halles

Ibis Lyon Part Dieu Les Halles is part of the Ibis hotel chain, known for its consistent quality and value. This hotel provides modern accommodations and essential amenities, catering to both business and leisure travelers.

Location

Address: 78 Rue de Bonnel, 69003 Lyon, France

Proximity:

Part-Dieu Train Station: Approximately a 5-minute walk – A major transportation hub with connections to national and international destinations.

Place Bellecour: About a 10-minute drive or a 15-minute tram ride – Lyon's central square, ideal for shopping and dining.

Vieux Lyon: Roughly a 15-minute drive or 20-minute tram ride – The historic district known for its Renaissance architecture and traboules.

Lyon-Saint Exupéry Airport: Around a 30-minute drive – Convenient for travelers flying in or out of the city.

Highlights

Convenient Location: Situated in the Part-Dieu district, close to the train station and shopping centers.

Modern Comfort: Offers contemporary rooms designed for comfort and relaxation.

Affordability: Provides good value for money, making it an attractive option for budget-conscious travelers.

Spa and Wellness

On-Site Spa: The hotel does not feature an on-site spa. Guests looking for wellness treatments can explore nearby spa facilities.

Fitness: The hotel does not have a fitness center, but guests can find local gyms in the vicinity.

Bars

On-Site Bar: The hotel features a bar where guests can enjoy a variety of drinks and light snacks. It provides a casual and comfortable setting for relaxation.

Events and Conferences

Meeting Rooms: Ibis Lyon Part Dieu Les Halles does not have dedicated conference or event spaces. For larger meetings or events, guests may need to use external venues or facilities nearby.

Nearby Options: Several business centers and event venues are available in the Part-Dieu area.

Basic Facilities and Amenities

Wi-Fi: Complimentary high-speed internet is available throughout the hotel.

Breakfast: A buffet breakfast is served daily, featuring a selection of pastries, fruits, cold cuts, and beverages.

Room Features: Rooms include air conditioning, flat-screen TVs, work desks, and in-room safes.

Reception: The front desk operates 24/7 to assist with check-in, check-out, and guest inquiries.

Laundry: Laundry and dry-cleaning services are available for an additional charge.

Opening and Closing Hours

Check-In: 12:00 PM

Check-Out: 12:00 PM

Breakfast: Typically served from 6:30 AM to 10:00 AM on weekdays and until 10:30 AM on weekends.

Price

Average Rate: Rates for a standard double room typically range from €80 to €120 per night, depending on the season, availability, and booking conditions.

Pros

Prime Location: Close to Part-Dieu Train Station and shopping centers, with easy access to public transport.

Comfortable Rooms: Modern, well-maintained rooms that provide a pleasant stay.

Affordable Rates: Offers good value for money in a central location.

Friendly Service: Helpful and accommodating staff providing consistent service.

Cons

No On-Site Spa or Fitness Center: Lack of wellness facilities may be a downside for guests seeking relaxation and fitness options.

Basic Amenities: Limited additional features compared to higher-end hotels; may not offer the same level of luxury or services.

Limited Meeting Facilities: No dedicated conference or event spaces on-site.

Local Tips

Explore the Part-Dieu Area: Take advantage of the hotel's location by exploring the nearby shopping centers, such as the Part-Dieu Mall.

Visit Place Bellecour: Enjoy the vibrant atmosphere of Place Bellecour, with its shops, restaurants, and landmarks.

Discover Vieux Lyon: Spend some time in the historic Vieux Lyon district to experience its unique architecture and local culture.

Use Public Transport: Utilize the nearby tram and bus services to easily navigate the city and reach various attractions.

5. Hôtel du Simplon

Hôtel du Simplon stands out for its warm, traditional ambiance combined with modern comforts. Its friendly service and central location make it an attractive option for both leisure and business travelers visiting Lyon.

Location

Address: 49 Boulevard des Brotteaux, 69006 Lyon, France

Proximity:

Part-Dieu Train Station: About a 10-minute walk – A major transportation hub connecting to various destinations.

Parc de la Tête d'Or: Approximately a 5-minute walk – A large city park ideal for leisurely strolls and outdoor activities.

Place Bellecour: Around a 15-minute tram ride or 20-minute walk – A central square with shopping and dining options.

Vieux Lyon: About a 20-minute tram ride – The historic district known for its Renaissance architecture and traboules.

Highlights

Traditional Charm: Offers a blend of classic decor and modern amenities in a historic setting.

Comfortable Rooms: Provides well-furnished rooms designed for relaxation and comfort.

Proximity to Attractions: Located near key attractions like Parc de la Tête d'Or and the Part-Dieu area.

Spa and Wellness

On-Site Spa: Hôtel du Simplon does not have an on-site spa. However, guests can access nearby wellness centers and spas for relaxation and treatments.

Fitness: The hotel does not feature a fitness center, but there are local gyms and fitness facilities available for guests.

Bars

On-Site Bar: The hotel does not have an on-site bar. Guests can explore nearby cafes and bars within walking distance for a variety of drinks and light snacks.

Events and Conferences

Meeting Rooms: Hôtel du Simplon does not offer dedicated conference or event spaces. For business meetings or events, guests may need to use external venues or facilities nearby.

Nearby Venues: Several business centers and conference venues are located in the Part-Dieu area.

Basic Facilities and Amenities

Wi-Fi: Free high-speed internet is available throughout the hotel.

Breakfast: A continental breakfast is served daily, featuring a selection of pastries, fruits, cold cuts, and beverages.

Room Features: Rooms include air conditioning, flat-screen TVs, work desks, and in-room safes.

Reception: The front desk operates 24/7 to assist with guest needs.

Laundry: Laundry and dry-cleaning services are available for an additional fee.

Opening and Closing Hours

Check-In: 2:00 PM

Check-Out: 12:00 PM

Breakfast: Typically served from 7:00 AM to 10:00 AM, but times may vary.

Price

Average Rate: Rates for a standard double room generally range from €90 to €130 per night, depending on the season, availability, and room type.

Pros

Charming Atmosphere: Offers a blend of traditional decor and modern comfort, creating a pleasant and welcoming environment.

Proximity to Attractions: Close to Parc de la Tête d'Or and Part-Dieu, providing easy access to local attractions.

Comfortable Rooms: Well-maintained rooms designed for a relaxing stay.

Friendly Service: Known for its attentive and helpful staff.

Cons

No On-Site Bar or Restaurant: Absence of an on-site bar or dining options may be a limitation for some guests.

No Spa or Fitness Center: Lack of wellness facilities means guests need to seek alternatives nearby.

Limited Event Facilities: No dedicated conference or event spaces on-site.

Local Tips

Explore Parc de la Tête d'Or: Take advantage of the hotel's proximity to this expansive city park, ideal for walking, jogging, or picnicking.

Visit the Part-Dieu Area: Check out the nearby shopping centers and dining options in the Part-Dieu district.

Discover Vieux Lyon: Take a tram or leisurely stroll to the historic Vieux Lyon district to experience its rich cultural heritage and unique architecture.

Public Transport: Utilize nearby tram and bus services to explore other parts of the city easily.

Budget Hotels

Budget hotels in Lyon offer economical accommodation options for travelers looking to save on their stay. These hotels provide basic yet comfortable amenities, ideal for those who prioritize cost savings while still enjoying a convenient and practical base for exploring the city. They are typically well-located, offering easy access to Lyon's main attractions and public transportation.

Top 5 Budget Hotels

1. **Ibis Lyon Part Dieu Les Halles**

Ibis Lyon Part Dieu Les Halles is part of the global Ibis hotel chain, renowned for its consistent quality and value. The hotel provides clean, modern rooms and essential amenities, making it suitable for both business and leisure travelers.

Location

Address: 78 Rue de Bonnel, 69003 Lyon, France

Proximity:

Part-Dieu Train Station: About a 5-minute walk – A major transportation hub with connections to various national and international destinations.

Place Bellecour: Approximately a 10-minute drive or a 15-minute tram ride – Lyon's central square, known for its shopping, dining, and cultural attractions.

Vieux Lyon: Around a 15-minute drive or a 20-minute tram ride – The historic district featuring Renaissance architecture and traboules.

Parc de la Tête d'Or: About a 10-minute walk – A large city park ideal for outdoor activities and leisurely strolls.

Lyon-Saint Exupéry Airport: Roughly a 30-minute drive – Convenient for travelers arriving by air.

Highlights

Central Location: Close to Part-Dieu Train Station and shopping areas, providing easy access to transportation and local attractions.

Modern Rooms: Offers clean and functional rooms with contemporary decor.

Affordability: Provides budget-friendly pricing, making it an attractive option for cost-conscious travelers.

Spa and Wellness

On-Site Spa: The hotel does not feature an on-site spa. Guests interested in wellness treatments can find local spa facilities in the vicinity.

Fitness: The hotel does not have a fitness center. Guests may look for nearby gyms or fitness options if needed.

Bars

On-Site Bar: The hotel includes a bar where guests can enjoy a range of beverages in a relaxed setting. It's a convenient place to unwind after a day of exploring Lyon.

Events and Conferences

Meeting Rooms: Ibis Lyon Part Dieu Les Halles does not offer dedicated conference or event spaces. For meetings or larger events, guests may need to use external venues or business centers nearby.

Nearby Facilities: Several business centers and conference facilities are located within the Part-Dieu area, offering additional options for event spaces.

Basic Facilities and Amenities

Wi-Fi: Complimentary high-speed internet is available throughout the hotel.

Breakfast: A buffet breakfast is served daily, featuring a selection of pastries, fruits, cold cuts, and beverages.

Room Features: Rooms come equipped with air conditioning, flat-screen TVs, work desks, and in-room safes.

Reception: The front desk operates 24/7 to assist with guest needs and inquiries.

Laundry: Laundry and dry-cleaning services are available for an additional charge.

Opening and Closing Hours

Check-In: 12:00 PM

Check-Out: 12:00 PM

Breakfast: Typically served from 6:30 AM to 10:00 AM on weekdays and until 10:30 AM on weekends.

Price

Average Rate: Rates for a standard double room typically range from €80 to €120 per night, depending on the season, availability, and booking conditions.

Pros

Convenient Location: Close to major transportation links, shopping, and dining options.

Affordable: Provides good value for money with competitive rates in a central area.

Modern and Clean: Offers contemporary and well-maintained rooms.

Friendly Service: Known for its helpful and attentive staff.

Cons

No On-Site Spa or Fitness Center: Absence of wellness facilities may be a drawback for guests seeking relaxation or fitness options.

Basic Amenities: Limited additional features compared to higher-end hotels; may not offer luxury amenities.

Limited Meeting Facilities: No dedicated conference or event spaces on-site.

Local Tips

Explore Parc de la Tête d'Or: Take advantage of the hotel's proximity to this large park for outdoor activities, picnicking, or a relaxing stroll.

Visit Place Bellecour: Enjoy shopping, dining, and sightseeing in Lyon's central square, easily accessible by tram or a short drive.

Discover Vieux Lyon: Take a tram or a short drive to the historic district to experience its unique architecture and cultural heritage.

Public Transport: Utilize the nearby tram and bus services to navigate the city efficiently and explore other attractions.

2. Hôtel Ibis Budget Lyon Confluence

Hôtel Ibis Budget Lyon Confluence is part of the Ibis Budget chain, known for its affordable and straightforward accommodations. The hotel offers essential amenities in a no-frills setting, focusing on delivering value for money in a central location.

Location

Address: 31 Cours de Verdun, 69002 Lyon, France

Proximity:

Lyon-Perrache Train Station: Approximately a 10-minute walk – A major transport hub with connections to various destinations within France and beyond.

Confluence Museum: About a 15-minute walk – An innovative museum offering exhibitions on science and anthropology.

Place Bellecour: Around a 10-minute tram ride – Lyon's central square, ideal for shopping, dining, and exploring.

Vieux Lyon: Roughly a 20-minute tram ride – The historic district known for its Renaissance buildings and traboules.

Parc de la Tête d'Or: About a 20-minute drive or 30 minutes by public transport – A large city park perfect for outdoor activities.

Highlights

Budget-Friendly: Offers economical rates, making it a great choice for travelers on a budget.

Central Location: Situated in the Confluence district, providing easy access to key attractions and public transportation.

Modern Rooms: Provides functional and clean accommodations with basic amenities.

Spa and Wellness

On-Site Spa: The hotel does not have an on-site spa. Guests seeking wellness treatments can explore nearby spa facilities in the Confluence area.

Fitness: No fitness center is available at the hotel; however, local gyms and fitness centers are accessible nearby.

Bars

On-Site Bar: The hotel does not feature a bar. Guests can visit nearby cafes and bars in the Confluence district for drinks and light refreshments.

Events and Conferences

Meeting Rooms: Hôtel Ibis Budget Lyon Confluence does not offer dedicated conference or event spaces. For business meetings or events, guests will need to utilize external venues in the area.

Nearby Facilities: Business centers and event spaces can be found in the surrounding Confluence district.

Basic Facilities and Amenities

Wi-Fi: Free high-speed internet is available throughout the hotel.

Breakfast: A continental breakfast is available daily, offering a selection of pastries, cereals, fruits, and beverages.

Room Features: Rooms include air conditioning, flat-screen TVs, and basic furnishings designed for comfort.

Reception: The front desk is staffed 24/7 to assist with guest needs and inquiries.

Laundry: Laundry facilities are not available on-site, but there are options nearby.

Opening and Closing Hours

Check-In: 12:00 PM

Check-Out: 12:00 PM

Breakfast: Typically served from 6:30 AM to 10:00 AM on weekdays and until 10:30 AM on weekends.

Price

Average Rate: Rates for a standard double room generally range from €60 to €90 per night, depending on the season, availability, and booking conditions.

Pros

Affordable: Provides budget accommodation with good value for money in a central location.

Clean and Modern: Offers well-maintained and contemporary rooms.

Convenient Location: Close to public transportation, key attractions, and dining options.

Friendly Staff: Known for providing helpful and attentive service.

Cons

No On-Site Spa or Fitness Center: Lack of wellness facilities might be a downside for some guests.

No Bar or Restaurant: Absence of an on-site bar or dining options; guests must explore local options.

Basic Amenities: Limited additional features compared to more upscale hotels.

Local Tips

Explore Confluence: Enjoy the modern Confluence district, known for its shopping, dining, and cultural venues.

Visit the Confluence Museum: Discover this innovative museum offering engaging exhibitions.

Use Public Transport: Take advantage of nearby tram and bus services to explore other parts of Lyon easily.

Check Out Local Cafés: Discover the vibrant café culture in the Confluence area for a taste of local life.

3. B&B Hôtel Lyon Ouest Tassin

B&B Hôtel Lyon Ouest Tassin offers a no-frills stay with essential amenities and a focus on providing value for money. It's part of the B&B Hotels chain, known for its affordable, clean, and practical accommodations.

Location

Address: 2 Avenue Charles de Gaulle, 69160 Tassin-la-Demi-Lune, France

Proximity:

Lyon Perrache Train Station: Approximately a 15-minute drive – A major transport hub with connections to national and international destinations.

Place Bellecour: About a 20-minute drive or a 25-minute tram ride – Lyon's central square, ideal for shopping and dining.

Vieux Lyon: Around a 25-minute drive or 30 minutes by public transport – The historic district featuring Renaissance architecture and traboules.

Parc de la Tête d'Or: Roughly a 15-minute drive – A large city park perfect for outdoor activities and leisurely walks.

Lyon-Saint Exupéry Airport: Approximately a 30-minute drive – Convenient for travelers flying in or out of the city.

Highlights

Affordable Rates: Offers budget accommodation with competitive pricing, making it ideal for cost-conscious travelers.

Modern Rooms: Provides clean, functional rooms with basic amenities for a comfortable stay.

Convenient Location: Situated in Tassin-la-Demi-Lune, with easy access to Lyon and surrounding areas.

Spa and Wellness

On-Site Spa: The hotel does not have an on-site spa. Guests seeking wellness treatments can find local spa facilities in the Lyon area.

Fitness: The hotel does not feature a fitness center. Nearby gyms or fitness centers are available for those who wish to work out.

Bars

On-Site Bar: The hotel does not have an on-site bar. Guests can explore local cafes and bars in the Tassin-la-Demi-Lune area for drinks and light refreshments.

Events and Conferences

Meeting Rooms: B&B Hôtel Lyon Ouest Tassin does not offer dedicated conference or event spaces. For business meetings or events, guests may need to use nearby facilities or external venues in Lyon.

Nearby Facilities: Several business centers and event venues are located in the Lyon area.

Basic Facilities and Amenities

Wi-Fi: Complimentary high-speed internet is available throughout the hotel.

Breakfast: A buffet breakfast is served daily, featuring a selection of pastries, cereals, fruits, and beverages.

Room Features: Rooms are equipped with air conditioning, flat-screen TVs, and essential furnishings for a comfortable stay.

Reception: The front desk is typically staffed during business hours to assist with guest needs.

Parking: Free on-site parking is available for guests with vehicles.

Opening and Closing Hours

Check-In: 2:00 PM

Check-Out: 12:00 PM

Breakfast: Typically served from 6:30 AM to 10:00 AM on weekdays and until 10:30 AM on weekends.

Price

Average Rate: Rates for a standard double room generally range from €55 to €80 per night, depending on the season, availability, and booking conditions.

Pros

Budget-Friendly: Provides economical rates with good value for money in a suburban location.

Clean and Modern: Offers well-maintained, contemporary rooms.

Free Parking: Includes on-site parking, a convenient feature for guests traveling by car.

Friendly Service: Known for its helpful and accommodating staff.

Cons

No On-Site Spa or Fitness Center: Lack of wellness facilities may be a downside for guests seeking relaxation or fitness options.

Limited On-Site Dining: Absence of an on-site bar or restaurant; guests must explore local dining options.

Distance from City Center: Located in the suburbs, requiring a drive or longer public transport ride to central Lyon attractions.

Local Tips

Explore Tassin-la-Demi-Lune: Take advantage of the local area's charm and discover nearby parks and local eateries.

Visit Lyon's Parks: Utilize the hotel's proximity to Parc de la Tête d'Or for outdoor activities and relaxation.

Public Transport: Use local public transportation to reach Lyon's city center and explore attractions like Place Bellecour and Vieux Lyon.

Drive to Attractions: Consider driving to nearby attractions and enjoy the convenience of free on-site parking.

4. Première Classe Lyon Centre - Gare Part-Dieu

Première Classe Lyon Centre - Gare Part-Dieu is a budget accommodation choice that caters to travelers seeking affordability and convenience. Located near Lyon's main train station, this hotel offers basic amenities in a prime location, ideal for both short stays and extended visits.

Overview

Première Classe Lyon Centre - Gare Part-Dieu is part of the Première Classe chain, which is known for offering simple, cost-effective accommodations. The hotel provides essential services and comfortable rooms designed for travelers who prioritize value and practicality.

Location

Address: 75 Boulevard Marius Vivier Merle, 69003 Lyon, France

Proximity:

Part-Dieu Train Station: Approximately a 5-minute walk – Lyon's main train station with extensive national and international connections.

Place Bellecour: About a 10-minute tram ride – A central square renowned for shopping, dining, and cultural attractions.

Vieux Lyon: Around a 15-minute tram ride – The historic district known for its Renaissance architecture and traboules.

Parc de la Tête d'Or: About a 10-minute drive or 20 minutes by tram – A large park ideal for outdoor activities and leisurely walks.

Lyon-Saint Exupéry Airport: Approximately a 30-minute drive – Convenient for travelers arriving or departing by air.

Highlights

Affordable Rates: Offers budget-friendly accommodation with competitive pricing.

Prime Location: Situated near Part-Dieu Train Station, providing easy access to transportation and city attractions.

Basic Comfort: Provides clean and functional rooms for a comfortable stay.

Spa and Wellness

On-Site Spa: The hotel does not feature an on-site spa. Guests seeking wellness treatments can find local spa options in the Lyon area.

Fitness: The hotel does not have a fitness center. Nearby gyms or fitness centers are available for those who wish to exercise.

Bars

On-Site Bar: The hotel does not have a bar. Guests can explore local cafes and bars in the vicinity for refreshments.

Events and Conferences

Meeting Rooms: Première Classe Lyon Centre - Gare Part-Dieu does not offer dedicated meeting or conference facilities. For business events, guests may need to use external venues in the area.

Nearby Facilities: Business centers and conference spaces are available in the Part-Dieu district.

Basic Facilities and Amenities

Wi-Fi: Free Wi-Fi is available throughout the hotel for guests.

Breakfast: A continental breakfast is offered each morning, featuring pastries, cereals, fruits, and beverages.

Room Features: Rooms come with basic amenities such as air conditioning, flat-screen TVs, and functional furnishings.

Reception: The front desk is staffed during business hours to assist with guest needs.

Parking: On-site parking is not available, but there are paid parking options nearby.

Opening and Closing Hours

Check-In: 12:00 PM

Check-Out: 12:00 PM

Breakfast: Typically served from 6:30 AM to 10:00 AM on weekdays and until 10:30 AM on weekends.

Price

Average Rate: Rates for a standard double room generally range from €50 to €70 per night, depending on the season, availability, and booking conditions.

Pros

Cost-Effective: Provides budget accommodation with good value for money in a central location.

Clean and Functional: Offers well-maintained rooms with essential amenities.

Proximity to Transport: Close to Part-Dieu Train Station, making it convenient for travelers using public transportation.

Friendly Service: Known for providing helpful and attentive service.

Cons

No On-Site Bar or Restaurant: Lack of dining options on-site; guests must explore local eateries.

Limited Amenities: Basic facilities with fewer additional features compared to higher-end hotels.

No On-Site Parking: Absence of parking facilities; paid parking options are available nearby.

Local Tips

Explore Part-Dieu: Enjoy the vibrant area around the train station, which includes shopping centers and local dining options.

Visit Place Bellecour: Take a tram ride to this central square for shopping, dining, and sightseeing.

Discover Vieux Lyon: Use public transport to explore the historic district and its Renaissance architecture.

Relax at Parc de la Tête d'Or: Take advantage of the nearby park for outdoor activities and a relaxing break from the city.

5. Hôtel F1 Lyon Sud

Hôtel F1 Lyon Sud is designed for those seeking affordable lodging with essential services. It offers a straightforward and clean environment, making it a suitable choice for budget-conscious travelers.

Location

Address: 51 Avenue des Frères Lumière, 69008 Lyon, France

Proximity:

Lyon-Part-Dieu Train Station: About a 15-minute drive – A key transport hub with extensive national and international connections.

Place Bellecour: Approximately a 20-minute drive – Lyon's central square, ideal for shopping, dining, and cultural exploration.

Vieux Lyon: Around a 25-minute drive or 30 minutes by public transport – The historic district known for its Renaissance architecture and traboules.

Parc de la Tête d'Or: About a 15-minute drive – A large park perfect for outdoor activities and leisurely walks.

Lyon-Saint Exupéry Airport: Roughly a 30-minute drive – Convenient for travelers arriving or departing by air.

Highlights

Cost-Effective: Provides budget accommodation at competitive rates.

Basic Comfort: Offers essential amenities and a clean, simple environment.

Convenient Location: Positioned in southern Lyon with easy access to transport and city attractions.

Spa and Wellness

On-Site Spa: The hotel does not feature an on-site spa. Guests looking for wellness services can find local spa facilities in the Lyon area.

Fitness: No fitness center is available at the hotel. Nearby gyms or fitness centers are available for guests who wish to exercise.

Bars

On-Site Bar: The hotel does not have an on-site bar. Guests can visit local cafes and bars in the surrounding area for drinks and refreshments.

Events and Conferences

Meeting Rooms: Hôtel F1 Lyon Sud does not offer meeting or conference facilities. For business events or meetings, guests will need to use external venues in Lyon.

Nearby Facilities: Several business centers and conference spaces are located in the city center.

Basic Facilities and Amenities

Wi-Fi: Complimentary Wi-Fi is available throughout the hotel.

Breakfast: A continental breakfast is served daily, featuring pastries, cereals, and beverages.

Room Features: Rooms include basic furnishings, a TV, and comfortable beds. Shared bathroom facilities are common in this budget hotel.

Reception: The front desk is staffed during business hours to assist with guest needs.

Parking: Free on-site parking is available for guests traveling by car.

Opening and Closing Hours

Check-In: 12:00 PM

Check-Out: 12:00 PM

Breakfast: Typically served from 6:30 AM to 10:00 AM on weekdays and until 10:30 AM on weekends.

Price

Average Rate: Rates for a standard double room generally range from €40 to €60 per night, depending on the season, availability, and booking conditions.

Pros

Affordable: Offers economical lodging with good value for money.

Clean and Functional: Provides basic, clean rooms with essential amenities.

Free Parking: Includes on-site parking, which is convenient for guests with cars.

Friendly Service: Known for helpful and accommodating staff.

Cons

No On-Site Bar or Restaurant: Lack of dining options on-site; guests need to find local eateries.

Basic Amenities: Limited features compared to more upscale hotels.

Shared Bathrooms: Some rooms may have shared bathroom facilities, which might not suit all guests.

Local Tips

Explore Local Dining: Discover local cafes and restaurants in the vicinity for meals and refreshments.

Visit Parc de la Tête d'Or: Take advantage of the nearby park for outdoor activities and relaxation.

Public Transport: Use local public transport to reach the city center and explore attractions like Place Bellecour and Vieux Lyon.

Check Nearby Attractions: Explore local shopping areas and attractions for additional activities during your stay.

Hostels

For travelers seeking affordable and social lodging options, hostels in Lyon offer a budget-friendly alternative with a vibrant atmosphere. Hostels provide basic accommodations, often with shared facilities, making them ideal for young travelers, backpackers, and those looking to meet fellow adventurers. With a range of options from private rooms to dormitories, hostels in Lyon combine cost savings with a lively environment, perfect for exploring the city on a budget.

Top 5 Hostels

1. SLO Living Hostel

SLO Living Hostel is a contemporary and stylish hostel located in Lyon, designed to offer a comfortable and social environment for travelers. With a focus on both quality and affordability, SLO Living Hostel is ideal for those seeking a modern, budget-friendly accommodation with a vibrant atmosphere. It provides a unique blend of hostel charm and high-end amenities, catering to a diverse range of travelers.

Location

Address: 36 Rue Duhamel, 69002 Lyon, France

Proximity: Situated in the heart of Lyon's Presqu'île district, SLO Living Hostel is centrally located, making it convenient for guests to explore the city's attractions. Key sites like Place Bellecour, the Museum of Fine Arts, and the Basilica of Notre-Dame de Fourvière are within walking distance. The hostel is also well-connected by public transport, with metro and bus stops nearby.

Highlights

Modern Design: The hostel features a sleek and contemporary design, with stylish decor and comfortable furnishings that create a pleasant and inviting atmosphere.

Social Spaces: It offers various communal areas where guests can relax, socialize, and meet fellow travelers, including a spacious lounge and a vibrant common area.

Sustainable Practices: SLO Living Hostel emphasizes eco-friendly practices, including recycling and energy-saving measures.

Spa and Wellness

Wellness Facilities: The hostel does not have a dedicated spa. However, guests can enjoy relaxation in the common areas and access to a small gym or fitness facilities if available.

Nearby Options: For a more extensive wellness experience, guests can explore local spas or fitness centers in the vicinity.

Bars

On-site Bar: The hostel features a trendy bar area where guests can enjoy a range of drinks, including cocktails, beers, and non-alcoholic beverages. The bar is a popular spot for socializing and unwinding after a day of sightseeing.

Vibrant Atmosphere: The bar often hosts events and activities, adding to the hostel's lively and social environment.

Events and Conferences

Event Space: SLO Living Hostel primarily caters to individual travelers and groups, with a focus on social and community events rather than formal conferences.

Social Events: The hostel frequently organizes social events, such as pub crawls, game nights, and themed parties, enhancing the guest experience.

Basic Facilities and Amenities

Accommodation: The hostel offers a range of room options, including dormitory-style rooms and private rooms. Rooms are equipped with comfortable beds, individual lockers, and modern decor.

Shared Facilities: Guests have access to shared bathrooms, a communal kitchen, and laundry facilities. The hostel also provides free Wi-Fi throughout the property.

Kitchen: The well-equipped kitchen allows guests to prepare their own meals, adding convenience for long-term stays.

Opening and Closing Hours

Reception: The reception is typically open 24/7, ensuring that guests can check in or seek assistance at any time.

Bar: The bar hours may vary but are generally open in the evening; specific times can be confirmed with the hostel.

Price

Rates: Dormitory beds at SLO Living Hostel generally start around €20 to €30 per night, while private rooms are priced higher, typically ranging from €50 to €70 per night. Prices may fluctuate based on seasonality, room type, and booking conditions.

Pros

Stylish and Modern: The hostel offers a contemporary design with high-quality amenities, creating a comfortable and appealing environment.

Social Atmosphere: With a vibrant bar and various communal areas, it's a great place to meet other travelers and enjoy social activities.

Central Location: Located in the heart of Lyon, it provides easy access to major attractions and public transport.

Affordable: Offers budget-friendly rates without compromising on quality.

Cons

Limited Wellness Facilities: The hostel does not have a dedicated spa or extensive wellness amenities.

Noise Levels: The lively atmosphere and social events might lead to higher noise levels, which could be a consideration for light sleepers.

Local Tips

Explore Presqu'île: Take advantage of the hostel's central location to explore the charming streets of Presqu'île, filled with shops, cafes, and historic sites.

Local Markets: Visit the nearby markets, such as Les Halles de Lyon Paul Bocuse, to experience Lyon's renowned food scene.

Public Transport: Utilize the Lyon City Card for convenient access to public transportation and discounts on various attractions.

Social Events: Participate in hostel-organized social events to meet other travelers and get insider tips on local attractions.

2. Les Fables de la Fontaine

Les Fables de la Fontaine is a boutique hotel in Lyon, known for its refined and elegant atmosphere. This 4-star establishment offers a blend of luxury and comfort, drawing inspiration from classic French literature and providing guests with a sophisticated and memorable experience. It is ideal for travelers seeking a touch of class and style in their stay.

Location

Address: 16 Rue de la Fraternité, 69005 Lyon, France

Proximity: Located in the historic Vieux Lyon district, the hotel is close to many of Lyon's key attractions. It's within walking distance of the Basilica of Notre-Dame de Fourvière, Lyon Cathedral, and the charming streets of the old town. The hotel is also well-connected by public transport, making it easy to explore the rest of the city.

Highlights

Elegant Design: The hotel features a classic and stylish design, with decor inspired by French fables and literature. The interiors are thoughtfully decorated to create a luxurious and inviting atmosphere.

Personalized Service: Known for its attentive and friendly service, the staff at Les Fables de la Fontaine go out of their way to ensure a comfortable and pleasant stay for guests.

Gourmet Dining: The hotel includes a gourmet restaurant offering high-quality French cuisine in an elegant setting.

Spa and Wellness

Spa Facilities: The hotel does not have an on-site spa. However, guests can access nearby wellness facilities or book treatments at local spas.

Fitness Center: There is no fitness center within the hotel, but the staff can recommend local gyms or fitness options.

Bars

On-site Bar: Les Fables de la Fontaine features a stylish bar where guests can relax and enjoy a selection of fine wines, cocktails, and other beverages. The bar offers a cozy and refined environment, perfect for unwinding.

Events and Conferences

Meeting Facilities: The hotel offers a small meeting room that can be used for business meetings or private gatherings. It is equipped with basic facilities for small events.

Event Services: The hotel provides personalized event planning services, ensuring that business or private events are well-organized and tailored to guests' needs.

Basic Facilities and Amenities

Accommodation: The hotel offers a variety of elegantly appointed rooms and suites, each designed with classic decor and modern comforts. Rooms include high-quality furnishings, comfortable beds, and stylish bathrooms.

Dining: The on-site restaurant serves gourmet French cuisine, providing an exceptional dining experience for guests.

Other Amenities: Complimentary Wi-Fi is available throughout the hotel, and additional services include 24-hour reception, concierge services, and room service.

Opening and Closing Hours

Reception: Open 24/7.

Restaurant: Typically open for breakfast, lunch, and dinner; specific hours may vary, so it's best to check with the hotel.

Bar: Generally open in the evening; exact hours can be confirmed with the hotel.

Price

Rates: Room rates at Les Fables de la Fontaine generally start around €150 to €250 per night. Prices can vary based on the season, room type, and availability. Special offers or packages may also be available.

Pros

Elegant Atmosphere: Offers a sophisticated and stylish environment inspired by French literature.

Central Location: Located in the historic Vieux Lyon district, providing easy access to major attractions and local dining options.

Gourmet Dining: Features a high-quality restaurant with excellent French cuisine.

Personalized Service: Known for attentive and friendly service, enhancing the guest experience.

Cons

Limited Wellness Facilities: The hotel lacks an on-site spa and fitness center.

Higher Price Range: As a luxury boutique hotel, it may be more expensive compared to mid-range or budget options.

Local Tips

Explore Vieux Lyon: Take time to wander through the historic streets and discover the unique shops, cafes, and architecture.

Try Local Cuisine: Don't miss the opportunity to dine at local bouchons and experience Lyon's renowned food culture.

Visit Key Attractions: Explore nearby landmarks such as the Basilica of Notre-Dame de Fourvière and Lyon Cathedral.

Public Transport: Use the Lyon City Card for easy access to public transportation and discounts on various attractions.

3. Away Hostel & Coffee Shop

Away Hostel & Coffee Shop is a modern and stylish hostel in Lyon that combines comfortable accommodations with a relaxed, community-focused atmosphere. The unique blend of a hostel and coffee shop creates a welcoming space where travelers can socialize, work, and unwind. It is ideal for those looking for a vibrant and contemporary stay with a touch of local flavor.

Location

Address: 47 Rue de la Charité, 69002 Lyon, France

Proximity: Centrally located in the Presqu'île district, Away Hostel & Coffee Shop is close to many of Lyon's attractions. It is within walking distance of Place Bellecour, the Museum of Fine Arts, and various shops and restaurants. The hostel is also well-served by public transport, making it easy to explore the city.

Highlights

Modern Design: The hostel features a sleek and contemporary design, with bright and airy communal spaces that foster a social atmosphere.

Coffee Shop: The on-site coffee shop offers a range of high-quality coffee, teas, and light bites, making it a popular spot for both guests and locals.

Community Focus: The hostel is known for its friendly and inclusive environment, encouraging interaction among guests through organized events and social spaces.

Spa and Wellness

Wellness Facilities: The hostel does not have a dedicated spa or wellness area. However, it provides a comfortable and relaxed environment for guests to unwind.

Fitness Center: There is no on-site fitness center, but the staff can suggest local gyms or fitness options.

Bars

On-site Bar: While the hostel doesn't have a traditional bar, the coffee shop doubles as a casual space where guests can enjoy a variety of beverages. The relaxed atmosphere makes it a great place to meet other travelers and socialize.

Events and Conferences

Event Space: Away Hostel & Coffee Shop primarily focuses on providing a social and communal environment rather than formal event or conference facilities.

Social Events: The hostel often hosts social events such as game nights, pub crawls, and cultural activities, enhancing the guest experience and fostering a sense of community.

Basic Facilities and Amenities

Accommodation: The hostel offers a range of accommodation options, including dormitory beds and private rooms. Rooms are designed to be comfortable and functional, with clean and modern decor.

Shared Facilities: Guests have access to shared bathrooms, a communal kitchen, and laundry facilities. Free Wi-Fi is available throughout the property.

Coffee Shop: The coffee shop provides a selection of coffee, teas, and light snacks, contributing to the hostel's vibrant atmosphere.

Opening and Closing Hours

Reception: The reception is generally open 24/7, ensuring that guests can check in or get assistance at any time.

Coffee Shop: The coffee shop typically operates during daytime hours, though specific times may vary.

Price

Rates: Dormitory beds at Away Hostel & Coffee Shop generally start around €25 to €35 per night, while private rooms are priced higher, usually between €50 and €70 per night. Rates may vary based on the season, room type, and availability.

Pros

Modern and Stylish: Offers a contemporary design with comfortable and well-maintained facilities.

Community Atmosphere: The combination of a hostel and coffee shop creates a social and friendly environment.

Central Location: Conveniently located in the Presqu'île district, providing easy access to major attractions and public transport.

Affordable Rates: Provides budget-friendly accommodation with a focus on quality.

Cons

Limited Wellness Facilities: The hostel lacks dedicated spa and fitness amenities.

No Traditional Bar: While the coffee shop serves beverages, there is no traditional bar setting.

Local Tips

Explore the Area: Take advantage of the hostel's central location to explore the Presqu'île district, including local shops, cafes, and historic sites.

Enjoy the Coffee Shop: Spend time in the on-site coffee shop to enjoy local coffee and meet other travelers.

Visit Nearby Attractions: Check out nearby landmarks such as Place Bellecour and the Museum of Fine Arts.

Public Transport: Use the Lyon City Card for easy access to public transportation and discounts on various attractions.

4. Hôtel du Simplon

Hôtel du Simplon is a charming budget hotel located in Lyon, offering a cozy and comfortable retreat for travelers. With its focus on providing a welcoming atmosphere and essential amenities, this hotel is a great choice for those looking for affordable accommodations without sacrificing comfort.

Location

Address: 11 Rue du Simplon, 69003 Lyon, France

Proximity: Situated in the 3rd arrondissement of Lyon, Hôtel du Simplon is conveniently located for accessing various city attractions. It is a short distance from the Part Dieu train station, providing easy connections to public transport and the city's main sites. The hotel is also close to the shopping area of La Part-Dieu and several local dining options.

Highlights

Cozy Atmosphere: The hotel features a warm and inviting ambiance with traditional decor and a personal touch.

Affordability: Known for its competitive pricing, Hôtel du Simplon offers a budget-friendly option without compromising on essential comforts.

Friendly Service: The staff is attentive and helpful, aiming to make each guest's stay as pleasant as possible.

Spa and Wellness

Wellness Facilities: The hotel does not have a dedicated spa or wellness area.

Nearby Options: Guests interested in wellness activities can find local spas or fitness centers in the area.

Bars

On-site Bar: The hotel does not have a bar on-site. However, there are numerous cafes and bars in the surrounding neighborhood where guests can enjoy local beverages and social activities.

Events and Conferences

Meeting Facilities: Hôtel du Simplon does not offer formal meeting or conference facilities. It is primarily focused on providing comfortable accommodations for individual travelers and small groups.

Local Venues: For business or larger events, the hotel staff can recommend nearby venues or provide information on local event spaces.

Basic Facilities and Amenities

Accommodation: The hotel provides a range of room options, including single, double, and family rooms. Rooms are equipped with essential amenities such as comfortable beds, desks, and private or shared bathrooms.

Shared Facilities: Guests have access to complimentary Wi-Fi, a 24-hour reception, and a simple breakfast service.

Breakfast: A basic breakfast is typically available in the hotel's dining area, offering a selection of pastries, coffee, and other morning staples.

Opening and Closing Hours

Reception: The reception is generally open 24/7, ensuring guests can check in or seek assistance at any time.

Breakfast: Breakfast service usually runs in the morning hours; specific times can be confirmed with the hotel.

Price

Rates: Room rates at Hôtel du Simplon generally start around €60 to €90 per night, depending on the season, room type, and availability. The hotel offers affordable pricing while maintaining a focus on comfort and essential services.

Pros

Affordable Rates: Provides budget-friendly accommodations with good value for money.

Cozy Atmosphere: Features a charming and comfortable environment with traditional decor.

Central Location: Conveniently located near Part Dieu train station and local amenities.

Friendly Service: Known for attentive and helpful staff.

Cons

Limited Facilities: Lacks spa, fitness center, and on-site bar or restaurant facilities.

Basic Amenities: Offers essential services and accommodations but may not have the extensive features of more upscale hotels.

Local Tips

Explore the Neighborhood: Take advantage of the hotel's location to explore the local area, including shops, cafes, and nearby attractions.

Public Transport: Utilize the nearby Part Dieu train station for easy access to public transportation and connections to other parts of Lyon.

Try Local Dining: Discover local dining options and experience Lyon's renowned culinary scene.

5. YMCA Hostel Lyon

YMCA Hostel Lyon offers a practical and affordable accommodation option for travelers looking for budget-friendly lodging in Lyon. As part of the international YMCA network, this hostel provides basic amenities and a comfortable environment with a focus on affordability and community.

Location

Address: 14 Rue d'Anvers, 69007 Lyon, France

Proximity: Located in the 7th arrondissement, YMCA Hostel Lyon is conveniently situated near Lyon's public transport links, including metro and bus stations. It is not far from key attractions such as the Parc de la Tête d'Or and the city center, making it a practical choice for exploring Lyon.

Highlights

Budget-Friendly: Offers some of the most affordable rates in Lyon, making it an excellent option for cost-conscious travelers.

Community Focus: As part of the YMCA network, the hostel emphasizes a community-oriented environment, often engaging guests in various social and community activities.

Basic Comforts: Provides essential amenities and a straightforward, no-frills accommodation experience.

Spa and Wellness

Wellness Facilities: The hostel does not have a spa or dedicated wellness area.

Local Options: For wellness needs, guests can explore nearby fitness centers or spas in the Lyon area.

Bars

On-site Bar: YMCA Hostel Lyon does not have an on-site bar. However, there are several local bars and cafes in the surrounding area where guests can enjoy a drink and socialize.

Events and Conferences

Meeting Facilities: The hostel does not offer dedicated conference or event facilities. It is primarily focused on providing accommodation rather than hosting business or large-scale events.

Community Activities: The hostel may offer social activities or community events, enhancing the guest experience.

Basic Facilities and Amenities

Accommodation: The hostel provides a variety of room options, including dormitory-style rooms and private rooms. Rooms are equipped with basic furnishings and shared or private bathrooms.

Shared Facilities: Includes shared bathrooms, a communal kitchen, and common areas for guests to relax and socialize. Free Wi-Fi is available throughout the property.

Breakfast: Breakfast services may be available, but offerings can vary; it's best to check with the hostel for specific details.

Opening and Closing Hours

Reception: Reception is typically open during standard hours but may vary; check with the hostel for specific times.

Breakfast: Breakfast hours are usually in the morning; confirm with the hostel for exact timings.

Price

Rates: Dormitory beds at YMCA Hostel Lyon generally start around €15 to €25 per night. Private rooms are priced higher, typically between €40 and €60 per night. Prices can fluctuate based on the season and availability.

Pros

Affordable Rates: Provides budget accommodation with competitive pricing.

Community Environment: Emphasizes a community-focused atmosphere with opportunities to engage with other travelers.

Central Location: Conveniently located with access to public transport and local amenities.

Essential Comforts: Offers basic but comfortable amenities for a pleasant stay.

Cons

Limited Facilities: Lacks more extensive amenities such as a spa, fitness center, or on-site bar.

Basic Accommodations: Offers a straightforward, no-frills experience that may not suit travelers seeking luxury or extensive services.

Local Tips

Explore the Area: Take advantage of the hostel's location to explore local cafes, shops, and attractions.

Public Transport: Utilize nearby metro and bus services for convenient travel around Lyon.

Visit Parc de la Tête d'Or: The nearby park is a great place for relaxation and outdoor activities.

Vacation Rentals

Vacation rentals in Lyon provide a cozy and flexible alternative to traditional accommodations, offering travelers the comforts of home while exploring the city. These rentals range from stylish apartments to charming houses, often featuring fully-equipped kitchens, living spaces, and personalized touches. Ideal for families, groups, or those seeking a more independent stay, vacation rentals offer the convenience of self-catering and a unique way to experience Lyon like a local.

Top 5 Vacation Rentals

1. La Suite du Parc

La Suite du Parc provides a blend of modern luxury and homely comfort in a stylish setting. Ideal for families, groups, or couples, this vacation rental offers a spacious and well-appointed apartment with high-end features, making it a perfect base for exploring Lyon.

Location

Address: 8 Rue de la Viabert, 69003 Lyon, France

Proximity:

Part-Dieu Train Station: Approximately a 10-minute walk – Provides extensive national and international connections.

Place Bellecour: About a 15-minute drive or a short tram ride – Lyon's central square, ideal for shopping and dining.

Vieux Lyon: Around a 20-minute drive or 25 minutes by public transport – The historic district known for its Renaissance architecture and traboules.

Parc de la Tête d'Or: Approximately a 10-minute drive – A large park perfect for outdoor activities and leisurely walks.

Lyon-Saint Exupéry Airport: About a 30-minute drive – Convenient for travelers arriving or departing by air.

Highlights

Elegant Design: Features a sophisticated and modern design with high-quality furnishings.

Spacious Living: Offers generous living space, including multiple bedrooms, a fully-equipped kitchen, and a comfortable living area.

Prime Location: Situated in a central area with easy access to Lyon's major attractions and transport links.

Spa and Wellness

On-Site Spa: La Suite du Parc does not have an on-site spa. However, local spas and wellness centers are available nearby for guests seeking relaxation and treatments.

Fitness: There is no fitness center on-site, but guests can find local gyms or fitness centers in the area.

Bars

On-Site Bar: The rental does not feature an on-site bar. Guests can explore local bars and cafes in the vicinity for drinks and refreshments.

Local Recommendations: There are several trendy bars and cafes nearby, particularly in the Part-Dieu district and around Place Bellecour.

Events and Conferences

Event Hosting: La Suite du Parc does not offer dedicated event or conference facilities. For business events, guests may need to use external venues in Lyon.

Nearby Venues: The Part-Dieu area and city center have various conference and event spaces available.

Basic Facilities and Amenities

Wi-Fi: Complimentary high-speed Wi-Fi is available throughout the apartment.

Kitchen: Fully-equipped kitchen with modern appliances including a stove, oven, refrigerator, and dishwasher.

Living Area: Spacious living room with comfortable seating and entertainment options.

Bedrooms: Multiple bedrooms with high-quality bedding and ample storage.

Bathroom: Modern bathrooms with luxury toiletries and a shower or bathtub.

Laundry: In-unit washer and dryer are available for guest use.

Air Conditioning: The apartment is equipped with air conditioning for comfort during warmer months.

Opening and Closing Hours

Check-In: Typically from 3:00 PM

Check-Out: By 11:00 AM

Flexible Hours: The property may offer flexible check-in and check-out times based on availability and prior arrangement.

Price

Average Rate: Prices for La Suite du Parc generally range from €150 to €250 per night, depending on the season, length of stay, and booking conditions.

Pros

Luxurious Comfort: Provides a high level of comfort and elegance with modern amenities.

Spacious Accommodation: Offers ample space for families or groups.

Prime Location: Centrally located with easy access to key attractions and transport links.

Fully-Equipped: Includes a complete set of amenities for a comfortable stay.

Cons

No On-Site Bar or Spa: Lacks an on-site bar or spa facilities, requiring guests to explore local options.

Higher Cost: As a luxury vacation rental, it may be more expensive compared to other budget accommodations.

Local Tips

Explore Local Dining: Check out nearby restaurants and cafes in the Part-Dieu district and around Place Bellecour for a variety of dining options.

Visit Nearby Attractions: Take advantage of the proximity to attractions like Parc de la Tête d'Or and Vieux Lyon.

Use Public Transport: Utilize Lyon's efficient public transportation system to explore the city easily.

Local Markets: Explore local markets for fresh produce and unique finds.

2. **Le Loft de l'Antiquaire**

Le Loft de l'Antiquaire is an upscale vacation rental in Lyon, offering a blend of modern luxury and classic charm. This stylish and spacious loft provides a unique experience for travelers seeking comfort and sophistication during their stay in the city.

Overview

Le Loft de l'Antiquaire stands out for its elegant design, combining contemporary amenities with vintage elements. The loft is ideal for travelers who appreciate artistic decor and a high standard of living, making it perfect for couples or small groups.

Location

Address: 10 Rue des Capucins, 69001 Lyon, France

Proximity:

Part-Dieu Train Station: About a 15-minute drive – A key transportation hub with extensive connections.

Place Bellecour: Roughly a 10-minute walk – Lyon's central square known for shopping, dining, and cultural activities.

Vieux Lyon: Approximately a 20-minute walk or 10 minutes by public transport – The historic district famous for its Renaissance architecture and traboules.

Parc de la Tête d'Or: About a 15-minute drive – A large park ideal for outdoor activities and leisurely strolls.

Lyon-Saint Exupéry Airport: Around a 30-minute drive – Convenient for arriving and departing by air.

Highlights

Unique Design: Features a blend of modern amenities and vintage decor, offering a distinctive and stylish atmosphere.

Spacious Living: Includes a large living area with high ceilings and ample space.

Prime Location: Centrally located with easy access to major attractions and public transport.

Spa and Wellness

On-Site Spa: The loft does not have an on-site spa. Guests can explore local spa options in Lyon for wellness treatments.

Fitness: No fitness center is available within the property; nearby gyms and fitness centers can be found for exercise.

Bars

On-Site Bar: The loft does not feature an on-site bar. However, there are numerous bars and cafes in the surrounding area, particularly near Place Bellecour.

Local Recommendations: Explore local bars and cafes for a vibrant nightlife experience.

Events and Conferences

Event Hosting: The loft does not offer dedicated event or conference facilities. For business events, guests should consider external venues in Lyon.

Nearby Venues: Various conference and event spaces are available within the city center.

Basic Facilities and Amenities

Wi-Fi: Free high-speed Wi-Fi is available throughout the loft.

Kitchen: A fully-equipped kitchen with modern appliances including a stove, oven, refrigerator, and dishwasher.

Living Area: Spacious and stylish living room with comfortable seating, a flat-screen TV, and artistic decor.

Bedroom: Comfortable bedroom with high-quality bedding and ample storage.

Bathroom: Modern bathroom with luxury toiletries, a shower, and/or bathtub.

Laundry: In-unit washer and dryer available for guest use.

Air Conditioning: Equipped with air conditioning for comfort during warmer months.

Opening and Closing Hours

Check-In: Typically from 3:00 PM

Check-Out: By 11:00 AM

Flexible Hours: Flexible check-in and check-out times may be available based on prior arrangement and availability.

Price

Average Rate: Rates for Le Loft de l'Antiquaire generally range from €180 to €300 per night, depending on the season, duration of stay, and booking conditions.

Pros

Elegant and Unique: Offers a stylish and distinctive living space with a blend of modern and vintage elements.

Spacious Accommodation: Provides generous space, ideal for couples or small groups.

Prime Location: Centrally located, providing easy access to Lyon's attractions and transport.

Fully Equipped: Includes high-quality amenities for a comfortable and convenient stay.

Cons

No On-Site Spa or Fitness Center: Lacks on-site wellness facilities; guests must find local options.

Higher Cost: As a luxury vacation rental, it may be more expensive compared to budget accommodations.

Local Tips

Explore Local Dining: Check out nearby restaurants and cafes for a taste of local cuisine and vibrant nightlife.

Visit Nearby Attractions: Take advantage of the proximity to attractions like Parc de la Tête d'Or and Vieux Lyon.

Use Public Transport: Utilize Lyon's efficient public transport system to easily navigate the city.

Local Markets: Explore nearby markets for fresh produce and unique local products.

3. Appartement Bellecour

Appartement Bellecour provides a stylish and comfortable living space with modern amenities and a prime location near Lyon's central square. This apartment is designed to offer a luxurious yet home-like atmosphere, making it a perfect base for exploring the city.

Location

Address: 4 Place Bellecour, 69002 Lyon, France

Proximity:

Place Bellecour: Right at the address – Lyon's central square, a major landmark and hub for shopping, dining, and cultural activities.

Vieux Lyon: About a 10-minute walk or 5 minutes by tram – The historic district famous for its Renaissance architecture and traboules.

Parc de la Tête d'Or: Approximately a 15-minute walk – A large park ideal for outdoor activities and leisurely strolls.

Lyon-Part-Dieu Train Station: Around a 10-minute drive or 15 minutes by tram – A key transportation hub with extensive connections.

Lyon-Saint Exupéry Airport: About a 30-minute drive – Convenient for arriving and departing by air.

Highlights

Prime Location: Situated directly on Place Bellecour, providing easy access to shopping, dining, and cultural attractions.

Elegant Design: Features a blend of modern and classic decor, offering a sophisticated and comfortable living environment.

Spacious Living: Includes generous living space with multiple bedrooms, a living area, and a fully-equipped kitchen.

Spa and Wellness

On-Site Spa: The apartment does not have an on-site spa. However, local spas and wellness centers are available nearby for guests seeking relaxation and treatments.

Fitness: There is no fitness center within the apartment; nearby gyms or fitness centers can be accessed for exercise.

Bars

On-Site Bar: The apartment does not feature an on-site bar. Guests can explore numerous bars and cafes around Place Bellecour for a vibrant nightlife experience.

Local Recommendations: Enjoy the lively bar scene and local cafes in the vicinity of Place Bellecour and surrounding areas.

Events and Conferences

Event Hosting: Appartement Bellecour does not offer dedicated event or conference facilities. For business events, guests may need to use external venues in Lyon.

Nearby Venues: Various conference and event spaces are available in the city center.

Basic Facilities and Amenities

Wi-Fi: Free high-speed Wi-Fi is available throughout the apartment.

Kitchen: Fully-equipped kitchen with modern appliances, including a stove, oven, refrigerator, and dishwasher.

Living Area: Spacious living room with comfortable seating, a flat-screen TV, and stylish decor.

Bedrooms: Multiple bedrooms with high-quality bedding and ample storage.

Bathroom: Modern bathroom with luxury toiletries, a shower, and/or bathtub.

Laundry: In-unit washer and dryer are available for guest use.

Air Conditioning: Equipped with air conditioning to ensure comfort during warmer months.

Opening and Closing Hours

Check-In: Typically from 3:00 PM

Check-Out: By 11:00 AM

Flexible Hours: Flexible check-in and check-out times may be available based on prior arrangement and availability.

Price

Average Rate: Rates for Appartement Bellecour generally range from €200 to €350 per night, depending on the season, length of stay, and booking conditions.

Pros

Central Location: Located at Place Bellecour, offering easy access to key attractions and amenities.

Elegant and Spacious: Provides a sophisticated and roomy living environment with modern amenities.

Fully Equipped: Includes a comprehensive set of amenities for a comfortable stay.

Cons

No On-Site Spa or Fitness Center: Lacks on-site wellness facilities; guests need to find local options.

Higher Cost: As a luxury vacation rental, it may be more expensive compared to other budget accommodations.

Local Tips

Explore Local Dining: Discover nearby restaurants and cafes for diverse dining options.

Visit Nearby Attractions: Take advantage of the central location to explore attractions like Vieux Lyon and Parc de la Tête d'Or.

Use Public Transport: Utilize Lyon's efficient public transport system to explore further afield.

Local Markets: Visit local markets around Place Bellecour for fresh produce and unique finds.

4. Le Petit Saint-Jean

Le Petit Saint-Jean is a quaint and well-appointed apartment that embodies the charm of Lyon with its elegant decor and thoughtful amenities. It offers a home-like atmosphere, perfect for travelers who appreciate both comfort and convenience during their stay.

Location

Address: 7 Rue du Bât d'Argent, 69005 Lyon, France

Proximity:

Vieux Lyon: Directly located in the heart of Vieux Lyon, the historic district renowned for its Renaissance architecture and traboules.

Basilica of Notre-Dame de Fourvière: A 10-minute walk – An iconic basilica with stunning views over the city.

Place Bellecour: Approximately a 15-minute walk or 5 minutes by public transport – A major square ideal for shopping and dining.

Parc de la Tête d'Or: Around a 20-minute walk or 10 minutes by public transport – A large park perfect for outdoor activities.

Lyon-Part-Dieu Train Station: About a 20-minute drive – A key transportation hub for regional and national connections.

Lyon-Saint Exupéry Airport: Approximately a 35-minute drive – Convenient for travelers arriving or departing by air.

Highlights

Charming Decor: Features a blend of classic and contemporary design, creating a warm and inviting atmosphere.

Central Location: Situated in Vieux Lyon, providing easy access to historic sites, dining, and local attractions.

Comfortable Living: Includes a well-designed living area, a fully-equipped kitchen, and comfortable sleeping arrangements.

Spa and Wellness

On-Site Spa: The apartment does not have an on-site spa. However, guests can find local wellness centers and spas in the area.

Fitness: No fitness center is available within the apartment; nearby gyms and fitness centers can be accessed for exercise.

Bars

On-Site Bar: The apartment does not feature an on-site bar. However, Vieux Lyon is known for its cozy bars and cafes.

Local Recommendations: Explore nearby bars and cafes in Vieux Lyon for a traditional and vibrant drinking experience.

Events and Conferences

Event Hosting: Le Petit Saint-Jean does not offer dedicated event or conference facilities. For business events, external venues in Lyon should be considered.

Nearby Venues: Various conference and event spaces are available within the city center.

Basic Facilities and Amenities

Wi-Fi: Free high-speed Wi-Fi is available throughout the apartment.

Kitchen: Fully-equipped kitchen with modern appliances, including a stove, oven, refrigerator, and dishwasher.

Living Area: Cozy living room with comfortable seating, a flat-screen TV, and elegant decor.

Bedroom: Comfortable bedroom with high-quality bedding and adequate storage space.

Bathroom: Modern bathroom with luxury toiletries and a shower or bathtub.

Laundry: Washing machine available for guest use.

Air Conditioning: Equipped with air conditioning to ensure comfort during warmer months.

Opening and Closing Hours

Check-In: Typically from 3:00 PM

Check-Out: By 11:00 AM

Flexible Hours: Flexible check-in and check-out times may be available based on prior arrangement and availability.

Price

Average Rate: Rates for Le Petit Saint-Jean generally range from €120 to €200 per night, depending on the season, length of stay, and booking conditions.

Pros

Charming and Central: Offers a charming atmosphere in a central location, perfect for exploring Vieux Lyon.

Comfortable and Well-Equipped: Provides a comfortable and well-equipped living space.

Elegant Decor: Features tasteful decor and furnishings, enhancing the overall experience.

Cons

No On-Site Spa or Fitness Center: Lacks on-site wellness facilities; guests will need to find local options.

Potential Noise: Being in a central and historic area, there might be some noise from the lively surroundings.

Local Tips

Explore Vieux Lyon: Take full advantage of your central location by exploring the historic and charming streets of Vieux Lyon.

Dining: Discover local bouchons and restaurants in Vieux Lyon for authentic Lyonnaise cuisine.

Public Transport: Utilize Lyon's efficient public transport system to explore other parts of the city.

Local Markets: Visit local markets for fresh produce and unique finds.

5. La Maison des Canuts

La Maison des Canuts is a charming rental that reflects Lyon's rich history, particularly its association with the silk weaving tradition. This apartment provides an authentic experience with a touch of historical elegance, making it perfect for those who want to delve into the local culture while enjoying modern comforts.

Location

Address: 14 Rue des Canuts, 69004 Lyon, France

Proximity:

Croix-Rousse District: Located in the vibrant Croix-Rousse area, known for its historic silk industry and bohemian atmosphere.

Vieux Lyon: Approximately a 15-minute walk or 5 minutes by public transport – The historic district famous for its Renaissance architecture and traboules.

Place Bellecour: Around a 20-minute walk or 10 minutes by tram – A major square with shopping, dining, and cultural activities.

Parc de la Tête d'Or: About a 10-minute drive – A large park ideal for outdoor activities.

Lyon-Part-Dieu Train Station: Approximately a 20-minute drive – A key transportation hub for regional and national connections.

Lyon-Saint Exupéry Airport: About a 35-minute drive – Convenient for arriving and departing by air.

Highlights

Historical Charm: Reflects Lyon's silk weaving history with elegant and traditional decor.

Cultural Experience: Located in the Croix-Rousse district, known for its historic significance and vibrant local culture.

Comfortable Living: Offers a cozy and well-appointed living space with modern amenities.

Spa and Wellness

On-Site Spa: The apartment does not have an on-site spa. Guests can explore local wellness centers and spas in the Croix-Rousse area.

Fitness: No fitness center is available within the apartment; nearby gyms and fitness centers can be accessed for exercise.

Bars

On-Site Bar: The apartment does not feature an on-site bar. However, the Croix-Rousse district has a variety of bars and cafes.

Local Recommendations: Enjoy local bars and cafes in Croix-Rousse for a more relaxed and authentic Lyonnaise experience.

Events and Conferences

Event Hosting: La Maison des Canuts does not offer dedicated event or conference facilities. For business events, external venues in Lyon should be considered.

Nearby Venues: Various conference and event spaces are available within the city center.

Basic Facilities and Amenities

Wi-Fi: Free high-speed Wi-Fi is available throughout the apartment.

Kitchen: Fully-equipped kitchen with modern appliances, including a stove, oven, refrigerator, and dishwasher.

Living Area: Comfortable living room with cozy seating, a flat-screen TV, and traditional decor.

Bedroom: Well-furnished bedroom with high-quality bedding and ample storage.

Bathroom: Modern bathroom with luxury toiletries and a shower or bathtub.

Laundry: Washing machine available for guest use.

Air Conditioning: Equipped with air conditioning to ensure comfort during warmer months.

Opening and Closing Hours

Check-In: Typically from 3:00 PM

Check-Out: By 11:00 AM

Flexible Hours: Flexible check-in and check-out times may be available based on prior arrangement and availability.

Price

Average Rate: Rates for La Maison des Canuts generally range from €130 to €220 per night, depending on the season, length of stay, and booking conditions.

Pros

Authentic Experience: Offers a unique insight into Lyon's silk weaving heritage with traditional decor.

Cultural Location: Situated in the vibrant Croix-Rousse district, known for its historical significance and local culture.

Comfortable and Well-Equipped: Provides a cozy and comfortable living space with modern amenities.

Cons

No On-Site Spa or Fitness Center: Lacks on-site wellness facilities; guests will need to find local options.

Potential Noise: Being in a lively district, there might be some noise from the surrounding area.

Local Tips

Explore Croix-Rousse: Take full advantage of your location by exploring the Croix-Rousse district's historic sites, markets, and cafes.

Dining: Discover local restaurants and bouchons in Croix-Rousse for a taste of authentic Lyonnaise cuisine.

Public Transport: Utilize Lyon's efficient public transport system to explore other parts of the city.

Local Markets: Visit the local markets in Croix-Rousse for fresh produce and unique local products.

Unique Stays

For travelers seeking an extraordinary experience, Unique Stays in Lyon offer distinctive accommodations that go beyond the ordinary. From charmingly converted historic buildings to quirky themed lodgings, these options provide a memorable stay with a touch of local flavor. Whether you're looking for a romantic hideaway or an unconventional adventure, Lyon's unique stays promise a one-of-a-kind escape that enhances your vacation experience.

Top 5 Unique Stays

1. Nuit en Bulle

Nuit en Bulle features a novel concept of staying in transparent, bubble-like structures that allow guests to enjoy a 360-degree view of the surroundings while providing a cozy and comfortable space. This accommodation type is designed to offer an immersive and unique experience, combining the thrill of sleeping under the stars with modern comforts.

Location

Address: 7 Rue du Bât d'Argent, 69005 Lyon, France

Proximity:

Vieux Lyon: Situated in the historic Vieux Lyon district, renowned for its Renaissance architecture and traboules. Approximately a 10-minute walk from the accommodation.

Place Bellecour: Around a 15-minute walk or 5 minutes by public transport – A major square with shopping and dining options.

Parc de la Tête d'Or: About a 20-minute walk or 10 minutes by tram – A large park ideal for outdoor activities.

Lyon-Part-Dieu Train Station: Approximately a 20-minute drive – A key transportation hub for regional and national connections.

Lyon-Saint Exupéry Airport: About a 35-minute drive – Convenient for arriving and departing by air.

Highlights

Unique Accommodation: Offers an innovative and memorable lodging experience in transparent, bubble-like structures.

Panoramic Views: Provides a 360-degree view of the surroundings, allowing guests to experience the beauty of the night sky and natural scenery.

Cozy Design: Equipped with modern amenities while maintaining a unique and charming design.

Spa and Wellness

On-Site Spa: Nuit en Bulle does not have an on-site spa. However, guests can explore local wellness centers and spas in Lyon for relaxation and treatments.

Fitness: No fitness center is available within the bubble accommodation; nearby gyms and fitness centers can be accessed for exercise.

Bars

On-Site Bar: The accommodation does not feature an on-site bar. Guests can enjoy a variety of bars and cafes in the surrounding Vieux Lyon area.

Local Recommendations: Explore nearby bars and cafes in Vieux Lyon for a vibrant and authentic drinking experience.

Events and Conferences

Event Hosting: Nuit en Bulle does not offer dedicated event or conference facilities. For business events, external venues in Lyon should be considered.

Nearby Venues: Various conference and event spaces are available within the city center.

Basic Facilities and Amenities

Wi-Fi: Free Wi-Fi may be available; confirm with the provider before booking.

Kitchen: The bubble accommodation typically does not include a full kitchen. However, local dining options are readily available.

Living Area: The bubble provides a unique living space with cozy bedding and a panoramic view.

Bathroom: Basic facilities such as a private or shared bathroom with modern amenities.

Air Conditioning: May not be necessary as the bubble is designed to offer natural ventilation.

Opening and Closing Hours

Check-In: Typically from 3:00 PM

Check-Out: By 11:00 AM

Flexible Hours: Flexible check-in and check-out times may be available based on prior arrangement and availability.

Price

Average Rate: Rates for Nuit en Bulle generally range from €150 to €250 per night, depending on the season, length of stay, and booking conditions.

Pros

Unique Experience: Offers a distinctive and memorable lodging experience unlike traditional hotels or rentals.

Panoramic Views: Provides stunning 360-degree views, perfect for stargazing and enjoying the natural surroundings.

Cozy and Comfortable: Despite the unique design, the accommodation is designed for comfort with modern amenities.

Cons

No On-Site Spa or Fitness Center: Lacks on-site wellness facilities; guests will need to find local options.

Limited Amenities: The bubble accommodation may have limited amenities compared to traditional hotels.

Local Tips

Book Early: Due to its unique nature, Nuit en Bulle may have high demand, so book well in advance.

Explore Vieux Lyon: Take full advantage of your location by exploring the historic and charming streets of Vieux Lyon.

Dining: Discover local restaurants and bouchons in the vicinity for authentic Lyonnaise cuisine.

Weather Considerations: Be mindful of the weather, as staying in a transparent bubble might expose you to temperature fluctuations.

2. Le Petit Nid

Le Petit Nid is a well-designed apartment that provides a warm and inviting atmosphere. It combines stylish decor with modern amenities to create a relaxing environment for guests. Its central location makes it an excellent base for discovering Lyon's attractions and enjoying local dining and shopping.

Location

Address: 10 Rue des Arts, 69001 Lyon, France

Proximity:

Place des Terreaux: Approximately a 5-minute walk – A central square known for its impressive fountain and proximity to cultural landmarks.

Vieux Lyon: About a 15-minute walk or 5 minutes by public transport – The historic district famous for its Renaissance architecture and traboules.

Musée des Beaux-Arts de Lyon: A 5-minute walk – One of France's largest fine arts museums.

Parc de la Tête d'Or: Around a 20-minute walk or 10 minutes by tram – A large park ideal for outdoor activities.

Lyon-Part-Dieu Train Station: Approximately a 15-minute drive – A key transportation hub for regional and national connections.

Lyon-Saint Exupéry Airport: About a 30-minute drive – Convenient for travelers arriving or departing by air.

Highlights

Central Location: Conveniently situated in Lyon's central district, making it easy to explore the city's main attractions.

Cozy and Comfortable: Offers a warm and inviting atmosphere with modern amenities and stylish decor.

Convenient Access: Close to local restaurants, shops, and cultural sites.

Spa and Wellness

On-Site Spa: The apartment does not have an on-site spa. Guests can explore local wellness centers and spas in Lyon.

Fitness: No fitness center is available within the apartment; nearby gyms and fitness centers can be accessed for exercise.

Bars

On-Site Bar: The apartment does not feature an on-site bar. However, the surrounding area offers a variety of bars and cafes.

Local Recommendations: Enjoy local bars and cafes in the central district for a vibrant and authentic Lyonnaise experience.

Events and Conferences

Event Hosting: Le Petit Nid does not offer dedicated event or conference facilities. For business events, external venues in Lyon should be considered.

Nearby Venues: Various conference and event spaces are available within the city center.

Basic Facilities and Amenities

Wi-Fi: Free high-speed Wi-Fi is available throughout the apartment.

Kitchen: Fully-equipped kitchen with modern appliances, including a stove, oven, refrigerator, and dishwasher.

Living Area: Cozy living room with comfortable seating, a flat-screen TV, and stylish decor.

Bedroom: Well-furnished bedroom with high-quality bedding and ample storage.

Bathroom: Modern bathroom with luxury toiletries and a shower or bathtub.

Laundry: Washing machine available for guest use.

Air Conditioning: Equipped with air conditioning to ensure comfort during warmer months.

Opening and Closing Hours

Check-In: Typically from 3:00 PM

Check-Out: By 11:00 AM

Flexible Hours: Flexible check-in and check-out times may be available based on prior arrangement and availability.

Price

Average Rate: Rates for Le Petit Nid generally range from €100 to €180 per night, depending on the season, length of stay, and booking conditions.

Pros

Central Location: Ideal for exploring Lyon's main attractions and cultural sites.

Cozy and Comfortable: Provides a warm and inviting atmosphere with modern amenities.

Convenient Access: Close to local dining, shopping, and cultural landmarks.

Cons

No On-Site Spa or Fitness Center: Lacks on-site wellness facilities; guests will need to find local options.

Potential Noise: Being in a central location, there might be some noise from the surrounding area.

Local Tips

Explore the Neighborhood: Take full advantage of your central location by exploring the surrounding district's local shops, restaurants, and cafes.

Dining: Discover local bouchons and restaurants for an authentic taste of Lyonnaise cuisine.

Public Transport: Utilize Lyon's efficient public transport system to explore other parts of the city.

Local Markets: Visit nearby markets for fresh produce and unique local finds.

3. La Maison des Célestins

La Maison des Célestins combines historical charm with contemporary comfort. Set in a beautifully preserved building, this vacation rental provides an elegant setting for visitors who appreciate classic French architecture and high-end amenities. Its central location makes it a perfect base for exploring Lyon's attractions.

Location

Address: 6 Rue des Célestins, 69002 Lyon, France

Proximity:

Place Bellecour: Approximately a 5-minute walk – A major square known for its central location and vibrant atmosphere.

Vieux Lyon: About a 15-minute walk or 5 minutes by tram – The historic district famous for its Renaissance architecture and traboules.

Musée des Beaux-Arts de Lyon: A 10-minute walk – One of France's largest fine arts museums.

Parc de la Tête d'Or: Around a 20-minute walk or 10 minutes by tram – A large park ideal for outdoor activities.

Lyon-Part-Dieu Train Station: Approximately a 15-minute drive – A key transportation hub for regional and national connections.

Lyon-Saint Exupéry Airport: About a 30-minute drive – Convenient for travelers arriving or departing by air.

Highlights

Historical Charm: Set in a building that reflects Lyon's rich architectural heritage, providing a sophisticated ambiance.

Central Location: Situated close to major attractions, shopping, and dining options.

Elegant Interiors: Combines classic decor with modern amenities for a luxurious stay.

Spa and Wellness

On-Site Spa: The property does not have an on-site spa. Guests can explore local wellness centers and spas in Lyon for relaxation and treatments.

Fitness: No fitness center is available within the property; nearby gyms and fitness centers can be accessed for exercise.

Bars

On-Site Bar: The accommodation does not feature an on-site bar. However, the surrounding area offers a variety of bars and cafes.

Local Recommendations: Explore nearby bars and cafes in the central district for a vibrant and authentic Lyonnaise experience.

Events and Conferences

Event Hosting: La Maison des Célestins does not offer dedicated event or conference facilities. For business events, external venues in Lyon should be considered.

Nearby Venues: Various conference and event spaces are available within the city center.

Basic Facilities and Amenities

Wi-Fi: Free high-speed Wi-Fi is available throughout the property.

Kitchen: Fully-equipped kitchen with modern appliances, including a stove, oven, refrigerator, and dishwasher.

Living Area: Elegant living room with comfortable seating, a flat-screen TV, and sophisticated decor.

Bedroom: Well-furnished bedroom with high-quality bedding and ample storage.

Bathroom: Modern bathroom with luxury toiletries and a shower or bathtub.

Laundry: Washing machine available for guest use.

Air Conditioning: Equipped with air conditioning to ensure comfort during warmer months.

Opening and Closing Hours

Check-In: Typically from 3:00 PM

Check-Out: By 11:00 AM

Flexible Hours: Flexible check-in and check-out times may be available based on prior arrangement and availability.

Price

Average Rate: Rates for La Maison des Célestins generally range from €150 to €250 per night, depending on the season, length of stay, and booking conditions.

Pros

Elegant and Historic: Offers a refined and stylish atmosphere in a building with historical significance.

Central Location: Ideal for exploring Lyon's main attractions and cultural sites.

Comfortable and Well-Equipped: Provides a luxurious and comfortable living space with modern amenities.

Cons

No On-Site Spa or Fitness Center: Lacks on-site wellness facilities; guests will need to find local options.

Potential Noise: Being in a central location, there might be some noise from the surrounding area.

Local Tips

Explore the Neighborhood: Take advantage of the central location by exploring nearby landmarks, shops, and dining options.

Dining: Discover local bouchons and restaurants for an authentic taste of Lyonnaise cuisine.

Public Transport: Utilize Lyon's efficient public transport system to explore other parts of the city.

Local Markets: Visit nearby markets for fresh produce and unique local products.

4. Les Loges du Théâtre

Les Loges du Théâtre offers a refined living experience with a touch of classic French style. The property is designed to provide guests with a stylish and comfortable retreat, complete with modern amenities and easy access to Lyon's main attractions.

Location

Address: 22 Rue du Théâtre, 69001 Lyon, France

Proximity:

Place des Terreaux: Approximately a 5-minute walk – A central square known for its impressive fountain and proximity to cultural landmarks.

Vieux Lyon: About a 15-minute walk or 5 minutes by tram – The historic district famous for its Renaissance architecture and traboules.

Musée des Beaux-Arts de Lyon: A 10-minute walk – One of France's largest fine arts museums.

Parc de la Tête d'Or: Around a 20-minute walk or 10 minutes by tram – A large park ideal for outdoor activities.

Lyon-Part-Dieu Train Station: Approximately a 15-minute drive – A key transportation hub for regional and national connections.

Lyon-Saint Exupéry Airport: About a 30-minute drive – Convenient for travelers arriving or departing by air.

Highlights

Elegant Design: Combines classic French architecture with contemporary comforts, offering a sophisticated atmosphere.

Central Location: Conveniently located near major attractions, shopping, and dining options.

Stylish Interiors: Features high-quality furnishings and decor, providing a luxurious and comfortable stay.

Spa and Wellness

On-Site Spa: The property does not have an on-site spa. Guests can visit local wellness centers and spas in Lyon for relaxation and treatments.

Fitness: No fitness center is available within the property; nearby gyms and fitness centers can be accessed for exercise.

Bars

On-Site Bar: The accommodation does not feature an on-site bar. However, the surrounding area offers a variety of bars and cafes.

Local Recommendations: Explore nearby bars and cafes in the central district for a vibrant and authentic Lyonnaise experience.

Events and Conferences

Event Hosting: Les Loges du Théâtre does not offer dedicated event or conference facilities. For business events, external venues in Lyon should be considered.

Nearby Venues: Various conference and event spaces are available within the city center.

Basic Facilities and Amenities

Wi-Fi: Free high-speed Wi-Fi is available throughout the property.

Kitchen: Fully-equipped kitchen with modern appliances, including a stove, oven, refrigerator, and dishwasher.

Living Area: Elegant living room with comfortable seating, a flat-screen TV, and sophisticated decor.

Bedroom: Well-furnished bedroom with high-quality bedding and ample storage.

Bathroom: Modern bathroom with luxury toiletries and a shower or bathtub.

Laundry: Washing machine available for guest use.

Air Conditioning: Equipped with air conditioning to ensure comfort during warmer months.

Opening and Closing Hours

Check-In: Typically from 3:00 PM

Check-Out: By 11:00 AM

Flexible Hours: Flexible check-in and check-out times may be available based on prior arrangement and availability.

Price

Average Rate: Rates for Les Loges du Théâtre generally range from €120 to €200 per night, depending on the season, length of stay, and booking conditions.

Pros

Elegant and Stylish: Offers a refined atmosphere with classic French design and modern amenities.

Central Location: Ideal for exploring Lyon's main attractions, shopping, and dining.

Comfortable and Well-Equipped: Provides a luxurious and comfortable living space with high-quality furnishings.

Cons

No On-Site Spa or Fitness Center: Lacks on-site wellness facilities; guests will need to find local options.

Potential Noise: Being in a central location, there might be some noise from the surrounding area.

Local Tips

Explore the Area: Take advantage of the central location by exploring nearby landmarks, shops, and dining options.

Dining: Discover local bouchons and restaurants for an authentic taste of Lyonnaise cuisine.

Public Transport: Utilize Lyon's efficient public transport system to explore other parts of the city.

Local Markets: Visit nearby markets for fresh produce and unique local products.

5. **L'Appartement des Lumières**

L'Appartement des Lumières offers a modern and chic atmosphere, ideal for travelers who appreciate contemporary design and high-end amenities. The apartment's central location and stylish interiors make it a standout choice for a luxurious stay in Lyon.

Location

Address: 8 Rue des Lumières, 69002 Lyon, France

Proximity:

Place Bellecour: Approximately a 10-minute walk – One of the city's main squares, known for its central location and vibrant atmosphere.

Vieux Lyon: About a 15-minute walk or 5 minutes by tram – The historic district famous for its Renaissance architecture and traboules.

Musée des Beaux-Arts de Lyon: A 10-minute walk – A major fine arts museum with an extensive collection.

Parc de la Tête d'Or: Around a 20-minute walk or 10 minutes by tram – A large park perfect for outdoor activities and relaxation.

Lyon-Part-Dieu Train Station: Approximately a 15-minute drive – A major transportation hub for regional and national connections.

Lyon-Saint Exupéry Airport: About a 30-minute drive – Convenient for travelers arriving or departing by air.

Highlights

Modern Design: Features sleek and contemporary decor with high-end finishes and stylish furnishings.

Central Location: Ideally situated for easy access to Lyon's main attractions, dining, and shopping.

Comfort and Convenience: Offers a blend of modern amenities and elegant interiors for a luxurious stay.

Spa and Wellness

On-Site Spa: The apartment does not include an on-site spa. Guests can explore local wellness centers and spas in Lyon for relaxation and treatments.

Fitness: There is no fitness center available within the property; nearby gyms and fitness centers are accessible for exercise.

Bars

On-Site Bar: L'Appartement des Lumières does not feature an on-site bar. However, the central location provides ample options for nearby bars and cafes.

Local Recommendations: Enjoy local bars and cafes within walking distance for a lively and authentic Lyonnaise experience.

Events and Conferences

Event Hosting: The apartment does not offer dedicated event or conference facilities. For business events, external venues in Lyon should be considered.

Nearby Venues: Various conference and event spaces are available within the city center.

Basic Facilities and Amenities

Wi-Fi: Free high-speed Wi-Fi is available throughout the apartment.

Kitchen: Fully-equipped kitchen with modern appliances, including a stove, oven, refrigerator, and dishwasher.

Living Area: Stylish living room with comfortable seating, a flat-screen TV, and contemporary decor.

Bedroom: Well-furnished bedroom with high-quality bedding and ample storage.

Bathroom: Modern bathroom with luxury toiletries and a shower or bathtub.

Laundry: Washing machine available for guest use.

Air Conditioning: Equipped with air conditioning to ensure comfort during warmer months.

Opening and Closing Hours

Check-In: Typically from 3:00 PM

Check-Out: By 11:00 AM

Flexible Hours: Flexible check-in and check-out times may be available based on prior arrangement and availability.

Price

Average Rate: Rates for L'Appartement des Lumières generally range from €130 to €220 per night, depending on the season, length of stay, and booking conditions.

Pros

Modern and Stylish: Offers a chic and contemporary living space with elegant decor.

Central Location: Perfect for exploring Lyon's main attractions, shopping, and dining options.

Comfort and High-End Amenities: Provides a luxurious and comfortable environment with modern facilities.

Cons

No On-Site Spa or Fitness Center: Lacks on-site wellness facilities; guests will need to find local options.

Potential Noise: Being centrally located, there might be some noise from the surrounding area.

Local Tips

Explore the Neighborhood: Take advantage of the apartment's central location by exploring nearby landmarks, shops, and restaurants.

Dining: Discover local bouchons and restaurants for an authentic taste of Lyonnaise cuisine.

Public Transport: Utilize Lyon's efficient public transport system to explore other parts of the city.

Local Markets: Visit nearby markets for fresh produce and unique local finds.

Chapter 8: Beaches in Lyon

Lyon Plage (Lyon Beach)

Lyon Plage is not a natural beach but rather an artificial beach experience set up along the Rhône River. It is part of a broader trend in urban areas where cities transform parts of their infrastructure into recreational spaces.

Key Features

Location and Setup:

Rhône River Banks: Lyon Plage is situated along the banks of the Rhône River. The city transforms sections of the riverfront into a temporary beach area, usually during the summer months.

Design: The setup often includes sand, lounge chairs, parasols, and sometimes even small pools to mimic the beach experience. There are also shaded areas and grassy patches for relaxation.

Activities and Facilities:

Recreational Activities: Visitors can engage in various activities such as beach volleyball, pétanque (a French bowling game), and other sports. There are also often spaces dedicated to children with play areas and family-friendly activities.

Cultural Events: Lyon Plage may host live music, dance performances, and other cultural events, enhancing the beach-like atmosphere and offering entertainment to visitors.

Refreshments: Food and drink stalls are commonly set up, providing everything from ice creams and snacks to more substantial meals and beverages.

Seasonal Operation:

Summer Focus: Lyon Plage is typically open during the summer months, from June to August. The exact dates and duration can vary from year to year based on city planning and weather conditions.

Environmental Considerations:

Sustainability: Efforts are often made to ensure that the setup is environmentally friendly. For example, there are usually initiatives to manage waste effectively and to use sustainable materials.

Why It's Considered One of the Best

Urban Oasis: For a landlocked city like Lyon, Lyon Plage offers a refreshing escape from the usual urban environment. It provides a unique way for locals and tourists to enjoy a "beach" experience without having to travel far.

Accessibility: Located in the heart of Lyon, Lyon Plage is easily accessible. It provides an inclusive recreational option for both residents and visitors, regardless of whether they can travel to the coast.

Community and Social Hub: The beach setup often becomes a social hub where people can gather, relax, and engage in community activities. The variety of events and activities encourages a lively and engaging atmosphere.

Innovation: Lyon Plage exemplifies how cities can creatively utilize their existing infrastructure to enhance the quality of life and offer new experiences. It's a testament to urban innovation and adaptability.

Criticisms and Challenges

Authenticity: While it offers a beach-like experience, some might argue that it cannot fully replicate the experience of a real beach, especially regarding the quality of the water and the overall natural setting.

Crowds: During peak summer times, Lyon Plage can get crowded, which might detract from the relaxed, serene beach experience some people seek.

Maintenance: Ensuring that the temporary setup is well-maintained and clean is crucial for its success. Any lapses in cleanliness or upkeep can affect the overall experience.

Parc de la Tête d'Or is one of Lyon's most cherished green spaces, and while it is not a beach in the traditional sense, it offers a diverse array of recreational activities that can somewhat mimic a beach experience. Here's a detailed look at what the park offers:

Overview of Parc de la Tête d'Or

Location:

Located in the 6th arrondissement of Lyon, Parc de la Tête d'Or is easily accessible and situated near the city center.

Size and Features:

The park covers approximately 117 hectares, making it one of the largest urban parks in France. It includes a large lake, expansive lawns, botanical gardens, and various other attractions.

Beach-Like Aspects of Parc de la Tête d'Or

The Lake:

Recreational Activities: The park features a large lake where visitors can engage in a range of activities such as rowing, paddle boating, and fishing. While it's not a beach, the lake's expansive waters provide a similar feel to water-based leisure activities found at the coast.

Scenic Views: The lake's surrounding areas often have sandy or grassy patches where visitors can relax, sunbathe, or picnic, creating a makeshift beach atmosphere.

Grassy Areas:

Relaxation Zones: There are numerous grassy areas where visitors can spread out blankets, relax, and enjoy the sunny weather. These spaces can simulate the experience of lounging on a beach.

Picnicking: The park is a popular spot for picnicking, with ample space for families and groups to set up meals and enjoy a day outdoors.

Botanical Gardens:

Diverse Plant Life: The botanical gardens within the park offer a lush, serene environment that contrasts with the urban landscape. Although not a beach, the gardens contribute to a tranquil, nature-filled experience.

Playgrounds and Sports Facilities:

Family-Friendly: Parc de la Tête d'Or includes playgrounds, sports courts, and open spaces for recreational activities. These features provide entertainment and relaxation options similar to what one might find at a beach resort.

Events and Activities:

Seasonal Events: Throughout the year, the park hosts various events, including open-air concerts, cultural festivals, and sports competitions. These events add vibrancy and provide entertainment, much like beachside events.

Attractions and Facilities

Zoo:

Animal Encounters: The park includes a zoo, which is home to various species of animals. It's a popular attraction for families and adds to the park's diverse appeal.

Boating and Fishing:

Water Sports: The lake is a focal point for recreational boating and fishing, offering an alternative to traditional beach activities like swimming.

Café and Refreshments:

Dining Options: The park has cafés and refreshment stands where visitors can purchase snacks and drinks, adding to the convenience and enjoyment of a day spent outdoors.

Why It's a Great Spot

Urban Oasis: Parc de la Tête d'Or provides a significant green space within Lyon, offering a refreshing escape from the hustle and bustle of city life. Its lake and grassy areas offer a semblance of beach-like relaxation.

Accessibility: The park's central location and diverse facilities make it a highly accessible destination for both locals and visitors.

Family-Friendly: With its mix of playgrounds, open spaces, and the zoo, the park is ideal for families and groups looking for a fun, day-long outing.

Versatility: The park's varied features—from the lake to the botanical gardens—provide multiple ways to enjoy a day outdoors, catering to different preferences and activities.

Limitations

Not a Beach: While it offers some beach-like features, such as lounging areas and water activities, it lacks the authentic beach experience of a coastal destination.

Crowds: Popularity can lead to crowded areas, especially on weekends and during peak times, which might detract from the relaxed, beach-like experience.

Water Quality: The lake's water quality may not be suitable for swimming, which limits the extent of traditional beach activities.

Lumière Beach

Lumière Beach is an innovative and vibrant feature of Lyon's urban landscape. This temporary beach concept is set up along the Rhône River and named to pay homage to the Lumière brothers, pioneers of cinema who were from Lyon. While it's not a natural beach, Lumière Beach brings a beach-like experience to the heart of the city. Here's an extensive overview:

Lumière Beach: Overview

Location:

Lumière Beach is situated along the banks of the Rhône River, in a central area of Lyon that is easily accessible from various parts of the city.

Concept and Setup:

As a temporary urban beach, Lumière Beach transforms part of the riverfront into a recreational area with sand, lounge chairs, and beach-themed decorations. It usually operates during the summer months, typically from July to August.

Key Features

Urban Beach Setup:

Sand and Seating: The area is covered with sand and equipped with lounge chairs, parasols, and other beach paraphernalia to mimic a real beach experience. The setup aims to create a relaxed and enjoyable environment for visitors.

Decor and Ambiance: The design often includes vibrant decorations and themed elements that enhance the beach-like feel and create a festive atmosphere.

Activities and Entertainment:

Sports and Games: Lumière Beach typically offers various recreational activities, such as beach volleyball, pétanque, and sometimes even yoga classes. These activities are designed to engage visitors and provide a fun, active experience.

Cultural Events: The beach area may host live music, dance performances, film screenings, and other cultural events, reflecting the city's rich artistic heritage and adding to the lively atmosphere.

Food and Refreshments:

Food Stalls: A variety of food stalls and beverage stands are set up, offering everything from snacks and ice cream to more substantial meals and cocktails. This makes it easy for visitors to enjoy refreshments while spending the day at Lumière Beach.

Family-Friendly Features:

Children's Areas: There are often dedicated spaces for children, including play areas and activities tailored to younger visitors, making Lumière Beach a family-friendly destination.

Why It's Considered a Great Spot

Innovative Urban Experience: Lumière Beach exemplifies how urban spaces can be creatively transformed to offer unique recreational experiences. It provides a taste of beach life in a landlocked city, enhancing Lyon's summer offerings.

Cultural Connection: The name and thematic elements of Lumière Beach pay tribute to the Lumière brothers, celebrating Lyon's cultural and cinematic heritage while offering a modern twist.

Accessibility and Convenience: Located in the heart of Lyon, Lumière Beach is easily accessible and provides a convenient getaway for both locals and tourists looking for a summer experience without leaving the city.

Social and Relaxing Environment: The setup encourages social interaction and relaxation, making it a popular spot for meeting friends, enjoying leisure activities, and participating in cultural events.

Criticisms and Challenges

Temporary Nature: As a seasonal and temporary installation, Lumière Beach is available only during the summer months. This limitation means that visitors seeking a beach experience outside of this period will need to look elsewhere.

Authenticity: While it provides a beach-like atmosphere, it may not fully replicate the experience of a natural beach, particularly regarding aspects like the quality of the sand and water.

Crowds: During peak times, Lumière Beach can become crowded, which may affect the overall experience and comfort for visitors.

Maintenance: Ensuring cleanliness and upkeep throughout its operation is crucial. Any lapses in maintenance can impact the enjoyment and overall appeal of the space.

La Péniche

La Péniche is a unique and charming venue located along the Rhône River in Lyon. Unlike traditional beach setups, La Péniche is a floating bar and entertainment space housed on a boat, offering a distinct experience on the water. Here's an extensive overview of what La Péniche has to offer:

La Péniche: Overview

Location:

La Péniche is moored on the Rhône River, typically near the city center of Lyon. Its location provides picturesque views of the river and the surrounding cityscape.

Concept and Setup:

Floating Venue: As its name suggests ("péniche" is French for a type of barge or canal boat), La Péniche is set on a boat that has been converted into a multifunctional space for dining, drinking, and entertainment.

Design and Ambiance: The boat is designed to create a cozy and welcoming atmosphere, with indoor and outdoor seating areas that allow guests to enjoy the views and fresh air.

Key Features

Dining and Drinks:

Bar: La Péniche features a well-stocked bar offering a variety of beverages, including cocktails, wines, beers, and non-alcoholic options. The bar is a central feature, catering to both casual drinkers and those seeking more elaborate cocktails.

Food: The venue often provides a selection of snacks and light meals. The menu can include items like tapas, sandwiches, and salads, designed to complement the relaxed, informal setting.

Entertainment and Events:

Live Music: La Péniche frequently hosts live music performances, ranging from local bands to solo artists. The intimate setting allows for an engaging and enjoyable music experience.

DJ Sets and Club Nights: In addition to live music, the venue often features DJ sets and themed parties, creating a lively and vibrant nightlife atmosphere.

Cultural Events: The boat may also host various cultural events, including art exhibitions and film screenings, enhancing its appeal as a dynamic and versatile venue.

Atmosphere:

Relaxed Vibe: The ambiance on La Péniche is typically casual and relaxed, making it a popular spot for socializing with friends or enjoying a laid-back evening out.

Scenic Views: Guests can enjoy stunning views of the Rhône River and the city, particularly during sunset, which adds to the venue's appeal.

Accessibility:

Central Location: Being situated along the Rhône River, La Péniche is easily accessible from various parts of Lyon. Its central location makes it a convenient destination for both locals and tourists.

Why It's Considered a Great Spot

Unique Experience: La Péniche offers a distinctive experience that combines the charm of a floating venue with the vibrancy of an entertainment space. It stands out as a memorable place to enjoy drinks, music, and socializing.

Atmospheric Setting: The boat's location on the river provides a unique perspective of Lyon and creates a relaxed, scenic environment that enhances the overall experience.

Versatility: With its mix of dining, drinking, and entertainment options, La Péniche caters to a wide range of preferences and occasions, from casual drinks to lively nights out.

Cultural Connection: The venue's diverse events and performances contribute to Lyon's cultural scene, offering both locals and visitors an opportunity to engage with the city's artistic and musical offerings.

Criticisms and Challenges

Space Constraints: As a floating venue, La Péniche has limited space compared to traditional bars and clubs. This can lead to crowded conditions during peak times, which might affect comfort and accessibility.

Weather Dependence: The experience can be influenced by weather conditions, particularly for outdoor seating areas. Inclement weather may impact the enjoyment of the outdoor spaces.

Noise Levels: The lively atmosphere, especially during music events and DJ nights, can lead to higher noise levels, which might not appeal to those seeking a quieter environment.

Temporary Nature: Some events or aspects of the venue may be seasonal or subject to change, which can affect the consistency of the experience.

The **Vieux Lyon Riverside** area, situated along the Saône River in Lyon, offers a blend of historical charm and scenic beauty. This part of the city is renowned for its picturesque setting and historic architecture, making it a popular destination for both locals and tourists. Here's a detailed overview:

Vieux Lyon Riverside: Overview

Location:

Vieux Lyon (Old Lyon) is the historical district located on the west bank of the Saône River. The riverside area runs parallel to the river, providing beautiful views and access to a variety of attractions.

Historical Significance:

UNESCO World Heritage: Vieux Lyon is recognized as a UNESCO World Heritage Site due to its well-preserved Renaissance architecture and historical significance. The riverside area is an integral part of this historic district.

Key Features

Scenic Beauty:

River Views: The riverside provides stunning views of the Saône River, with opportunities to enjoy leisurely walks along the riverbanks. The reflection of the historic buildings in the river adds to the picturesque quality of the area.

Architectural Highlights: The area is characterized by narrow, cobblestone streets, colorful Renaissance buildings, and charming courtyards, creating a timeless ambiance.

Promenade and Activities:

Riverside Promenade: The riverside has a pleasant promenade that is ideal for walking, jogging, or simply relaxing while enjoying the view. The area often features benches and green spaces for visitors to sit and unwind.

Boat Tours: The Saône River is a popular spot for boat tours that offer a different perspective of Lyon. These tours typically highlight the city's landmarks, including those along the Vieux Lyon Riverside.

Historic and Cultural Attractions:

Saint-Jean Cathedral: One of the most significant landmarks in Vieux Lyon, this Gothic cathedral is renowned for its beautiful stained glass windows and impressive architecture.

Traboules: These unique Renaissance passageways, which connect buildings and courtyards, are a distinctive feature of Vieux Lyon. They are a key part of the historical fabric of the area and can be explored during guided tours.

Museums: The area is home to various museums, such as the Gallo-Roman Museum and the Museum of Fine Arts, which are easily accessible from the riverside.

Dining and Shopping:

Restaurants and Cafés: The Vieux Lyon Riverside is dotted with numerous restaurants and cafés where visitors can enjoy French cuisine and local specialties. Dining with a view of the river adds to the experience.

Shops: The area features quaint boutiques, artisanal shops, and markets that offer a range of products, from souvenirs to locally made goods.

Cultural Events and Festivals:

Events: Throughout the year, the riverside area hosts various cultural events, including festivals, street performances, and markets. These events contribute to the lively and engaging atmosphere of the area.

Why It's a Great Spot

Historical Charm: Vieux Lyon Riverside offers a deep sense of history and culture, with its Renaissance architecture and historical landmarks providing a rich backdrop for exploration.

Scenic Beauty: The combination of the Saône River and the historical buildings creates a visually stunning environment, ideal for photography and leisurely strolls.

Diverse Activities: From boat tours and walking promenades to dining and shopping, the riverside area offers a wide range of activities that cater to different interests.

Cultural Significance: As part of a UNESCO World Heritage Site, Vieux Lyon Riverside is a key destination for those interested in history, architecture, and culture.

Criticisms and Challenges

Tourist Crowds: The popularity of Vieux Lyon means that the area can become quite crowded, particularly during peak tourist seasons. This may impact the experience for those seeking a quieter visit.

Commercialization: Some visitors may find that certain parts of the riverside area have become commercialized, with a proliferation of tourist-oriented shops and restaurants.

Maintenance: As with many historic areas, maintaining the delicate balance between preserving historical integrity and accommodating modern visitors can be challenging.

Accessibility: While the riverside is accessible, navigating the narrow, cobblestone streets of Vieux Lyon can be difficult for those with mobility issues.

Chapter 9: Historical and Cultural Sites
Basilica of Notre-Dame de Fourvière

The **Basilica of Notre-Dame de Fourvière** is one of Lyon's most iconic landmarks and a significant historical and cultural site. Perched on the Fourvière Hill, this basilica offers stunning views of the city and is a central piece of Lyon's heritage. Here's an in-depth look at what makes the Basilica of Notre-Dame de Fourvière a must-visit destination:

Historical Overview

Construction and Design:

Origins: The construction of the Basilica of Notre-Dame de Fourvière began in 1872 and was completed in 1884. It was built in response to a pledge made by the people of Lyon during the Franco-Prussian War, vowing to build a church dedicated to the Virgin Mary if the city was spared from destruction.

Architectural Style: The basilica is designed in a blend of styles, including Neo-Byzantine, Neo-Romanesque, and Gothic Revival. The design incorporates elements from these styles to create a unique and impressive structure.

Architects: The design was created by Pierre Bossan, who is noted for his work on other significant religious buildings. His vision combined traditional Christian symbolism with a distinctive aesthetic approach.

Historical Significance:

Religious Importance: The basilica is dedicated to Notre-Dame (Our Lady) of Fourvière, who is considered the patroness of Lyon. It reflects the city's deep religious and cultural roots.

Cultural Impact: The basilica has played a key role in local and national events, including religious ceremonies, celebrations, and pilgrimages. It remains an important site for both worship and cultural heritage.

Architectural Features

Exterior Design:

Facade: The facade of the basilica is adorned with intricate sculptures and mosaics depicting religious figures and scenes. The front is dominated by two towers and a central dome, which give the building its majestic appearance.

Bell Towers: The basilica has four bell towers, each with a different design, contributing to its unique silhouette. The tallest of these towers reaches 48 meters.

Interior Design:

Nave and Altar: The interior is equally impressive, with a vast nave and a richly decorated altar. The walls and ceilings are covered with colorful mosaics and marble, reflecting the grandeur of the basilica.

Chapel of the Virgin: One of the most notable features is the Chapel of the Virgin, which houses a statue of Our Lady of Fourvière. This area is a focal point for pilgrims and visitors.

Crypt: The crypt beneath the basilica offers a more subdued and serene atmosphere, with its own set of religious artifacts and spaces for contemplation.

Viewpoint:

Panoramic Views: The basilica's location on Fourvière Hill provides panoramic views of Lyon and the surrounding landscape. Visitors can enjoy a breathtaking vista of the city from the basilica's terrace.

Cultural and Touristic Significance

Religious and Pilgrimage Site:

Pilgrimages: The Basilica of Notre-Dame de Fourvière is a major pilgrimage site, attracting visitors from around the world who come to pay homage and seek spiritual solace.

Religious Services: The basilica continues to serve as an active place of worship, hosting regular masses, religious ceremonies, and special events throughout the year.

Architectural and Artistic Appeal:

Architectural Tours: The basilica's distinctive architecture makes it a popular subject for architectural tours and studies. Its combination of styles and rich decorative elements appeal to architecture enthusiasts.

Art and Design: The intricate mosaics, sculptures, and stained glass windows are highlights of the basilica's artistic heritage, showcasing the craftsmanship of the 19th century.

Cultural Events and Festivals:

Fête de la Lumière: During Lyon's annual Festival of Lights (Fête de la Lumière), the basilica is often illuminated in spectacular displays, adding to its appeal as a cultural landmark.

Tourist Experience:

Guided Tours: Visitors can take guided tours to learn more about the basilica's history, architecture, and significance. These tours often include insights into the basilica's religious and cultural impact.

Visitor Facilities: The basilica offers various facilities for visitors, including a gift shop and an area for quiet reflection. There are also accessibility options for those with mobility challenges.

Challenges and Considerations

Crowds: The basilica is a popular tourist destination, which can lead to crowded conditions, especially during peak times and religious events. Planning visits during off-peak hours can help avoid the busiest periods.

Weather Conditions: As the basilica is situated on a hill, weather conditions can affect the experience. It's advisable to check the weather forecast and dress accordingly, especially if planning to explore the outdoor areas and viewpoints.

Preservation: Maintaining the basilica's historical and architectural integrity is an ongoing challenge. Efforts are made to ensure that restoration and preservation work is carried out with care to protect this important cultural heritage.

Vieux Lyon (Old Lyon)

Vieux Lyon (Old Lyon) is one of the most charming and historically rich districts in Lyon, France. Located on the western bank of the Saône River, this area is renowned for its well-preserved Renaissance architecture, narrow medieval streets, and vibrant cultural scene. It is a UNESCO World Heritage Site and offers a wealth of experiences for visitors. Here's an in-depth exploration of Vieux Lyon:

Historical Overview

Origins and Development:

Roman Foundations: Vieux Lyon's history dates back to Roman times, with the area originally known as Lugdunum. While the majority of the Renaissance architecture is from the 15th and 16th centuries, the area has been continuously inhabited since ancient times.

Renaissance Flourish: The district flourished during the Renaissance, a period when Lyon became a major center for trade and commerce. Wealthy merchants and bankers built grand townhouses, many of which still stand today.

UNESCO World Heritage Status:

Designation: In 1998, Vieux Lyon was designated a UNESCO World Heritage Site for its exceptional preservation of Renaissance architecture and its role in the city's historical development.

Preservation Efforts: The designation has led to significant efforts to maintain and restore the district's historic buildings and public spaces.

Architectural and Cultural Highlights

Renaissance Architecture:

Colorful Facades: The buildings in Vieux Lyon are characterized by their vibrant, colorful facades and ornate decorations. Many structures feature wooden balconies, carved stonework, and elaborate doorways.

Townhouses: Notable examples include the Hôtel de Gadagne and the Hôtel de la Chancellerie, which showcase the grandeur of Renaissance design.

Traboules:

Definition: Traboules are unique passageways that connect different buildings and courtyards. Originally designed for practical purposes, such as transporting goods and avoiding bad weather, they are now a fascinating architectural feature.

Exploration: Some traboules are open to the public and can be explored through guided tours. They offer a glimpse into the historical layout of the district and the lives of its past residents.

Saint-Jean Cathedral:

Location: Situated in the heart of Vieux Lyon, Saint-Jean Cathedral (Cathédrale Saint-Jean-Baptiste) is a stunning example of Gothic architecture.

Features: The cathedral is known for its intricate stained glass windows, beautiful rose windows, and impressive astronomical clock.

Museums:

Gadagne Museum: Housed in the Hôtel de Gadagne, this museum complex includes the Museum of Lyon History and the Museum of Puppetry. It offers insights into the city's history and the art of puppetry, a traditional form of entertainment in Lyon.

Musée Miniature et Cinéma: This museum, located in the heart of Vieux Lyon, showcases miniature scenes and film sets, offering a unique look at cinematic craftsmanship and the art of miniature modeling.

Culinary and Shopping Experiences

Restaurants and Cafés:

Local Cuisine: Vieux Lyon is renowned for its traditional Lyonnaise cuisine. The district is home to many "bouchons," traditional Lyonnais eateries known for their hearty dishes such as quenelles, andouillette, and coq au vin.

Cafés: The area's charming cafés provide a perfect setting to enjoy a coffee or a glass of wine while soaking in the ambiance of the historic streets.

Shops and Markets:

Boutiques: The district features a range of boutiques selling artisanal goods, antiques, and souvenirs. These shops often occupy historic buildings, adding to the district's charm.

Local Markets: The nearby Saint-Antoine Market, while not directly in Vieux Lyon, is easily accessible and offers fresh produce, local specialties, and other goods.

Cultural and Recreational Activities

Festivals and Events:

Fête de la Lumière: The annual Festival of Lights (Fête de la Lumière) is a major event in Lyon, during which the city is illuminated with artistic light displays. Vieux Lyon is a central part of the festival, with many buildings and streets participating in the light show.

Local Festivals: The district also hosts various local festivals, cultural events, and street performances throughout the year.

Walking Tours:

Guided Tours: Walking tours of Vieux Lyon offer an opportunity to explore its historical and architectural landmarks with knowledgeable guides who provide insights into the district's past.

Self-Guided Exploration: Visitors can also enjoy self-guided exploration, wandering through the narrow streets, discovering hidden traboules, and taking in the historical atmosphere.

Challenges and Considerations

Tourist Crowds:

Popularity: Vieux Lyon is a popular tourist destination, which can lead to crowded conditions, particularly during peak travel seasons and major events. Visiting early in the day or during off-peak times can help avoid the busiest crowds.

Cobblestone Streets:

Mobility: The district's cobblestone streets and uneven surfaces can be challenging for those with mobility issues. Comfortable walking shoes are recommended, and accessibility options may be limited in some areas.

Preservation vs. Modernization:

Balance: Balancing the preservation of historic structures with the needs of modern infrastructure can be a challenge. Efforts are ongoing to ensure that development does not compromise the district's historical integrity.

Lyon Cathedral (Cathédrale Saint-Jean-Baptiste)

The **Cathédrale Saint-Jean-Baptiste**, commonly known as Lyon Cathedral, is a prominent and historic landmark in Lyon, France. Situated in the heart of the Vieux Lyon (Old Lyon) district, the cathedral is renowned for its architectural splendor and historical significance. Here's an extensive overview of this remarkable site:

Historical Background

Origins and Construction:

Founding: The site of Lyon Cathedral has been a place of Christian worship since the early Christian period. The current structure began construction in the 12th century and was completed in the 15th century.

Architectural Evolution: The cathedral is a blend of Romanesque and Gothic architectural styles, reflecting the changes and developments in architecture over several centuries.

Historical Significance:

Religious Importance: As the seat of the Archdiocese of Lyon, the cathedral has been a central place of worship and religious authority in the region. It has hosted numerous significant religious ceremonies, including papal visits and royal events.

Cultural Impact: The cathedral is a key element of Lyon's historical and cultural heritage, and it has played an important role in the city's religious and civic life.

Architectural Features

Exterior Design:

Facade: The facade of the cathedral is an impressive example of Gothic architecture, characterized by its intricate stone carvings, large rose windows, and pointed arches. The facade features both Romanesque and Gothic elements, showcasing the architectural transition over time.

Towers: The cathedral has two asymmetric towers, which are distinctive features of its skyline. The towers are adorned with decorative elements and contribute to the cathedral's imposing presence.

Interior Design:

Nave and Chancel: The interior of Lyon Cathedral is spacious, with a grand nave and chancel. The nave is flanked by aisles and features vaulted ceilings supported by ribbed arches.

Astronomical Clock: One of the most famous features of the cathedral is its astronomical clock, located in the south transept. The clock, dating from the 14th century, is a remarkable piece of medieval craftsmanship that displays not only the time but also astronomical information and religious dates.

Stained Glass Windows: The cathedral's stained glass windows are notable for their vibrant colors and intricate designs. They depict various religious scenes and figures, contributing to the cathedral's overall aesthetic.

Additional Features:

Chapels: The cathedral houses several chapels, each with its own unique artwork and religious artifacts. These chapels provide spaces for prayer and reflection.

Treasury: The cathedral's treasury contains a collection of religious relics, manuscripts, and liturgical objects of historical and artistic value.

Cultural and Touristic Significance

Religious and Pilgrimage Site:

Religious Services: Lyon Cathedral continues to serve as a place of worship, hosting regular masses, special liturgical events, and ceremonies. It remains an important center for the Catholic community in Lyon.

Pilgrimages: The cathedral attracts pilgrims and visitors from around the world, drawn by its religious significance and historical importance.

Architectural and Artistic Appeal:

Guided Tours: Visitors can take guided tours to learn about the cathedral's history, architecture, and art. These tours often include insights into the construction process, architectural styles, and the significance of various features.

Photography and Exploration: The cathedral's stunning architecture and interior make it a popular subject for photography. Visitors can explore the various parts of the cathedral, including the nave, chapels, and cloisters.

Cultural Events:

Concerts and Performances: The cathedral occasionally hosts concerts and musical performances, taking advantage of its excellent acoustics and grand setting.

Festivals and Ceremonies: The cathedral is a central venue for major religious festivals and civic ceremonies, contributing to its vibrant cultural life.

Challenges and Considerations

Tourist Crowds:

Popularity: The cathedral is a major tourist attraction, which can lead to large crowds, particularly during peak travel seasons and religious events. Visiting during quieter times can enhance the experience.

Preservation and Maintenance:

Conservation Efforts: Maintaining the cathedral's historical and architectural integrity is an ongoing challenge. Conservation efforts are necessary to preserve the building's features and ensure its longevity.

Restoration Work: Periodic restoration work may affect accessibility to certain areas of the cathedral, so visitors should check for any ongoing maintenance activities before planning their visit.

Accessibility:

Navigation: The cathedral's historical design includes uneven surfaces and narrow passageways, which can be challenging for visitors with mobility issues. It's advisable to check accessibility options and plan accordingly.

Musée des Beaux-Arts de Lyon

The **Musée des Beaux-Arts de Lyon** (Lyon Museum of Fine Arts) is one of the most important and prestigious art museums in France. Located in the heart of Lyon, this museum is renowned for its extensive collection of artworks spanning several centuries and artistic styles. Here's an in-depth look at what makes the Musée des Beaux-Arts de Lyon a must-visit destination:

Historical Background

Origins and Development:

Foundation: The Musée des Beaux-Arts de Lyon was founded in 1803 during the French Revolutionary period. It was established to house and preserve artworks that had been confiscated from religious institutions and private collections.

Building: The museum is housed in the former Benedictine convent of Saint-Pierre, a historic building that dates back to the 17th century. The convent's architecture, with its elegant courtyards and cloisters, provides a stunning backdrop for the museum's collections.

Collections and Exhibitions

Permanent Collections:

Paintings: The museum boasts an impressive collection of paintings from the 14th to the 20th century. Highlights include works by famous artists such as Pierre-Auguste Renoir, Claude Monet, Edgar Degas, and Vincent van Gogh. The collection spans various movements, including Renaissance, Baroque, Rococo, Neoclassical, Romanticism, and Impressionism.

Sculptures: The sculpture collection features masterpieces from different periods, including works by renowned sculptors such as Rodin and Barye. The museum's sculpture garden and courtyards showcase both classical and modern pieces.

Antiquities: The museum has a significant collection of antiquities, including Egyptian, Greek, and Roman artifacts. These collections offer insights into ancient civilizations and their art forms.

Decorative Arts: The museum's collection of decorative arts includes ceramics, textiles, furniture, and objets d'art. These items reflect the evolution of design and craftsmanship over the centuries.

Temporary Exhibitions:

Special Exhibitions: The museum regularly hosts temporary exhibitions that focus on specific artists, artistic movements, or themes. These exhibitions often include loans from other institutions and private collections, offering visitors a chance to see rare and exceptional works.

Collaborations: The museum collaborates with other institutions and museums to present diverse and innovative exhibitions. These collaborations contribute to the museum's dynamic program and enhance its cultural offerings.

Architectural Features

Building Design:

Historic Architecture: The museum's building is a prime example of classical architecture, featuring elegant facades, spacious galleries, and serene courtyards. The former convent's architecture creates a tranquil environment for viewing art.

Interior Spaces: The museum's interior includes a series of grand halls and intimate galleries, each designed to complement the artworks on display. The layout facilitates both large-scale exhibitions and smaller, focused displays.

Museum Gardens:

Courtyards: The museum's courtyards and gardens provide peaceful spaces for visitors to relax and reflect. These outdoor areas often feature sculptures and fountains, enhancing the museum experience.

Educational and Cultural Activities

Educational Programs:

Workshops and Tours: The museum offers a range of educational programs, including guided tours, workshops, and lectures. These programs are designed for various audiences, including school groups, families, and art enthusiasts.

Publications: The museum publishes catalogs, books, and scholarly articles related to its collections and exhibitions. These publications provide valuable insights into the museum's holdings and art history.

Cultural Events:

Lectures and Symposia: The museum hosts lectures, symposia, and artist talks that provide deeper understanding and context for the artworks on display. These events feature contributions from scholars, artists, and curators.

Cultural Partnerships: The museum collaborates with local and international cultural organizations to enhance its programming and reach a wider audience.

Visitor Experience

Facilities:

Visitor Services: The museum offers various services for visitors, including a café, museum shop, and accessibility options. The museum shop features art-related books, prints, and souvenirs.

Accessibility: The museum is committed to providing access for all visitors, with facilities and services tailored to accommodate different needs.

Admission and Hours:

Tickets: Admission fees vary depending on exhibitions and visitor categories. The museum often offers free admission on specific days or for certain groups.

Opening Hours: The museum is generally open to the public several days a week, with specific hours that may vary. It is advisable to check the museum's website for current opening hours and ticket information.

Challenges and Considerations

Crowds:

Popularity: The museum's extensive collection and special exhibitions can attract large numbers of visitors, particularly during peak tourist seasons. Planning a visit during quieter times or early in the day can help avoid crowds.

Restoration and Maintenance:

Conservation Efforts: Maintaining and restoring artworks is a critical part of the museum's operations. Ongoing conservation efforts ensure that the museum's collections are preserved for future generations.

Temporary Closures:

Exhibitions and Renovations: The museum may have temporary closures or restricted access due to special exhibitions, renovations, or maintenance work. It is advisable to check the museum's schedule in advance.

Gallo-Roman Museum of Lyon-Fourvière

The **Gallo-Roman Museum of Lyon-Fourvière** (Musée Gadagne or Musée des Antiquités Romaines) is a significant archaeological museum located in Lyon, France. It is dedicated to the Gallo-Roman history of the city and provides extensive insights into Lyon's ancient past. Here's an in-depth look at what makes this museum a must-visit destination:

Historical Background

Origins and Development:

Foundation: The Gallo-Roman Museum was established in 1921 and is situated on the Fourvière Hill, where ancient Lyon (Lugdunum) once stood. The museum's location is significant, as it is close to the ruins of the Roman city.

Architecture: The museum building was designed by architect Jean-Marie Chémetov and completed in 1975. Its design is modern and complements the historical artifacts it houses.

Collections and Exhibitions

Permanent Collections:

Roman Artifacts: The museum's collections include a vast array of Roman artifacts, such as sculptures, mosaics, ceramics, and everyday objects. These artifacts offer a glimpse into daily life, religious practices, and artistic achievements in ancient Lyon.

Archaeological Finds: The museum features significant archaeological finds from the Roman city of Lugdunum, including remnants of public buildings, bathhouses, and theaters.

Statues and Reliefs: Notable pieces include statues of Roman deities, emperors, and mythological figures, as well as reliefs depicting scenes from Roman life and mythology.

Temporary Exhibitions:

Special Exhibitions: The museum regularly hosts temporary exhibitions that focus on specific aspects of Gallo-Roman history or broader themes related to ancient civilizations. These exhibitions often feature artifacts from other collections or temporary loans.

Educational Displays: Temporary exhibitions may include interactive displays and educational materials designed to engage visitors and enhance their understanding of the ancient world.

Architectural and Design Features

Building Design:

Modern Architecture: The museum's architecture is characterized by its modern design, featuring clean lines and extensive use of glass. This contemporary approach contrasts with the ancient artifacts and highlights the museum's role in bridging the past and present.

Integration with Ruins: The museum is designed to integrate with the surrounding Roman ruins and the natural landscape of Fourvière Hill. It offers panoramic views of Lyon and its historical sites.

Exhibition Spaces:

Gallery Layout: The museum's galleries are arranged to provide a chronological and thematic exploration of Roman history. Artifacts are displayed in context, with informative labels and multimedia presentations that enhance the visitor experience.

Restoration Workshop: The museum includes a restoration workshop where visitors can observe conservation efforts and learn about the processes involved in preserving ancient artifacts.

Cultural and Educational Activities

Educational Programs:

Workshops and Tours: The museum offers a range of educational programs, including guided tours, workshops for schools, and family activities. These programs are designed to provide deeper insights into Gallo-Roman history and engage visitors of all ages.

Lectures and Seminars: The museum hosts lectures and seminars on topics related to Roman history, archaeology, and art. These events often feature experts and scholars who share their knowledge and research.

Publications:

Catalogs and Books: The museum publishes catalogs, books, and research papers related to its collections and exhibitions. These publications provide valuable resources for researchers and enthusiasts interested in Gallo-Roman history.

Visitor Experience

Facilities:

Visitor Services: The museum provides various services for visitors, including a café, museum shop, and amenities for families. The museum shop offers a range of books, souvenirs, and replicas related to Roman history.

Accessibility: The museum is equipped with facilities for visitors with disabilities, including ramps, elevators, and accessible restrooms.

Admission and Hours:

Tickets: Admission fees vary depending on exhibitions and visitor categories. The museum often offers reduced prices for groups, students, and seniors.

Opening Hours: The museum is open to the public several days a week, with specific hours that may vary. It is advisable to check the museum's website for the most up-to-date information on opening hours and ticket prices.

Challenges and Considerations

Tourist Crowds:

Popularity: The museum's significant collections and location make it a popular destination, particularly during peak tourist seasons. Visiting during off-peak times can enhance the experience and provide a more leisurely exploration of the exhibits.

Preservation and Conservation:

Maintenance: Preserving ancient artifacts is a critical aspect of the museum's operations. Ongoing conservation efforts ensure that the collections are maintained and protected for future generations.

Educational Engagement:

Interactive Elements: While the museum offers educational programs, incorporating more interactive and digital elements could further enhance visitor engagement and understanding.

Chapter 10: Outdoor Activities

Exploring Parc de la Tête d'Or

Parc de la Tête d'Or (Golden Head Park) is Lyon's largest and most renowned public park, offering a diverse array of outdoor activities and natural beauty. Covering 117 hectares in the 6th arrondissement of Lyon, it serves as a central recreational space for both locals and visitors. Here's an extensive look at what makes Parc de la Tête d'Or one of the best outdoor destinations in Lyon:

Historical Background

Origins and Development:

Creation: The park was created in the mid-19th century, with its development beginning in 1856. It was designed by the landscape architect Denis Bühler and was influenced by the English garden style, which emphasizes naturalistic landscapes and open spaces.

Name: The name "Tête d'Or" (Golden Head) is believed to derive from a local legend involving a golden statue or a golden head found in the area, though the exact origin of the name is somewhat ambiguous.

Key Features and Attractions

Botanical Gardens:

Diverse Flora: The park's botanical gardens showcase a vast collection of plants, including exotic species, medicinal herbs, and ornamental flowers. The gardens are organized into different sections, each with its own theme and plant varieties.

Greenhouses: The park houses several greenhouses that display tropical and subtropical plants. These structures provide a controlled environment for plants that would not thrive in the local climate.

Lake and Boating:

Artificial Lake: The park features a large artificial lake, which is a central attraction. The lake is used for various recreational activities, including boating and paddle boating.

Paddle Boats: Visitors can rent paddle boats to explore the lake, enjoying a peaceful and scenic experience. The lake's calm waters and picturesque surroundings make it a popular spot for families and couples.

Zoo:

Animal Exhibits: The park includes a free-to-enter zoo, which houses a variety of animals from around the world. The zoo focuses on conservation and education, featuring species such as lions, giraffes, monkeys, and birds.

Educational Programs: The zoo offers educational programs and activities for children and families, providing opportunities to learn about wildlife and conservation efforts.

Rose Garden:

Beautiful Blooms: The rose garden is a highlight of the park, featuring thousands of rose bushes arranged in various designs. The garden is particularly vibrant during the blooming season, offering a colorful and fragrant experience.

Seasonal Displays: The rose garden often hosts seasonal events and exhibitions, showcasing different varieties of roses and floral arrangements.

Playgrounds and Sports Facilities:

Play Areas: The park is equipped with several playgrounds and play areas for children. These facilities include swings, slides, and climbing structures, making it a family-friendly destination.

Sports Facilities: The park features sports facilities, including tennis courts, basketball courts, and a cycling path. These amenities provide opportunities for physical activity and recreation.

Walking and Cycling Paths:

Trails: The park offers extensive walking and cycling paths that wind through its various landscapes. These trails are ideal for leisurely strolls, jogging, or cycling.

Scenic Routes: The paths pass through wooded areas, open lawns, and along the lake, providing diverse and scenic routes for outdoor enthusiasts.

Picnic Areas and Gardens:

Picnic Spots: The park has numerous picnic areas equipped with tables and benches. These spots are perfect for enjoying a meal in a natural setting, whether you bring your own food or purchase refreshments from nearby vendors.

Garden Spaces: The park's open lawns and garden areas offer ample space for picnicking, relaxing, or playing outdoor games.

Cultural and Community Events

Festivals and Markets:

Seasonal Events: Parc de la Tête d'Or hosts various festivals and markets throughout the year. These events include flower festivals, craft markets, and cultural celebrations.

Outdoor Performances: The park often features outdoor performances, such as concerts, theater productions, and dance events. These performances add to the park's vibrant cultural atmosphere.

Educational and Family Activities:

Workshops and Classes: The park offers workshops and classes for all ages, including nature-related activities, art classes, and educational programs about plants and animals.

Family-Friendly Events: The park's amenities and activities make it a popular destination for families. Special family-oriented events and activities are frequently organized.

Visitor Experience

Facilities:

Refreshments: The park has several cafés and kiosks where visitors can purchase food and drinks. These establishments offer a range of refreshments, from snacks to full meals.

Restrooms: The park is equipped with restrooms for visitor convenience.

Accessibility:

Public Transport: The park is accessible via public transport, with several bus and tram lines stopping nearby. It is also within walking distance from central areas of Lyon.

Wheelchair Accessibility: The park's paths and facilities are designed to be accessible to visitors with disabilities, ensuring that everyone can enjoy the park's features.

Admission:

Free Entry: Most areas of the park, including the lake, botanical gardens, and playgrounds, are free to enter. The zoo is also free of charge, though donations are encouraged to support its conservation efforts.

Challenges and Considerations

Crowds:

Popularity: Parc de la Tête d'Or is a popular destination, particularly on weekends and during public holidays. Visitors may encounter larger crowds during peak times, so planning a visit during quieter periods can enhance the experience.

Maintenance and Conservation:

Ongoing Efforts: Maintaining the park's extensive grounds and facilities requires ongoing effort. Some areas may be under maintenance or renovation, which can temporarily affect accessibility.

Weather:

Seasonal Changes: Weather conditions can impact outdoor activities. The park is most enjoyable during pleasant weather, and visitors should be prepared for varying conditions, especially if planning to engage in outdoor sports or picnicking.

Hiking and Walking in Fourvière Hill

Fourvière Hill in Lyon is a prominent and historically significant location that offers excellent opportunities for hiking and walking. Overlooking the city, this hill provides stunning panoramic views, rich historical context, and a variety of trails and paths for outdoor enthusiasts. Here's an extensive guide to hiking and walking in Fourvière Hill:

Historical and Cultural Significance

Historical Background:

Ancient Roots: Fourvière Hill, known as the "hill of the god Fourvius" in Roman times, was the site of the ancient Roman city of Lugdunum. It was a major center of administration and culture during the Roman Empire.

Religious Heritage: The hill is home to several significant religious sites, including the Basilica of Notre-Dame de Fourvière, which was built in the late 19th century and is a major pilgrimage site.

Key Hiking and Walking Trails

Fourvière Hill Trails:

Fourvière Hill Walk: This trail offers a circular route around the hill, providing access to major landmarks such as the Basilica of Notre-Dame de Fourvière, the Gallo-Roman Museum, and the Roman theaters. The path includes both paved and natural surfaces, with some steep sections.

Roman Ruins Trail: This trail takes visitors through the ancient Roman ruins on Fourvière Hill, including the Odeon and the Roman Theater. It's an opportunity to explore Lyon's historical heritage while enjoying a walk through well-preserved archaeological sites.

Panoramic Views Trail:

Viewpoints: The trail includes several viewpoints that offer spectacular vistas of Lyon and the surrounding region. Popular spots include the terrace of the Basilica, which provides sweeping views of the city and the Rhône-Alpes region.

Photography Spots: The panoramic views make this trail an excellent choice for photography enthusiasts. Early morning or late afternoon light can provide the best conditions for capturing the cityscape.

Nature and Scenic Trails:

Forest Path: Some trails on Fourvière Hill wind through wooded areas, offering a more natural experience. These paths provide a respite from the urban environment and allow walkers to enjoy the serene beauty of the local flora.

Garden Walks: The area around the Basilica includes landscaped gardens and terraced green spaces. Walking through these areas provides a blend of natural beauty and historical ambiance.

Attractions and Points of Interest

Basilica of Notre-Dame de Fourvière:

Architectural Marvel: This basilica is a key highlight of Fourvière Hill, known for its ornate architecture and stunning mosaics. It's a major destination for both religious pilgrims and tourists.

Observation Deck: The basilica's observation deck offers some of the best panoramic views of Lyon.

Roman Theaters:

Ancient Theaters: The Roman theaters, including the Grand Theater and the Odeon, are important archaeological sites that date back to the 1st century AD. They offer insight into Lyon's Roman past and are integral to the hiking experience.

Gallo-Roman Museum of Lyon-Fourvière:

Museum Visit: Located near the Roman ruins, this museum provides context for the artifacts and ruins seen on the trails. It's a valuable resource for understanding the history of Lugdunum.

Saint-Just Cathedral:

Historic Church: Located nearby, this cathedral is worth a visit for its historical and architectural significance. It adds to the rich tapestry of Fourvière Hill's cultural offerings.

Visitor Experience

Preparation:

Footwear: Wear comfortable hiking shoes or walking boots, as some trails can be steep and uneven.

Weather: Check the weather forecast before heading out. Some trails may be slippery in wet conditions, so be cautious during rainy weather.

Facilities:

Cafés and Restaurants: There are several cafés and restaurants on Fourvière Hill where visitors can stop for a meal or a drink. These establishments offer a chance to relax and enjoy the views after a hike.

Rest Areas: The hill features several rest areas with benches and shaded spots where visitors can take a break.

Accessibility:

Steep Sections: Some trails on Fourvière Hill are steep and may not be suitable for those with mobility issues. It's advisable to choose paths that match your fitness level and physical capabilities.

Public Transport: Fourvière Hill is accessible by public transport, including funicular trains that connect the hill with the city center.

Safety:

Stay on Marked Trails: To ensure safety and protect the environment, stick to marked trails and avoid wandering off the paths.

Hydration: Bring water and stay hydrated, especially during warmer months.

Challenges and Considerations

Crowds:

Popularity: Fourvière Hill is a popular tourist destination, and certain spots, especially around the Basilica, can be crowded. Visiting early in the morning or later in the afternoon can help avoid the busiest times.

Weather Conditions:

Seasonal Variations: The trails can be more challenging in adverse weather conditions. Snow or heavy rain may make some paths difficult to navigate.

Conservation:

Protecting Heritage: As an area with significant historical and archaeological value, it's important to respect the sites and contribute to their preservation by avoiding vandalism and littering.

Cycling Along the Rhône and Saône Rivers

Cycling along the Rhône and Saône rivers in Lyon is a fantastic way to explore the city's scenic beauty, rich history, and vibrant culture. Both rivers offer dedicated cycling paths that are well-maintained and provide a safe, enjoyable experience for cyclists of all levels. Here's an extensive guide to cycling along the Rhône and Saône rivers:

Overview

Rivers and Routes:

Rhône River: The Rhône flows south from Lake Geneva to the Mediterranean Sea, and its path through Lyon offers a picturesque route with urban and natural landscapes.

Saône River: The Saône, a tributary of the Rhône, flows north from the French Alps, and its route through Lyon complements the Rhône path, offering additional scenic views and attractions.

Cycling Routes and Highlights

Cycling Along the Rhône River:

North of Lyon:

Parc de la Tête d'Or to Quai de la Pêcherie: Starting at the Parc de la Tête d'Or, cyclists can head south along the Rhône riverbanks, passing through scenic areas and parks. The route follows the Quai de la Pêcherie and offers views of the city's landmarks and waterfront.

Lyon's Riverside Promenades: The path along the Rhône includes promenades and bridges, such as the Pont de la Guillotière and the Pont Wilson, which connect different parts of the city and offer varied views of the river.

South of Lyon:

Quai de Serbie to Confluence: This section of the Rhône path leads to the Confluence area, where the Rhône meets the Saône. It includes modern architectural landmarks like the Musée des Confluences and the Confluence shopping center.

Urban and Nature Mix: The route features both urban landscapes and natural scenery, including parks, gardens, and open spaces. It's ideal for combining city sightseeing with relaxing riverside views.

Cycling Along the Saône River:

North of Lyon:

Vieux Lyon to Pont Lafayette: Starting from the historic Vieux Lyon, cyclists can follow the Saône path northwards, passing through charming old neighborhoods and historic buildings. The route includes views of the Basilica of Notre-Dame de Fourvière and the old city's architecture.

Saône Riverside Parks: The route includes several parks and green spaces along the Saône, such as the Parc de la Tête d'Or and Parc des Berges du Rhône, offering places to rest and enjoy the surroundings.

South of Lyon:

Confluence to Gerland: The southern section of the Saône path leads to the Gerland area, known for its modern urban development and sports facilities. It includes views of Lyon's dynamic and evolving cityscape.

Cultural and Historical Landmarks: This route offers access to cultural landmarks and museums, such as the Musée des Confluences and various historical sites along the riverbanks.

Attractions and Points of Interest

Historical Sites:

Vieux Lyon: Cycling through Vieux Lyon provides a chance to explore the city's Renaissance heritage and historic architecture.

Basilica of Notre-Dame de Fourvière: Views of this iconic basilica can be enjoyed from various points along the rivers, offering a blend of historical and architectural interest.

Modern Architecture:

Musée des Confluences: Located at the confluence of the Rhône and Saône, this striking museum offers contemporary architecture and exhibitions on science and society.

Confluence District: This modern district features innovative architecture and urban design, visible from the riverside paths.

Green Spaces:

Parc de la Tête d'Or: One of Lyon's largest parks, it offers expansive green areas, botanical gardens, and a large lake.

Parc des Berges du Rhône: This park features walking and cycling paths, gardens, and recreational areas along the Rhône.

Practical Tips for Cyclists

Bike Rentals:

Public Bike Sharing: Lyon offers a public bike-sharing system called Vélo'v, which provides convenient rental options for exploring the city.

Local Rentals: Numerous bike rental shops around Lyon offer a range of bicycles, including electric bikes, for more comfortable rides.

Cycling Infrastructure:

Dedicated Paths: Both the Rhône and Saône rivers have dedicated cycling paths that are well-marked and separated from vehicle traffic.

Bridges and Crossings: There are several bridges connecting the two rivers and providing access to various parts of the city.

Safety and Etiquette:

Helmet and Gear: While helmets are not mandatory for adults in France, they are recommended for safety. Ensure your bike is in good condition and equipped with lights if cycling in low-light conditions.

Respecting Pedestrians: The riverside paths are popular with pedestrians, so be mindful and courteous to others using the paths.

Weather Considerations:

Check Forecast: Lyon's weather can be variable, so check the forecast before heading out. Rain or strong winds may impact cycling conditions.

Dress Accordingly: Dress in layers and be prepared for changes in weather, especially if cycling long distances.

Hydration and Refreshments:

Bring Water: Carry water and stay hydrated, especially during warm weather.

Refreshment Stops: There are cafés and restaurants along the rivers where you can stop for a break and enjoy refreshments.

Challenges and Considerations

Crowds:

Busy Times: The riverside paths can be busy, particularly on weekends and during peak tourist seasons. Cycling early in the morning or later in the day can help avoid the busiest times.

Urban Environment:

Traffic: While the cycling paths are well-maintained, be prepared for occasional intersections and crossings with vehicle traffic. Exercise caution at these points.

Maintenance:

Path Conditions: While generally well-maintained, sections of the path may experience wear and tear or temporary closures for maintenance. Check local updates if planning a longer ride.

Boat Tours on the Saône and Rhône Rivers

Boat tours on the Saône and Rhône rivers in Lyon offer a unique and picturesque way to explore the city's landscapes, historic sites, and vibrant atmosphere. These tours provide a different perspective of Lyon, highlighting its architectural landmarks, scenic beauty, and historical significance. Here's an extensive guide to boat tours on these rivers:

Overview of Boat Tours

Rivers and Routes:

Saône River: The Saône flows through the heart of Lyon, offering routes that highlight the city's historical architecture, charming neighborhoods, and cultural landmarks.

Rhône River: The Rhône runs alongside Lyon, providing routes that showcase modern developments, green spaces, and panoramic views of the city.

Types of Boat Tours

Sightseeing Cruises:

Classic City Tours: These cruises provide a general overview of Lyon's main attractions. They typically cover key sites along both the Saône and Rhône rivers, such as the Basilica of Notre-Dame de Fourvière, Vieux Lyon, and the Confluence district.

Duration: Sightseeing cruises usually last between 1 to 2 hours and are often available throughout the day.

Dinner Cruises:

Gourmet Experience: Dinner cruises offer a refined dining experience with a view. Guests can enjoy a multi-course meal prepared by chefs while cruising along the rivers.

Evening Views: These cruises often take place in the evening, providing a chance to see the city illuminated by night, with highlights such as illuminated bridges and buildings.

Themed Cruises:

Cultural Tours: Some boat tours focus on specific themes, such as Lyon's history, gastronomy, or wine. These tours may include commentary, presentations, or tastings related to the theme.

Seasonal Events: Themed cruises may be offered during special events or seasons, such as festivals, holidays, or summer events.

Private Charters:

Customized Tours: Private boat charters are available for those who prefer a personalized experience. These charters can be customized to include specific routes, meals, or entertainment.

Occasions: Private charters are ideal for celebrations, corporate events, or intimate gatherings.

Key Highlights and Attractions

Historic Landmarks:

Vieux Lyon: Cruises along the Saône provide views of the historic district of Vieux Lyon, known for its Renaissance architecture and narrow, winding streets.

Basilica of Notre-Dame de Fourvière: The basilica's striking facade and panoramic views of the city are visible from both rivers, offering an impressive sight from the water.

Modern Developments:

Confluence District: The Rhône river route includes views of the Confluence district, featuring modern architecture, such as the Musée des Confluences and the Confluence shopping center.

Green Spaces: The riverside parks and promenades along the Rhône provide a glimpse of Lyon's commitment to urban green spaces and recreational areas.

Scenic Views:

Panoramic Perspectives: Boat tours offer unique vantage points for appreciating Lyon's skyline, bridges, and natural surroundings. Views of the city from the water are particularly striking during sunset or nighttime.

Architectural Features:

Bridges and Quays: Lyon's bridges, such as the Pont Lafayette and Pont de la Guillotière, and quays along the rivers are architectural highlights that are beautifully showcased from the boat.

Practical Tips for Boat Tours

Booking and Reservations:

Advance Booking: It's advisable to book boat tours in advance, especially during peak tourist seasons or for popular tours. Online reservations are often available and convenient.

Tour Providers: Various companies operate boat tours in Lyon, such as Les Bateaux Lyonnais and Lyon City Boat. Research and compare options to find the tour that best suits your preferences.

Clothing and Comfort:

Dress Appropriately: Wear comfortable clothing and consider layering, as weather conditions on the river can vary. Bring a light jacket or sweater, especially for evening cruises.

Footwear: Comfortable shoes are recommended, particularly if you'll be boarding and disembarking the boat.

Accessibility:

Wheelchair Access: Many boat tours are wheelchair accessible, but it's a good idea to confirm with the tour provider in advance to ensure that they can accommodate specific needs.

Weather Considerations:

Check Forecast: Lyon's weather can be variable, so check the forecast before your tour. Most boats have covered areas or indoor seating in case of rain.

Dining and Refreshments:

Meals: For dinner cruises, verify the menu options and dietary restrictions in advance. Some tours offer a selection of meals and beverages, while others may provide a more casual dining experience.

Drinks: Most boat tours offer drinks, but you may also bring your own refreshments if allowed by the tour provider.

Challenges and Considerations

Crowds:

Busy Times: Boat tours can be popular, particularly during peak tourist seasons or special events. Consider scheduling your tour during off-peak times to avoid large crowds.

Pricing:

Cost: Boat tours vary in price based on duration, type, and included amenities. Compare different options to find a tour that fits your budget and preferences.

Timing:

Tour Duration: Plan accordingly based on the duration of the tour and any additional activities or attractions you want to visit in Lyon.

Visiting Parc des Hauteurs

Parc des Hauteurs is a beautiful and historically significant park located on the Fourvière Hill in Lyon. Offering stunning views, green spaces, and a blend of natural and cultural attractions, it is a great spot for both relaxation and exploration. Here's an extensive guide to visiting Parc des Hauteurs:

Overview

Location and Access:

Location: Parc des Hauteurs is situated on Fourvière Hill, which is a prominent hill overlooking the city of Lyon. The park is part of the larger Fourvière area, known for its historical significance and panoramic views.

Access: The park is accessible by foot, with several walking paths leading up from the city. Visitors can also use public transportation, such as buses or the funicular railway, which connects the lower city to the top of Fourvière Hill.

Key Features and Attractions

Scenic Views:

Panoramic Vistas: The park offers some of the best panoramic views of Lyon, including sights of the Rhône and Saône rivers, the city's skyline, and the surrounding landscapes. The viewpoints provide excellent opportunities for photography and sightseeing.

Basilica of Notre-Dame de Fourvière: From the park, visitors can enjoy views of the iconic basilica, which dominates the hill and is a key feature of Lyon's skyline.

Historical Monuments:

Roman Ruins: Parc des Hauteurs is located near significant Roman archaeological sites, including the ancient Roman theaters and the Gallo-Roman Museum. While the park itself is more focused on green space, the nearby historical sites can be explored in conjunction with a visit to the park.

Fourvière Basilica: The basilica, a major historical and architectural landmark, is closely associated with the park. Its impressive facade and detailed mosaics are visible from various points in the park.

Green Spaces and Gardens:

Landscaped Areas: The park features beautifully landscaped gardens and open green spaces, ideal for leisurely walks, picnics, or simply relaxing in a serene environment.

Flower Beds and Trees: The park is adorned with flower beds and mature trees, creating a pleasant and tranquil setting.

Walking Paths and Trails:

Paths and Trails: The park includes several walking paths that meander through its green spaces and offer different vantage points of the city and surrounding areas. The paths are well-maintained and suitable for casual strolling.

Hiking Trails: For those interested in more vigorous exercise, there are trails leading up from the city to the park, providing both a workout and the chance to explore the natural beauty of the area.

Cultural and Educational Aspects:

Educational Signage: Some areas of the park include informational signage about the history and significance of the surrounding landmarks, providing educational insights to visitors.

Cultural Events: The park occasionally hosts cultural events, such as outdoor concerts, festivals, and art exhibitions. Checking local listings for any events during your visit can enhance your experience.

Practical Tips for Visiting

Preparation:

Comfortable Footwear: Wear comfortable walking shoes, as the park and its surrounding areas include both paved and natural surfaces.

Weather: Check the weather forecast before your visit. Lyon can experience varying weather conditions, and it's best to be prepared for sunshine, rain, or cooler temperatures.

Facilities:

Refreshments: There are no major dining facilities within the park itself, but there are cafés and restaurants in the nearby area where you can enjoy a meal or refreshments before or after your visit.

Rest Areas: The park has benches and shaded spots where you can rest and enjoy the surroundings.

Accessibility:

Wheelchair Access: The park's paths are generally accessible, but some areas may have steeper inclines. It's advisable to check the specific accessibility details if you have mobility concerns.

Public Transportation:

Funicular Railway: The funicular railway from the city center to Fourvière Hill provides a convenient and scenic way to reach the park. The ride offers beautiful views of Lyon as you ascend the hill.

Buses: Several bus routes serve the Fourvière area, providing additional options for reaching the park.

Safety and Etiquette:

Respect the Environment: Follow park rules and regulations, and respect the natural environment. Avoid littering and stay on designated paths to protect the park's flora and fauna.

Safety: While the park is generally safe, it's always wise to be aware of your surroundings and secure personal belongings, especially if visiting during less busy times.

Challenges and Considerations

Crowds:

Popularity: The park can be popular, especially on weekends and during tourist season. Visiting early in the day or during weekdays can help avoid larger crowds.

Inclines:

Hilly Terrain: The park's location on Fourvière Hill means that there are some steep areas and inclines. Be prepared for a bit of a climb if approaching on foot.

Limited Amenities:

Facilities: While the park offers a beautiful setting, amenities like restrooms and dining options are limited within the park itself. Plan accordingly and consider visiting nearby areas for additional facilities.

Exploring the Traboules in Croix-Rousse offers a fascinating journey into one of Lyon's most unique and historically rich neighborhoods. Traboules are hidden passageways that weave through the buildings of Lyon, particularly in the Croix-Rousse district. These passages provide a glimpse into the city's past and offer a distinctive way to experience Lyon's architectural and cultural heritage. Here's an extensive guide to exploring the traboules in Croix-Rousse:

Overview of Traboules

Definition and Purpose:

Traboules: The term "traboule" comes from the Latin "transambulare," meaning "to walk through." These are narrow, covered passageways that allow pedestrians to traverse through buildings and courtyards, connecting streets and often providing shortcuts.

Historical Use: Traboules were originally used by silk workers in the 19th century to transport their wares between workshops and residences, often to protect them from the weather. They also provided practical routes in the densely built areas of Lyon.

Croix-Rousse District

Historical Background:

Silk Industry: Croix-Rousse, known as the "Canut" district, was the heart of Lyon's silk-weaving industry. The area's traboules are closely associated with this industrial heritage, reflecting the historical importance of the silk trade in Lyon's economy and culture.

Architectural Features: The traboules in Croix-Rousse are notable for their distinctive architecture, including spiral staircases, vaulted passageways, and charming courtyards.

Key Traboules to Explore

Traboule de la Cour des Voraces:

Location: Found at 9-11 Rue des Voraces.

Description: This traboule is famous for its impressive spiral staircase and grand entrance. It was an important site for silk workers and remains one of the most notable examples of traboules in Croix-Rousse.

Traboule de la Maison des Canuts:

Location: Accessible from 16-18 Rue de la Croix-Rousse.

Description: This traboule connects different courtyards and offers insights into the daily life of Lyon's silk workers. The Maison des Canuts, a museum dedicated to the silk industry, is nearby and provides additional context about the traboules.

Traboule du 3 Rue Imbert-Colomès:

Location: 3 Rue Imbert-Colomès.

Description: A less crowded traboule, this passageway features a charming courtyard and traditional architecture. It provides a quieter experience compared to some of the more frequented traboules.

Traboule de la Cour des Annonciades:

Location: 14-16 Rue des Fantasques.

Description: This traboule is noted for its elegant design and historical significance. It offers a glimpse into the architectural style of the period and connects various parts of the Croix-Rousse district.

Practical Tips for Exploring Traboules

Guided Tours:

Historical Tours: Many guided tours are available that focus on the traboules and the history of Croix-Rousse. These tours provide valuable insights and historical context that enhance the experience.

Self-Guided Tours: For those who prefer exploring on their own, several online maps and resources are available that detail the locations and features of key traboules.

Access and Etiquette:

Respect Privacy: Traboules are often private property, so be mindful of residents and follow any posted rules or guidelines. Many traboules are accessible through courtyards and doorways, but it's important to respect people's homes and personal spaces.

Quiet Exploration: Keep noise levels down and avoid disturbing the residents. Some traboules may have restricted access, so be prepared to turn back if a passageway is closed or not open to the public.

Clothing and Footwear:

Comfortable Shoes: Wear comfortable walking shoes, as exploring traboules involves navigating narrow, sometimes uneven passageways and stairs.

Weather Considerations: Since traboules are often covered and can be damp, appropriate clothing for variable weather conditions is advisable.

Safety:

Be Cautious: While generally safe, be cautious in less well-lit or unfamiliar areas. Keep personal belongings secure and be aware of your surroundings.

Nearby Attractions

Maison des Canuts:

Museum: This museum provides an in-depth look at Lyon's silk industry and the role of traboules in the city's history. It's a great complement to exploring the traboules and offers historical exhibits and demonstrations.

Place des Terreaux:

Square: Located at the base of Croix-Rousse, this square is home to the impressive Hôtel de Ville (City Hall) and the Bartholdi Fountain. It's a central landmark worth visiting before or after exploring the traboules.

Croix-Rousse Market:

Local Market: The market on Boulevard de la Croix-Rousse is vibrant and offers a range of local produce, crafts, and culinary delights. It provides a lively contrast to the historical and serene atmosphere of the traboules.

Challenges and Considerations

Navigation:

Complex Layout: The traboules can be confusing due to their labyrinthine layout. Using a map or a guided tour can help navigate the area more easily.

Accessibility:

Varied Access: Some traboules may have restricted access or may not be open to the public. Be prepared to explore alternative passages or return at another time if access is limited.

Crowds:

Popularity: Popular traboules and tourist spots can get crowded, particularly during peak tourist seasons. Visiting during off-peak times can provide a more relaxed experience.

Rock Climbing at Mur de Lyon

Rock climbing at the Mur de Lyon offers a thrilling and accessible climbing experience in one of Lyon's urban settings. The Mur de Lyon, often referred to as the "Lyon Wall," is a prominent climbing wall that caters to both beginners and experienced climbers. Here's an extensive guide to rock climbing at Mur de Lyon:

Overview

Location:

Mur de Lyon: Located in the heart of Lyon, the Mur de Lyon is situated in the **Parc de la Tête d'Or**, one of the city's largest and most popular parks. The climbing wall is an integral part of this recreational area, offering climbers easy access to both urban and natural surroundings.

Features:

Climbing Wall: The Mur de Lyon is known for its large, outdoor climbing wall that features a variety of routes and difficulty levels. The wall is designed to accommodate climbers of different skill levels and provides an excellent opportunity for practice and training.

Key Features of the Mur de Lyon

Diverse Routes:

Difficulty Levels: The climbing wall offers routes ranging from beginner to advanced levels, catering to climbers with varying skills. Routes are graded to help climbers select appropriate challenges.

Variety: The wall features a range of climbing styles, including overhangs, vertical sections, and technical routes, providing a comprehensive climbing experience.

Facilities and Equipment:

Climbing Gear: Climbers are expected to bring their own climbing gear, including harnesses, climbing shoes, and ropes. The park does not provide rental equipment, so it's important to come prepared.

Safety: The climbing wall is equipped with safety features such as safety mats and secure anchors. However, climbers should ensure they follow safety guidelines and procedures to avoid accidents.

Training and Coaching:

Climbing Courses: The Mur de Lyon occasionally offers climbing courses and workshops for beginners and advanced climbers. These sessions provide instruction on climbing techniques, safety practices, and route management.

Local Climbing Clubs: There are local climbing clubs and organizations that offer group climbs, training sessions, and events at the Mur de Lyon. Joining a club can enhance your climbing experience and provide opportunities for socializing with other climbers.

Practical Tips for Rock Climbing at Mur de Lyon

Preparation:

Bring Equipment: Ensure you have all necessary climbing gear, including a harness, climbing shoes, and rope. Check your equipment before heading out to ensure it's in good condition.

Clothing: Wear comfortable, moisture-wicking clothing that allows for ease of movement. Consider layering, as weather conditions can change.

Safety:

Check Safety Measures: Before climbing, familiarize yourself with the safety measures in place. Use climbing helmets if provided or recommended, and always double-check your gear.

Warm-Up: Perform a proper warm-up before climbing to prevent injuries. Stretch and engage in light exercise to prepare your muscles.

Weather Considerations:

Check Forecast: The Mur de Lyon is an outdoor climbing wall, so weather conditions can impact your climbing plans. Check the weather forecast before your visit and be prepared for changes in weather.

Rain and Wet Conditions: Avoid climbing if the wall is wet or if rain is expected, as wet conditions can increase the risk of accidents.

Respect and Etiquette:

Follow Rules: Adhere to any posted rules and guidelines for using the climbing wall. Respect other climbers and take turns on popular routes.

Clean Up: Leave the area clean and dispose of any trash properly. Respect the natural environment and the park's facilities.

Accessibility:

Public Transportation: The Mur de Lyon is easily accessible by public transportation, including buses and trams. The park is well-connected to the city's transportation network.

Parking: There are parking facilities near the park, but availability can vary. Consider using public transportation or cycling to the park if parking is limited.

Nearby Attractions

Parc de la Tête d'Or:

Additional Activities: While at the park, you can enjoy other recreational activities such as walking, jogging, or picnicking. The park also features a large lake, botanical gardens, and playgrounds.

Relaxation: After climbing, relax in one of the park's many green spaces or visit a café within the park for refreshments.

Lyon's Historic Sites:

Vieux Lyon: Explore Lyon's historic district, Vieux Lyon, known for its Renaissance architecture, traboules, and charming streets.

Basilica of Notre-Dame de Fourvière: Visit this iconic basilica for panoramic views of the city and a glimpse into Lyon's architectural heritage.

Local Climbing Shops:

Gear and Advice: Nearby climbing shops can provide additional gear, advice, and information about local climbing routes and events.

Challenges and Considerations

Crowds:

Busy Times: The climbing wall can be popular, particularly during weekends and peak times. Arrive early or visit during off-peak hours to avoid large crowds.

Skill Levels:

Varied Routes: While the wall caters to various skill levels, some routes may be more challenging than others. Be prepared to select routes that match your climbing experience and skill level.

Maintenance:

Wall Condition: The climbing wall is generally well-maintained, but it's always good to check for any updates or maintenance notices that might affect climbing conditions.

Chapter 11: Shopping in Lyon

Markets

Exploring the markets in Lyon offers a vibrant and immersive way to experience the city's culture, gastronomy, and local life. Lyon is renowned for its rich culinary traditions and diverse market offerings, making its markets essential destinations for any visitor. Here's an extensive guide on how to best explore Lyon's markets:

Overview of Lyon's Markets

Lyon boasts a range of markets, each with its unique character and offerings. The most notable markets include:

Marché Les Halles de Lyon-Paul Bocuse

Marché de la Croix-Rousse

Marché Saint-Antoine

Marché de Monplaisir

Marché de la Gare de Vaise

1. Marché Les Halles de Lyon-Paul Bocuse

Location: 102 Cours Lafayette, 69003 Lyon

Overview:

Description: Known as Lyon's premier indoor market, Les Halles de Lyon-Paul Bocuse is a gourmet paradise. It features a wide array of high-quality food products, from fresh produce to artisanal cheeses and charcuterie.

History: Named after the famous Lyonnais chef Paul Bocuse, the market is a testament to Lyon's reputation as the culinary capital of France.

What to Explore:

Gourmet Delights: Explore stalls offering a variety of French delicacies, including foie gras, truffles, pastries, and local wines. The market is renowned for its excellent quality and variety.

Local Specialties: Sample Lyonnais specialties like quenelles (dumplings), and andouillette (sausage), and enjoy freshly baked breads and pastries.

Dining Options: The market also features small dining areas where you can enjoy ready-to-eat dishes prepared by local chefs.

Practical Tips:

Timing: Visit during weekdays to avoid the weekend crowds. The market is open from Tuesday to Saturday.

Cash: While many vendors accept credit cards, carrying some cash can be useful for small purchases.

2. Marché de la Croix-Rousse

Location: Boulevard de la Croix-Rousse, 69004 Lyon

Overview:

Description: This open-air market is located in the bohemian Croix-Rousse district and is famous for its lively atmosphere and diverse offerings.

History: The market is situated in a historical area known for its silk-weaving heritage.

What to Explore:

Fresh Produce: Browse through stalls selling seasonal fruits and vegetables, often directly sourced from local farms.

Local Products: Discover artisanal cheeses, meats, and bread. The market also features crafts, flowers, and other non-food items.

Cultural Experience: The market has a vibrant, community-oriented vibe, making it a great place to experience local life and culture.

Practical Tips:

Timing: The market operates on Tuesday, Thursday, and Saturday mornings.

Negotiation: Don't hesitate to engage with vendors and ask questions about their products. It's a great way to learn more about Lyon's culinary traditions.

3. Marché Saint-Antoine

Location: Quai Saint-Antoine, 69002 Lyon

Overview:

Description: This market is located along the Saône River, offering picturesque views and a charming shopping experience. It's known for its range of fresh produce and local goods.

History: Situated in the heart of the city, the market has a long history and is a key part of Lyon's daily life.

What to Explore:

Seafood and Produce: Explore stalls specializing in fresh seafood, fruits, and vegetables. The market is known for its high-quality products and scenic setting.

Local Artisans: Find unique items such as homemade jams, pickles, and regional wines. The market often features local artisans showcasing their crafts.

Practical Tips:

Timing: Visit on Tuesday, Thursday, and Saturday mornings.

Location: Enjoy a stroll along the river after your market visit. The area around Quai Saint-Antoine is scenic and perfect for exploring on foot.

4. Marché de Monplaisir

Location: Boulevard des Belges, 69008 Lyon

Overview:

Description: This market is situated in the Monplaisir district and offers a more local and intimate market experience compared to some of the larger, more tourist-oriented markets.

History: The market reflects the character of the residential neighborhood, providing a genuine taste of local life.

What to Explore:

Diverse Offerings: Browse through a range of fresh produce, meats, cheeses, and baked goods. The market is known for its friendly atmosphere and quality products.

Local Interaction: Engage with local vendors and residents to gain insights into everyday life in Lyon.

Practical Tips:

Timing: The market operates on Wednesday and Saturday mornings.

Local Vibe: Embrace the local ambiance and take the time to chat with vendors to learn about their products and local recommendations.

5. Marché de la Gare de Vaise

Location: Place du Pont, 69009 Lyon

Overview:

Description: Located near the Vaise train station, this market serves both locals and travelers. It offers a variety of fresh foods and local specialties.

History: The market is situated in a bustling area known for its mix of residential and commercial spaces.

What to Explore:

Convenience: Ideal for travelers looking to pick up fresh produce, snacks, or ingredients for a meal. The market's location makes it a convenient stop for visitors passing through the area.

Local Flavor: Discover a range of regional products, including cheeses, charcuterie, and baked goods.

Practical Tips:

Timing: Visit on Tuesday and Friday mornings.

Accessibility: The market's proximity to the train station makes it easily accessible for those traveling through Lyon.

General Tips for Market Exploration

Plan Your Visit:

Market Days: Verify the operating days and hours for each market, as they may vary. Most markets operate in the mornings and close by early afternoon.

Local Events: Check if there are any special events, festivals, or seasonal markets taking place during your visit.

Engage with Vendors:

Ask Questions: Engage with vendors to learn more about their products and seek recommendations. Many vendors are passionate about their offerings and are happy to share their knowledge.

Tasting: Take advantage of free samples or small tastings, especially at specialty food stalls.

Cash and Payment:

Bring Cash: While many vendors accept credit cards, some may only accept cash. Having some cash on hand ensures a smoother shopping experience.

Small Change: Carry small denominations for easier transactions.

Cultural Etiquette:

Respect Local Customs: Follow local customs and etiquette while shopping. Be polite, and avoid touching products without permission.

Photography: If you wish to take photos, ask for permission, especially in areas where vendors may prefer not to be photographed.

Timing and Crowds:

Avoid Peak Times: To avoid large crowds, visit markets early in the morning or during weekdays if possible. This will allow for a more relaxed experience.

Language:

Basic French Phrases: While many vendors in Lyon speak English, knowing a few basic French phrases can enhance your interaction and show respect for local culture.

Shopping Districts

Lyon boasts several vibrant shopping districts, each offering a unique shopping experience that caters to a variety of tastes and preferences. Here's an extensive guide to the main shopping districts in Lyon, including their features, key attractions, and practical tips for visitors:

1. Presqu'île

Location: The area between the Rhône and Saône rivers, covering the central part of Lyon.

Overview:

Description: Presqu'île is Lyon's main shopping district, known for its upscale boutiques, department stores, and charming pedestrian streets. It's the heart of Lyon's commercial activity and offers a blend of high-end and high-street shopping.

Historical Context: The district features a mix of historical architecture and modern retail spaces, making it a picturesque area for shopping.

Key Attractions:

Rue de la République: One of Lyon's primary shopping streets, lined with international brands, high-street fashion, and flagship stores. It's a bustling area with a variety of shops and eateries.

Place Bellecour: One of Europe's largest squares, which is surrounded by major shopping avenues and offers a central location for exploring nearby shops.

Les Galeries Lafayette: A renowned French department store offering a wide range of fashion, cosmetics, and home goods.

Practical Tips:

Public Transport: Easily accessible via metro and bus. The Bellecour metro station (Lines A and D) is centrally located.

Walking: The district is best explored on foot to fully enjoy its pedestrian-friendly streets and historical architecture.

2. Part-Dieu

Location: In the 3rd arrondissement, northeast of the city center.

Overview:

Description: Part-Dieu is Lyon's modern shopping district, known for its large shopping centers and business hub. It offers a more contemporary shopping experience compared to the historic Presqu'île.

Historical Context: Originally an industrial and business district, Part-Dieu has evolved into a major commercial area with a focus on convenience and modern retail.

Key Attractions:

La Part-Dieu Shopping Center: One of the largest shopping centers in Lyon, featuring a wide range of stores, including fashion, electronics, and home goods. It also has dining options and entertainment facilities.

Cité Internationale: A complex that includes shopping options, restaurants, and cultural venues. It's a modern area offering a variety of experiences.

Practical Tips:

Public Transport: The Part-Dieu train station is a major transport hub, connecting to various parts of Lyon and beyond. Metro Line B and several bus lines serve the area.

Parking: Ample parking is available at the shopping center, making it convenient for visitors traveling by car.

3. Croix-Rousse

Location: On the northern hill of Lyon, in the 4th arrondissement.

Overview:

Description: Croix-Rousse is known for its bohemian atmosphere and distinctive shopping experience. The area is famous for its independent boutiques, local markets, and artisanal shops.

Historical Context: Historically a center for silk-weaving, Croix-Rousse retains its artisan charm and is home to a variety of unique and locally-produced goods.

Key Attractions:

Marché de la Croix-Rousse: A popular market offering fresh produce, local specialties, and artisanal products. It's a great place to explore Lyon's culinary heritage.

Boutiques: Explore independent shops selling handmade goods, vintage clothing, and unique crafts. The area is known for its creative and eclectic offerings.

Practical Tips:

Public Transport: Accessible by metro (Line C) and several bus lines. The area is also walkable, though hilly terrain may require comfortable shoes.

Local Experience: Embrace the local vibe by visiting cafes and interacting with vendors at the market.

4. Confluence

Location: At the confluence of the Rhône and Saône rivers, in the 2nd arrondissement.

Overview:

Description: Confluence is a modern, newly developed district that blends shopping with contemporary architecture and urban planning. It offers a fresh shopping experience with a focus on sustainability and innovation.

Historical Context: The district is part of a major urban renewal project aimed at revitalizing the area with modern amenities and sustainable design.

Key Attractions:

Les Docks – Village de Mode: A shopping center housed in a converted warehouse, featuring a mix of high-end and boutique stores, as well as restaurants and cafes.

Centre Commercial Confluence: A large shopping mall with a variety of stores, dining options, and entertainment facilities. It's known for its modern design and waterfront location.

Practical Tips:

Public Transport: Accessible via tram (Line T1) and metro (Line D). The area is well-connected and easy to navigate.

Scenic Views: Enjoy the waterfront location and modern architecture, making it a pleasant area for strolling and exploring.

5. Monplaisir

Location: In the 8th arrondissement, southeast of the city center.

Overview:

Description: Monplaisir is a residential area known for its local shops, markets, and a more relaxed shopping environment compared to the bustling central districts.

Historical Context: The area has a more suburban feel, with a focus on community and everyday shopping needs.

Key Attractions:

Marché de Monplaisir: A local market offering fresh produce, cheeses, meats, and baked goods. It's a great place to experience local life and shop for everyday items.

Local Shops: Explore small boutiques and stores offering a variety of products, from fashion to home goods.

Practical Tips:

Public Transport: Accessible via tram (Line T2) and bus lines. The area is also easily navigable by bike or on foot.

Community Vibe: Enjoy a more relaxed shopping experience and engage with local residents.

General Shopping Tips

Opening Hours:

Typical Hours: Most shops in Lyon open around 10:00 AM and close by 7:00 PM. Some may have extended hours or stay open late on certain days.

Payment Methods:

Credit Cards: Most shops accept credit cards, but it's a good idea to carry some cash for smaller vendors or markets.

Language:

French Phrases: While many shopkeepers speak English, learning a few basic French phrases can enhance your shopping experience and interactions.

Bargaining:

Markets: Bargaining is not typically practiced in fixed-price stores, but it's often acceptable in markets and with local artisans.

Transportation:

Public Transit: Lyon's public transportation system is efficient and connects all major shopping districts. Consider purchasing a day pass for unlimited travel.

Local Customs:

Etiquette: Be polite and respectful when shopping, and follow any specific rules or customs of the shop or market.

Souvenirs and Local Products

Exploring Lyon offers an excellent opportunity to find unique souvenirs and local products that reflect the city's rich culture, history, and gastronomy. Here's a comprehensive guide to the best souvenirs and local products you can find in Lyon, along with tips for selecting and purchasing them:

1. Culinary Delights

a. Local Specialties

Quenelles:

Description: Lyonnais quenelles are light, dumpling-like dishes made from fish or meat, often served in a creamy sauce. Although you can't bring the dish itself home, you can buy ready-made or frozen quenelles from local markets or specialty food shops.

Where to Buy: Specialty food stores like Les Halles de Lyon-Paul Bocuse.

Andouillette:

Description: This distinctive Lyonnais sausage is made from pork and is known for its strong flavor. It's a great gift for food enthusiasts who appreciate traditional French charcuterie.

Where to Buy: Local butcher shops and markets, such as Marché de la Croix-Rousse.

Salmon and Other Preserved Fish:

Description: Lyon's markets offer a variety of preserved fish, including smoked salmon, which can be a tasty souvenir.

Where to Buy: Les Halles de Lyon-Paul Bocuse or Marché Saint-Antoine.

b. Gourmet Products

Lyonnais Mustard:

Description: Lyon is known for its mustard, which makes a flavorful and practical souvenir. Look for local brands that offer traditional and artisanal varieties.

Where to Buy: Grocery stores, gourmet shops, or markets.

Local Wines and Beverages:

Description: The region around Lyon produces excellent wines, such as Beaujolais and Côtes du Rhône. Local liqueurs and spirits, such as Cointreau or Chartreuse, are also popular.

Where to Buy: Wine shops, local markets, or specialty stores.

French Pastries and Chocolates:

Description: Bring home delectable French pastries or artisanal chocolates from local patisseries and chocolatiers.

Where to Buy: Renowned patisseries like Maison Troisgros or chocolate shops such as Bernachon.

2. Artisan Crafts

a. Silk Products

Silk Scarves and Accessories:

Description: Lyon has a rich history in silk weaving. High-quality silk scarves, ties, and other accessories are exquisite souvenirs that highlight the city's heritage.

Where to Buy: Shops in the Croix-Rousse district, where the tradition of silk weaving is still alive.

Silk Prints and Fabrics:

Description: For a unique and luxurious gift, consider silk prints or fabric pieces that showcase Lyon's historic silk designs.

Where to Buy: Specialty stores and boutiques in Croix-Rousse.

b. Pottery and Ceramics

Local Pottery:

Description: Handcrafted pottery and ceramics are lovely souvenirs that capture the essence of local craftsmanship.

Where to Buy: Artisan shops and markets.

Decorative Items:

Description: Look for decorative ceramics such as hand-painted plates, bowls, and vases.

Where to Buy: Local artisan shops and markets.

3. Regional Products

a. Lyonnais Cookbooks

French Cookbooks:

Description: Cookbooks featuring Lyonnais recipes and French cuisine offer a taste of the city's culinary traditions that you can recreate at home.

Where to Buy: Bookstores, gourmet shops, and markets.

b. Regional Spices and Herbs

Herbs de Provence:

Description: A blend of herbs commonly used in French cooking, perfect for adding a touch of Lyon's culinary style to your dishes at home.

Where to Buy: Markets and gourmet stores.

4. Unique Gifts

a. Lyon-themed Souvenirs

Miniature Landmarks:

Description: Small replicas of famous Lyon landmarks, such as the Basilica of Notre-Dame de Fourvière or the Lyon Cathedral, make for memorable souvenirs.

Where to Buy: Souvenir shops and tourist stores.

Local Art:

Description: Purchase prints or artworks from local artists that capture the beauty and essence of Lyon.

Where to Buy: Art galleries and local markets.

Shopping Tips

Authenticity:

Verify Authenticity: When purchasing artisanal or gourmet products, especially expensive items like silk or wines, ensure they are authentic and sourced from reputable vendors.

Packaging:

Check Packaging: For edible souvenirs, ensure they are well-packaged and suitable for travel. Some products may need special handling or customs declarations.

Language:

Basic French Phrases: Knowing a few basic French phrases can help you interact with vendors and make purchases more smoothly.

Local Markets:

Visit Markets: Markets like Marché Les Halles de Lyon-Paul Bocuse or Marché de la Croix-Rousse are excellent places to find local products and souvenirs.

Payment Methods:

Cash and Cards: While many places accept credit cards, having some cash on hand can be useful, especially in smaller shops or markets.

Bargaining:

Negotiation: Bargaining is generally not practiced in fixed-price stores but may be acceptable in markets or with artisans.

Boutiques and Designer Shops

Lyon offers a sophisticated and diverse shopping experience with its boutiques and designer shops. The city's shopping scene combines luxury with local flair, featuring a range of high-end designer stores, independent boutiques, and unique fashion outlets. Here's a comprehensive guide to exploring Lyon's boutiques and designer shops:

1. Presqu'île District

Overview:

Description: Presqu'île, the central district of Lyon, is home to many of the city's high-end boutiques and designer shops. This area is renowned for its chic streets and historic architecture, making it an ideal location for luxury shopping.

Key Boutiques and Designer Shops:

Le Printemps

Location: 48 Boulevard de la République, 69002 Lyon

Overview: A high-end department store offering a range of luxury brands, including fashion, cosmetics, and home goods. It features collections from top designers and international labels.

Highlight: Known for its elegant shopping environment and diverse selection of premium products.

Galeries Lafayette

Location: 9 Rue du Président Edouard Herriot, 69001 Lyon

Overview: Another prestigious department store with a wide range of designer fashion, accessories, and beauty products. The store is renowned for its stylish layout and high-quality merchandise.

Highlight: Offers a curated selection of luxury brands and often features exclusive collections.

Café Couture

Location: 34 Rue de la Charité, 69002 Lyon

Overview: A boutique offering high-end fashion and accessories, with a focus on French and international designers. The store combines contemporary style with classic elegance.

Highlight: Known for its personalized shopping experience and unique designer pieces.

Mademoiselle YéYé

Location: 14 Rue du Palais Grillet, 69002 Lyon

Overview: A boutique specializing in vintage and designer clothing. It offers a curated selection of stylish pieces from both past and contemporary collections.

Highlight: Perfect for finding unique vintage items and designer garments.

2. Croix-Rousse District

Overview:

Description: The Croix-Rousse district is known for its bohemian vibe and artisan spirit. Here you'll find a mix of independent boutiques and local designers offering unique fashion and handcrafted items.

Key Boutiques and Designer Shops:

Avenue des Alpes

Location: 29 Boulevard de la Croix-Rousse, 69004 Lyon

Overview: A boutique offering contemporary fashion from emerging designers and local artisans. It features a selection of stylish clothing and accessories with a focus on originality.

Highlight: Great for discovering new and unique fashion trends.

La Maison des Artistes

Location: 18 Rue des Fantasques, 69004 Lyon

Overview: A boutique showcasing works from local artists and designers. It offers a variety of handmade clothing, accessories, and art pieces.

Highlight: Ideal for finding one-of-a-kind items and supporting local talent.

3. Part-Dieu District

Overview:

Description: Part-Dieu is Lyon's modern shopping hub, featuring large shopping centers and designer stores. This district is known for its contemporary retail environment and is perfect for luxury shopping.

Key Boutiques and Designer Shops:

La Part-Dieu Shopping Center

Location: 17 Rue du Dr Bouchut, 69003 Lyon

Overview: A large shopping center that includes several high-end fashion stores and luxury boutiques. The center offers a wide range of designer brands and high-quality products.

Highlight: Features an extensive selection of international and French designer labels.

Michael Kors

Location: Inside La Part-Dieu Shopping Center

Overview: A boutique offering stylish American fashion and accessories. Known for its modern and elegant designs.

Highlight: Perfect for high-end handbags, watches, and apparel.

4. Confluence District

Overview:

Description: The Confluence district is known for its modern architecture and innovative design. It features contemporary boutiques and designer shops that reflect the district's cutting-edge style.

Key Boutiques and Designer Shops:

Les Docks – Village de Mode

Location: 7 Rue Duc, 69002 Lyon

Overview: A stylish shopping complex housed in a converted warehouse, featuring a mix of designer boutiques and contemporary fashion stores.

Highlight: Combines shopping with a vibrant social atmosphere and modern design.

The Kooples

Location: Inside Les Docks – Village de Mode

Overview: A boutique offering trendy French fashion with a rock-chic aesthetic. Known for its edgy designs and stylish apparel.

Highlight: Great for finding contemporary and fashionable clothing.

5. Monplaisir District

Overview:

Description: Monplaisir offers a more relaxed shopping experience with local boutiques and specialty shops. It's a great place to explore unique finds and local fashion.

Key Boutiques and Designer Shops:

Boutique Le Bonheur

Location: 24 Boulevard des Belges, 69008 Lyon

Overview: A boutique offering a range of stylish clothing and accessories from both local and international designers.

Highlight: Known for its personalized service and unique selection.

Les Enfants du Rhône

Location: 22 Avenue de Saxe, 69008 Lyon

Overview: A boutique specializing in children's fashion and accessories. It offers high-quality, stylish clothing for kids.

Highlight: Perfect for finding chic and comfortable clothing for children.

Shopping Tips

Opening Hours:

Typical Hours: Most boutiques and designer shops open from 10:00 AM to 7:00 PM. Some stores may have extended hours, especially in busy districts like Presqu'île.

Tax-Free Shopping:

VAT Refund: Non-EU visitors can claim a VAT refund on purchases over a certain amount. Make sure to ask for a tax-free form when making a purchase.

Language:

Basic French Phrases: While many staff members in upscale boutiques speak English, learning a few basic French phrases can enhance your shopping experience.

Payment Methods:

Credit Cards: Most boutiques accept major credit cards. It's still a good idea to carry some cash for smaller purchases or less formal shops.

Bargaining:

Fixed Prices: Bargaining is generally not practiced in high-end boutiques and designer stores. Prices are fixed, reflecting the quality and exclusivity of the items.

Flea Markets

Lyon's flea markets offer a fascinating glimpse into the city's eclectic mix of vintage, antique, and second-hand treasures. These markets are a great way to discover unique finds, from antique furniture and vintage clothing to rare collectibles and eclectic knick-knacks. Here's a comprehensive guide to exploring the flea markets in Lyon:

1. Marché aux Puces de Lyon – Villeurbanne

Overview:

Location: 108 Avenue des Frères Lumière, 69100 Villeurbanne (a suburb of Lyon)

Description: One of the largest and most popular flea markets in the Lyon metropolitan area, located just a short distance from the city center. It offers a wide variety of antiques, vintage items, and second-hand goods.

Highlights:

Antiques and Collectibles: Discover a diverse range of antiques, from vintage furniture and art to rare collectibles and memorabilia.

Vintage Clothing: Find unique clothing items and accessories from past decades, perfect for fashion enthusiasts and collectors.

Furniture: Browse through an assortment of vintage and antique furniture pieces, including restored and original items.

Tips:

Opening Hours: Typically open on weekends, with varying hours. Check the market's schedule before visiting.

Bargaining: Haggling is common, so don't hesitate to negotiate prices with vendors.

2. Marché de la Croix-Rousse

Overview:

Location: Place de la Croix-Rousse, 69004 Lyon

Description: While primarily known as a food market, the Croix-Rousse market also features a selection of vintage and second-hand items. It's a vibrant market with a mix of fresh produce, local goods, and eclectic finds.

Highlights:

Vintage Goods: Find a range of vintage items including clothing, accessories, and household goods.

Local Flavor: Enjoy the lively atmosphere of the market, which reflects the bohemian spirit of the Croix-Rousse district.

Tips:

Opening Hours: Generally open on Tuesdays and Saturdays. Visit in the morning for the best selection.

Local Experience: Combine your visit with a stroll around the Croix-Rousse district, known for its artistic and bohemian vibe.

3. Marché de Saint-Antoine

Overview:

Location: Quai de Bondy, 69005 Lyon

Description: This market, located along the Saône River, is known for its fresh produce and local goods but also features stalls selling antiques and vintage items. It's a picturesque location with a charming riverside setting.

Highlights:

Antique Finds: Look for antique books, vintage postcards, and other collectible items.

Scenic Setting: Enjoy the scenic beauty of the Saône River while exploring the market.

Tips:

Opening Hours: Usually open on Fridays and Saturdays. Check for specific hours and vendor schedules.

Photography: The riverside location provides excellent photo opportunities, so bring a camera.

4. Marché de Brocante – Lyon 7th Arrondissement

Overview:

Location: Rue de la Villette, 69007 Lyon

Description: A smaller, less frequented flea market that offers a selection of second-hand goods and antiques. It's a great place to find hidden gems without the crowds.

Highlights:

Hidden Treasures: Explore a variety of second-hand items, including vintage clothing, antiques, and curiosities.

Local Atmosphere: Experience a more laid-back and local shopping experience compared to larger markets.

Tips:

Opening Hours: Typically open on weekends. Visit early for the best selection.

Local Knowledge: Engage with local vendors who may offer insights and recommendations on other nearby markets.

5. La Part-Dieu Market

Overview:

Location: 17 Rue du Dr Bouchut, 69003 Lyon

Description: While primarily a modern shopping center, La Part-Dieu Market occasionally hosts flea market events and pop-up sales featuring vintage and antique items.

Highlights:

Occasional Events: Check for special flea market events or pop-up markets held within the shopping center.

Variety of Goods: Explore a mix of modern and vintage items during these special events.

Tips:

Check Schedules: Look for event announcements and schedules to plan your visit around these special flea market events.

Shopping Experience: Combine your visit with shopping at the Part-Dieu Shopping Center for a diverse retail experience.

General Tips for Flea Market Visits

Arrive Early:

Best Selection: Arriving early gives you the best chance to find unique items before they are picked over.

Cash and Change:

Payment: Bring cash and small change, as many vendors may not accept credit cards.

Bargaining:

Negotiation: Don't be afraid to negotiate prices. Flea markets are often open to haggling.

Comfortable Attire:

Dress Comfortably: Wear comfortable shoes and clothing, as you may be walking and browsing for extended periods.

Inspection:

Check Items: Inspect items carefully for condition and authenticity, especially when buying antiques or valuable collectibles.

Local Knowledge:

Ask Locals: Engage with locals and vendors for recommendations on other markets or hidden gems.

Chapter 12: Food and Drink

1. **Quenelles de Brochet**

Quenelles de Brochet is a quintessential Lyonnaise dish celebrated for its refined texture and delicate flavor. Originating from the region's rich culinary tradition, this dish is a perfect example of Lyon's sophisticated approach to traditional French cuisine. Quenelles de Brochet are essentially pike dumplings, often served in a creamy sauce, and are a must-try for anyone visiting Lyon.

Main Ingredient

Pike: The primary ingredient in Quenelles de Brochet is pike, a freshwater fish known for its mild flavor and firm texture. The pike is usually blended into a smooth mousse or pâté.

Binding Agents: To achieve the desired texture, the pike mousse is combined with ingredients like eggs and flour, which help bind the mixture and give it a light, airy consistency.

Accompaniments

Sauce Nantua: Traditionally, Quenelles de Brochet is served with Sauce Nantua, a rich and creamy sauce made from butter, cream, and crayfish or shrimp. This sauce enhances the delicate flavor of the quenelles.

Vegetables: The dish is often accompanied by seasonal vegetables or a side of rice to balance out the richness of the sauce.

Potatoes: Sometimes, quenelles are served with potatoes, either mashed or roasted, as a hearty complement.

What Makes Quenelles de Brochet Special?

Unique Texture: The smooth, airy texture of the quenelles is a result of the pike being finely ground and then mixed with binding agents to create a light, fluffy consistency.

Flavor Profile: The mild flavor of the pike, combined with the rich and creamy Sauce Nantua, offers a delicate balance that highlights the freshness of the fish without overpowering it.

Historical Significance: Quenelles de Brochet is deeply rooted in Lyonnaise culinary tradition, showcasing the city's history of elevating simple ingredients into sophisticated dishes.

Where to Try Quenelles de Brochet in Lyon

Le Café des Fédérations

Address: 8 Rue du Garet, 69001 Lyon, France

Overview: A classic Lyonnaise bouchon known for its traditional dishes, including Quenelles de Brochet. The restaurant offers a warm, authentic atmosphere and a menu that celebrates regional specialties.

La Mère Brazier

Address: 12 Rue Royale, 69001 Lyon, France

Overview: A historic restaurant that has been a cornerstone of Lyonnaise cuisine since 1921. La Mère Brazier is renowned for its refined approach to traditional dishes, including its celebrated quenelles.

Le Bouchon des Filles

Address: 20 Rue Sergent Blandan, 69001 Lyon, France

Overview: A charming bouchon offering a cozy environment and a menu featuring classic Lyonnaise fare. Quenelles de Brochet is often highlighted as one of their specialties.

Restaurant Paul Bocuse

Address: 40 Quai de la Plage, 69660 Collonges-au-Mont-d'Or, France (a short drive from Lyon)

Overview: A prestigious restaurant by the legendary chef Paul Bocuse, known for its high-end takes on traditional French dishes, including quenelles.

Le Sud

Address: 3 Place de la Bourse, 69002 Lyon, France

Overview: A well-regarded restaurant offering a contemporary twist on classic Lyonnaise dishes, including a refined version of Quenelles de Brochet.

Tips for Enjoying Quenelles de Brochet

Pair with Wine: Complement your quenelles with a glass of white wine or a light red wine. A crisp Chardonnay or a light Beaujolais works well with the creamy texture of the dish.

Enjoy with Sauce: Make sure to savor the quenelles with plenty of Sauce Nantua. The creamy sauce is essential for enhancing the flavor and richness of the dish.

Ask for Recommendations: When dining in a traditional bouchon or restaurant, ask the staff for their recommendations on the best way to enjoy the quenelles. They may offer variations or suggestions based on their specialties.

2. Andouillette

Andouillette is a traditional French sausage known for its distinctive and robust flavor, making it a notable dish in Lyonnaise cuisine. With its origins rooted in French culinary history, this sausage is particularly celebrated in Lyon, where it is a staple of the local food culture. Made from pork and seasoned with a variety of spices, Andouillette offers a unique and hearty taste that appeals to adventurous eaters.

Main Ingredient

Pork: The primary ingredient in Andouillette is pork, specifically the intestines or tripe of the pig. This gives the sausage its characteristic flavor and texture.

Seasonings: The sausage is seasoned with a mix of spices and herbs, such as pepper, garlic, and sometimes white wine or cognac. These seasonings add depth and complexity to the flavor profile.

Accompaniments

Mustard: Andouillette is often served with Dijon mustard or other local mustards, which complement its strong flavor and add a tangy contrast.

Sauces: It can also be served with a variety of sauces, including a red wine reduction or a rich gravy.

Vegetables: Common accompaniments include sautéed or roasted vegetables, such as potatoes, carrots, and onions, which balance the richness of the sausage.

Bread: A side of crusty French bread is also a traditional accompaniment, ideal for soaking up any sauces.

What Makes Andouillette Special?

Distinctive Flavor: The use of pork intestines or tripe gives Andouillette a unique and robust flavor that is both rich and savory. Its strong taste is an acquired one, often cherished by those with a taste for bold and traditional foods.

Textural Experience: The texture of Andouillette is coarse and somewhat chewy, providing a distinctive mouthfeel that contrasts with more conventional sausages.

Culinary Tradition: Andouillette is deeply rooted in French culinary tradition, particularly in Lyon, where it reflects the region's history of making use of all parts of the pig and crafting flavorful dishes from humble ingredients.

Where to Try Andouillette in Lyon

Le Café des Fédérations

Address: 8 Rue du Garet, 69001 Lyon, France

Overview: A traditional Lyonnaise bouchon known for its authentic and hearty Lyonnaise dishes, including Andouillette.

La Mère Brazier

Address: 12 Rue Royale, 69001 Lyon, France

Overview: This historic restaurant offers a refined take on traditional Lyonnaise cuisine, including expertly prepared Andouillette.

Les Fines Gueules

Address: 18 Rue de l'Ancienne Préfecture, 69002 Lyon, France

Overview: A contemporary bistro known for its high-quality traditional French dishes, including Andouillette.

Le Bouchon des Filles

Address: 20 Rue Sergent Blandan, 69001 Lyon, France

Overview: A cozy bouchon with a reputation for serving classic Lyonnaise fare, including a well-regarded Andouillette.

Le Sud

Address: 3 Place de la Bourse, 69002 Lyon, France

Overview: A restaurant offering a modern twist on classic Lyonnaise cuisine, including their version of Andouillette.

Tips for Enjoying Andouillette

Be Open-Minded: Andouillette has a strong and distinct flavor that may be different from other sausages. Approach it with an open mind and a willingness to explore traditional French tastes.

Pair with a Strong Wine: The bold flavor of Andouillette pairs well with robust red wines such as a Beaujolais or a Syrah, which can stand up to the sausage's intensity.

Ask for Recommendations: When dining in a traditional bouchon or restaurant, ask the staff for their advice on the best way to enjoy Andouillette. They may offer suggestions on preparation styles or complementary sides.

3. **Salade Lyonnaise**

Salade Lyonnaise is a quintessential dish of Lyonnaise cuisine, reflecting the city's reputation for rich and flavorful food. This traditional French salad is known for its combination of fresh greens, crispy bacon, and a poached egg, all brought together with a tangy vinaigrette. It's a perfect example of how Lyonnaise cuisine turns simple ingredients into a delightful and hearty dish.

Main Ingredients

Frisée Lettuce: The base of Salade Lyonnaise is frisée, a curly, slightly bitter lettuce that adds a distinctive texture and flavor.

Bacon Lardons: Crispy bacon or lardons (small strips of pork belly) provide a savory, smoky element to the salad.

Poached Egg: A poached egg is a key component, adding richness and creaminess when its yolk is broken over the salad.

Vinaigrette: The salad is typically dressed with a simple vinaigrette made from Dijon mustard, red wine vinegar, and olive oil. Sometimes, the vinaigrette includes a touch of shallots or garlic.

Accompaniments

Croutons: Some variations of Salade Lyonnaise include crunchy croutons, which add additional texture to the dish.

Onions: Thinly sliced onions or shallots can be added for extra flavor and a bit of sharpness.

Herbs: Fresh herbs such as chives or parsley might be sprinkled on top for added freshness and color.

What Makes Salade Lyonnaise Special?

Balance of Flavors: Salade Lyonnaise expertly balances the bitter greens of frisée with the rich, smoky flavor of bacon and the creamy texture of the poached egg. The vinaigrette adds a tangy contrast that ties all the components together.

Texture Contrast: The combination of crisp lettuce, crunchy bacon, and a runny poached egg creates a satisfying contrast of textures in every bite.

Traditional Simplicity: The salad embodies the Lyonnaise philosophy of using high-quality, simple ingredients to create a dish that is both flavorful and satisfying.

Where to Try Salade Lyonnaise in Lyon

Le Café des Fédérations

Address: 8 Rue du Garet, 69001 Lyon, France

Overview: A classic Lyonnaise bouchon known for its traditional dishes, including an authentic Salade Lyonnaise.

La Mère Brazier

Address: 12 Rue Royale, 69001 Lyon, France

Overview: A historic restaurant offering refined Lyonnaise cuisine, including a well-executed Salade Lyonnaise.

Les Fines Gueules

Address: 18 Rue de l'Ancienne Préfecture, 69002 Lyon, France

Overview: A contemporary bistro that serves high-quality traditional dishes, including a fresh and flavorful Salade Lyonnaise.

Le Bouchon des Filles

Address: 20 Rue Sergent Blandan, 69001 Lyon, France

Overview: A cozy bouchon that serves classic Lyonnaise fare, including their take on Salade Lyonnaise.

Le Sud

Address: 3 Place de la Bourse, 69002 Lyon, France

Overview: Known for its modern take on traditional Lyonnaise cuisine, including a creative version of Salade Lyonnaise.

Tips for Enjoying Salade Lyonnaise

Perfect Poached Egg: For the best experience, ensure the poached egg is cooked so the yolk is runny, adding a rich, creamy texture to the salad.

Fresh Ingredients: Use the freshest frisée lettuce and high-quality bacon to enhance the flavors of the salad.

Customize the Dressing: Adjust the vinaigrette to your taste by balancing the tanginess of the vinegar with the richness of the mustard.

4. **Gratin Dauphinois**

Gratin Dauphinois is a beloved French dish known for its creamy, cheesy goodness and comforting texture. Originating from the Dauphiné region in southeastern France, this dish has become a staple in French cuisine and is especially popular in Lyonnaise gastronomy. The gratin is made from thinly sliced potatoes baked in a rich, creamy mixture of cream, milk, and cheese, creating a deliciously indulgent side dish.

Main Ingredients

Potatoes: The core ingredient of Gratin Dauphinois is potatoes, typically Yukon Gold or another starchy variety. They are thinly sliced to ensure they cook evenly and absorb the creamy mixture.

Cream and Milk: The creamy base is made from a combination of heavy cream and milk, which gives the gratin its rich and velvety texture.

Cheese: Gruyère cheese is traditionally used, providing a nutty flavor and a gooey, melted texture. Some variations also include Parmesan cheese for added richness and a golden crust.

Garlic and Nutmeg: Garlic is often rubbed on the baking dish to impart subtle flavor, while nutmeg adds a hint of warmth and depth to the dish.

Butter: The baking dish is typically buttered to prevent sticking and to enhance the flavor of the gratin.

Accompaniments

Meats: Gratin Dauphinois pairs wonderfully with roasted meats such as beef, pork, or lamb. It's a rich side dish that complements hearty main courses.

Vegetables: It can be served alongside steamed or roasted vegetables, which help balance the richness of the gratin.

Salads: A fresh green salad can provide a refreshing contrast to the creamy gratin, adding a light and crisp element to the meal.

What Makes Gratin Dauphinois Special?

Creamy Texture: The combination of cream and milk creates a luxurious, velvety texture that makes every bite indulgent and satisfying.

Flavorful Cheese: The use of Gruyère cheese adds a distinct, nutty flavor and helps create a beautifully golden, crispy top layer.

Comforting Dish: Gratin Dauphinois is the epitome of comfort food, offering a rich and hearty addition to any meal.

Where to Try Gratin Dauphinois in Lyon

Le Café des Fédérations

Address: 8 Rue du Garet, 69001 Lyon, France

Overview: A traditional Lyonnaise bouchon known for its classic dishes, including Gratin Dauphinois. The restaurant offers a hearty and authentic experience.

La Mère Brazier

Address: 12 Rue Royale, 69001 Lyon, France

Overview: This historic restaurant provides refined versions of classic French dishes, including a luxurious Gratin Dauphinois.

Les Fines Gueules

Address: 18 Rue de l'Ancienne Préfecture, 69002 Lyon, France

Overview: A contemporary bistro that serves high-quality French cuisine, including a well-executed Gratin Dauphinois.

Le Bouchon des Filles

Address: 20 Rue Sergent Blandan, 69001 Lyon, France

Overview: Known for its traditional Lyonnaise fare, including comforting dishes like Gratin Dauphinois.

Le Sud

Address: 3 Place de la Bourse, 69002 Lyon, France

Overview: A restaurant offering a modern twist on traditional dishes, including Gratin Dauphinois.

Tips for Enjoying Gratin Dauphinois

Use Starchy Potatoes: For the best texture, use starchy potatoes like Yukon Gold, which will hold their shape and become tender during baking.

Preheat Your Oven: Ensure your oven is preheated to achieve a perfectly golden and crispy top layer.

Layer Evenly: Arrange the potato slices in an even layer for consistent cooking and a uniform texture.

5. **Tarte Tatin**

Tarte Tatin is a classic French dessert known for its delightful combination of caramelized apples and buttery pastry. Originating from the Tatin sisters' hotel in Lamotte-Beuvron, France, this upside-down tart has become a staple in French patisserie and is celebrated for its rich flavor and elegant simplicity. The tart is typically served warm, making it a comforting and indulgent treat.

Main Ingredients

Apples: The main ingredient is apples, preferably a variety that holds its shape during cooking, such as Granny Smith or Golden Delicious. These apples are caramelized before being topped with pastry.

Butter: Unsalted butter is used to make the caramel and for the pastry, contributing to the tart's rich flavor.

Sugar: Granulated sugar is caramelized with butter to create the sweet and slightly bitter caramel that coats the apples.

Pastry: A simple shortcrust pastry or pâte brisée is used as the base, which is placed on top of the caramelized apples before baking.

Accompaniments

Crème Fraîche: Tarte Tatin is often served with a dollop of crème fraîche, which adds a tangy contrast to the sweet and caramelized apples.

Whipped Cream: A classic accompaniment is lightly sweetened whipped cream, which complements the richness of the tart.

Vanilla Ice Cream: For a decadent touch, serve Tarte Tatin with a scoop of vanilla ice cream, adding a creamy contrast to the warm tart.

What Makes Tarte Tatin Special?

Caramelized Apples: The apples are cooked in butter and sugar until they are deeply caramelized, creating a rich and complex flavor.

Upside-Down Technique: The tart is baked upside down, allowing the apples to cook in the caramel and absorb its sweetness. Once baked, it's inverted to reveal a glossy, caramelized topping.

Simple Ingredients: Despite its sophisticated taste, Tarte Tatin is made with basic ingredients, showcasing how simple elements can be transformed into an elegant dessert.

Where to Try Tarte Tatin in Lyon

Bouchon Les Fines Gueules

Address: 18 Rue de l'Ancienne Préfecture, 69002 Lyon, France

Overview: This contemporary bistro offers high-quality French cuisine, including a delicious Tarte Tatin.

La Mère Brazier

Address: 12 Rue Royale, 69001 Lyon, France

Overview: A historic restaurant known for its refined French dishes, La Mère Brazier serves an exquisite Tarte Tatin as part of its dessert offerings.

Le Café des Fédérations

Address: 8 Rue du Garet, 69001 Lyon, France

Overview: A traditional Lyonnaise bouchon that serves classic French fare, including a well-loved Tarte Tatin.

Le Sud

Address: 3 Place de la Bourse, 69002 Lyon, France

Overview: Known for its modern take on traditional French cuisine, Le Sud offers a delightful version of Tarte Tatin.

Les Gourmands Disent

Address: 9 Rue des Quatre Chapeaux, 69002 Lyon, France

Overview: A charming patisserie that specializes in classic French desserts, including a delectable Tarte Tatin.

Tips for Enjoying Tarte Tatin

Serve Warm: Tarte Tatin is best enjoyed warm, as the caramel and apples are at their most flavorful and the pastry remains tender.

Invert Carefully: When inverting the tart, do so carefully to avoid disturbing the caramelized apples and ensure a beautiful presentation.

Pair with Creamy Accompaniments: Complement the tart with a dollop of crème fraîche, whipped cream, or a scoop of vanilla ice cream for a balanced and indulgent dessert experience.

Markets and Food Halls

Lyon is renowned for its vibrant culinary scene, and its markets and food halls are central to this reputation. Whether you're a food enthusiast, a local ingredient hunter, or simply looking for a delightful culinary experience, Lyon's markets and food halls offer a sensory feast of flavors, aromas, and local specialties.

1. Les Halles de Lyon-Paul Bocuse

Overview: Often considered the flagship food market of Lyon, Les Halles de Lyon-Paul Bocuse is a must-visit for anyone interested in high-quality French produce. Named after the famous chef Paul Bocuse, this covered market is home to an array of gourmet stalls and is a testament to Lyon's status as the gastronomic capital of France.

Highlights:

Wide Variety: Offers everything from fresh seafood, meats, and cheeses to pastries, fruits, and vegetables.

Local Specialties: Try local delicacies such as Lyonnaise sausages, pâtés, and freshly baked breads.

Gourmet Products: Discover high-end products like truffles, foie gras, and artisanal chocolates.

Location: 102 Cours Lafayette, 69003 Lyon, France

Opening Hours:

Monday to Saturday: 7:00 AM – 2:00 PM

Closed on Sundays

Price Range: Varies by vendor, but expect premium pricing for high-quality products.

Local Tips:

Visit Early: For the freshest produce and to avoid crowds, visit early in the morning.

Sample and Chat: Don't hesitate to sample products and ask vendors for recommendations on local specialties.

2. Marché de la Croix-Rousse

Overview: Located in the lively Croix-Rousse district, this market is known for its vibrant atmosphere and diverse selection of local produce. It's a favorite among locals for its authenticity and variety.

Highlights:

Fresh Produce: From fruits and vegetables to herbs and spices, the market offers a wide selection of fresh, seasonal produce.

Local Vendors: Engage with local farmers and artisans who bring a personal touch to their products.

Prepared Foods: Enjoy ready-to-eat options such as pastries, cheeses, and hot food stalls.

Location: Place de la Croix-Rousse, 69004 Lyon, France

Opening Hours:

Tuesday and Friday: 6:00 AM – 1:00 PM

Saturday: 6:00 AM – 1:30 PM

Closed on Sundays and Mondays

Price Range: Generally affordable, with prices varying depending on the vendor and product.

Local Tips:

Bring Cash: Many vendors prefer cash payments.

Explore the Area: The Croix-Rousse district is also known for its traboules and historic architecture, making it a great area to explore.

3. Marché Saint-Antoine

Overview: Situated near the Saône River, this market is known for its picturesque setting and high-quality offerings. It caters to both locals and tourists, providing a delightful shopping experience with a view.

Highlights:

Scenic Location: Enjoy shopping with views of the Saône River and the Basilica of Notre-Dame de Fourvière.

Artisan Goods: Find a variety of artisan products including cheeses, meats, and bread.

Local Atmosphere: Experience the vibrant local market culture in a scenic and historical setting.

Location: Quai Saint-Antoine, 69002 Lyon, France

Opening Hours:

Tuesday to Sunday: 7:00 AM – 1:30 PM

Closed on Mondays

Price Range: Prices are moderate, with a range of options for different budgets.

Local Tips:

Enjoy the Surroundings: Take a stroll along the river after visiting the market to enjoy the scenic beauty of Lyon.

4. Marché des Capucins

Overview: Known as one of the oldest markets in Lyon, Marché des Capucins offers a traditional market experience with a focus on local and artisanal products.

Highlights:

Traditional Market: Experience the charm of a traditional Lyonnaise market with a wide selection of local goods.

Local Specialties: Sample traditional Lyonnaise products such as quenelles and pralines.

Artisanal Goods: Discover unique, handcrafted items from local artisans.

Location: 4 Rue des Capucins, 69001 Lyon, France

Opening Hours:

Tuesday to Saturday: 7:00 AM – 1:00 PM

Closed on Sundays and Mondays

Price Range: Generally affordable, with a range of products to suit different budgets.

Local Tips:

Try Local Dishes: Ask vendors for recommendations on traditional Lyonnaise dishes to try.

5. Marché de Monplaisir

Overview: Located in the Monplaisir district, this market is known for its friendly atmosphere and diverse range of products. It offers a more relaxed shopping experience compared to the larger markets.

Highlights:

Diverse Selection: Offers fresh produce, meats, cheeses, and baked goods.

Community Feel: Enjoy a more intimate and community-focused market experience.

Local Favorites: Discover local favorites and specialty items from nearby vendors.

Location: 50 Avenue des Frères Lumière, 69008 Lyon, France

Opening Hours:

Wednesday and Saturday: 7:00 AM – 1:00 PM

Closed on Sundays and Mondays

Price Range: Generally affordable, with a variety of options for different budgets.

Local Tips:

Relax and Enjoy: The smaller size of the market makes it a great place to relax and enjoy a leisurely shopping experience.

Final Tips

Bring Reusable Bags: Many markets will provide bags, but bringing your own helps reduce waste and makes carrying purchases easier.

Sample Local Delicacies: Don't miss the opportunity to sample local specialties and ask vendors for recommendations.

Check Market Days: Some markets operate only on specific days, so it's a good idea to check their schedule before visiting.

Exploring Lyon's markets and food halls is a delightful way to experience the city's culinary culture and enjoy fresh, high-quality products. Whether you're stocking up on ingredients, trying local specialties, or simply soaking in the vibrant atmosphere, Lyon's markets offer something for every food lover.

Cafés and Bakeries

Lyon, renowned for its rich gastronomic heritage, offers an impressive array of cafés and bakeries that cater to every taste. From charming patisseries to cozy coffee shops, these establishments are perfect for enjoying a leisurely breakfast, a mid-day coffee, or a sweet treat. Here's a guide to some of the best cafés and bakeries in Lyon:

1. Boulangerie du Palais

Overview: Boulangerie du Palais is a celebrated bakery known for its artisanal breads and delectable pastries. Located in the heart of Lyon, it's a popular spot for both locals and visitors.

Highlights:

Artisan Breads: Freshly baked bread, including traditional baguettes and sourdough.

Pastries: Enjoy a selection of pastries such as croissants, pain au chocolat, and éclairs.

Cakes and Tarts: A variety of cakes and tarts made with high-quality ingredients.

Location: 17 Rue des Capucins, 69001 Lyon, France

Opening Hours:

Monday to Saturday: 7:00 AM – 7:00 PM

Closed on Sundays

Price Range: Affordable to moderate, with a range of options for different budgets.

Local Tips:

Try the Croissants: The croissants are highly recommended for their buttery, flaky texture.

Visit Early: Arrive early for the freshest bread and pastries.

2. Café du Soleil

Overview: Café du Soleil is a charming café offering a cozy atmosphere and a selection of French classics. It's a great place to relax with a coffee or enjoy a light meal.

Highlights:

Coffee: High-quality coffee and espresso drinks.

Breakfast: Enjoy a range of breakfast options including croissants, omelets, and fresh juices.

Lunch: Light lunch options such as quiches, salads, and sandwiches.

Location: 10 Place des Jacobins, 69002 Lyon, France

Opening Hours:

Monday to Friday: 8:00 AM – 6:00 PM

Saturday: 9:00 AM – 6:00 PM

Closed on Sundays

Price Range: Moderate, with a focus on quality ingredients and classic French fare.

Local Tips:

Enjoy the Terrace: When the weather is nice, the outdoor seating area offers a pleasant spot for people-watching.

3. Maison Troisgros

Overview: Maison Troisgros is a renowned bakery and pâtisserie, known for its sophisticated pastries and exceptional quality. It's a part of the famous Troisgros family, known for its Michelin-starred restaurants.

Highlights:

Gourmet Pastries: Try their elegant pastries, including éclairs, macarons, and fruit tarts.

Breads and Viennoiseries: A selection of artisanal breads and viennoiseries.

Chocolate: Luxurious chocolates and confectioneries.

Location: 17 Rue de la Charité, 69002 Lyon, France

Opening Hours:

Monday to Saturday: 8:00 AM – 7:00 PM

Closed on Sundays

Price Range: Higher-end, reflecting the quality and craftsmanship of the products.

Local Tips:

Sample the Macarons: The macarons are highly praised and make a perfect gift or treat.

4. Café des Fédérations

Overview: A beloved café and brasserie in Lyon, Café des Fédérations offers a traditional Lyonnaise café experience. It's known for its warm atmosphere and hearty fare.

Highlights:

Coffee and Tea: Classic coffee and tea options, including French press and specialty teas.

Local Specialties: Traditional Lyonnaise dishes and pastries.

Atmosphere: Cozy and authentic, reflecting Lyon's rich culinary tradition.

Location: 8 Rue du Major Martin, 69001 Lyon, France

Opening Hours:

Monday to Saturday: 7:30 AM – 7:00 PM

Closed on Sundays

Price Range: Moderate, with a focus on traditional Lyonnaise cuisine.

Local Tips:

Try the Local Pastries: The bakery offers a range of traditional Lyonnaise pastries.

5. La Mère Brazier

Overview: La Mère Brazier is a historic café and bakery offering a blend of traditional French pastries and modern culinary delights. It's named after the famous French chef Eugénie Brazier.

Highlights:

Pastries: A wide selection of pastries, including tarts, cakes, and éclairs.

Breakfast and Brunch: Offers a range of breakfast and brunch options, from fresh pastries to savory dishes.

Elegant Setting: Stylish and comfortable atmosphere.

Location: 12 Rue Royale, 69001 Lyon, France

Opening Hours:

Monday to Saturday: 8:00 AM – 6:00 PM

Closed on Sundays

Price Range: Moderate to high, reflecting the quality and heritage of the establishment.

Local Tips:

Enjoy the Brunch Menu: The brunch menu offers a delightful range of options for a leisurely meal.

Final Tips

Explore Local Specialties: Lyon is known for its pastries and local specialties, so make sure to try regional treats.

Consider Opening Hours: Many bakeries and cafés close early, so plan your visits accordingly.

Check for Seasonal Specials: Some establishments offer seasonal items, so keep an eye out for limited-time treats.

Lyon's cafés and bakeries are integral to its culinary landscape, offering everything from traditional pastries to gourmet delights. Whether you're starting your day with a croissant or enjoying a leisurely afternoon coffee, these spots are perfect for savoring the flavors of Lyon.

Wine and Cocktail Bars

Lyon's reputation as a gastronomic hub extends to its vibrant wine and cocktail scene. The city boasts a diverse range of bars where you can savor exquisite wines, innovative cocktails, and crafted drinks in stylish settings. Here's a guide to some of the best wine and cocktail bars in Lyon:

1. Les Fines Gueules

Overview: Les Fines Gueules is a chic wine bar offering a curated selection of French wines and an inviting atmosphere. It's known for its knowledgeable staff and comfortable setting.

Highlights:

Wine Selection: Features a broad range of French wines, including rare and local varieties.

Tasting Menu: Offers wine tasting flights and paired snacks.

Atmosphere: Elegant yet relaxed, perfect for enjoying a glass of wine with friends.

Location: 11 Rue des Marronniers, 69002 Lyon, France

Opening Hours:

Monday to Saturday: 5:00 PM – 1:00 AM

Closed on Sundays

Price Range: Moderate to high, depending on the wine selection.

Local Tips:

Ask for Recommendations: The staff is knowledgeable and can recommend wines based on your preferences.

Pair with Small Plates: Enjoy a selection of small plates to complement your wine.

2. Le Verre à Soi

Overview: Le Verre à Soi is a stylish cocktail bar known for its creative cocktails and sophisticated ambiance. It's an excellent spot for cocktail enthusiasts looking for something unique.

Highlights:

Signature Cocktails: Features a menu of innovative cocktails crafted by skilled mixologists.

Ambiance: Modern and elegant, with a focus on creating a refined drinking experience.

Special Events: Hosts cocktail-making workshops and special events.

Location: 20 Rue du Bât d'Argent, 69001 Lyon, France

Opening Hours:

Monday to Saturday: 6:00 PM – 2:00 AM

Closed on Sundays

Price Range: Moderate to high, reflecting the quality and creativity of the cocktails.

Local Tips:

Try the Signature Drinks: Don't miss out on their unique cocktails, which are a highlight of the menu.

Enjoy the Atmosphere: The bar's chic decor and ambiance make it a great place for a special night out.

3. La Cave à Jules

Overview: La Cave à Jules is a charming wine bar with a focus on natural wines and a cozy, rustic atmosphere. It's perfect for a relaxed evening with a focus on quality wines.

Highlights:

Natural Wines: Offers a selection of natural and organic wines from various regions.

Comfortable Setting: Features a warm and inviting environment with wooden interiors.

Cheese and Charcuterie: Accompany your wine with a variety of cheeses and charcuterie.

Location: 7 Rue des Trois Maries, 69003 Lyon, France

Opening Hours:

Tuesday to Saturday: 4:00 PM – 11:00 PM

Closed on Sundays and Mondays

Price Range: Moderate, with a focus on high-quality, natural wines.

Local Tips:

Sample the Cheese Plate: The cheese and charcuterie plates are excellent for pairing with the wines.

Explore Natural Wines: If you're new to natural wines, the staff can help you choose a selection.

4. Le Bistrot du Vin

Overview: Le Bistrot du Vin is a cozy wine bar that offers a relaxed environment and an extensive selection of wines, making it a great spot for casual sipping and socializing.

Highlights:

Wine List: Features a diverse range of local and international wines.

Casual Atmosphere: A friendly and informal setting that's perfect for an easy-going evening.

Small Plates: Offers a selection of light bites and tapas to complement the wine.

Location: 32 Rue de la Charité, 69002 Lyon, France

Opening Hours:

Monday to Saturday: 5:00 PM – 12:00 AM

Closed on Sundays

Price Range: Affordable to moderate, catering to a range of budgets.

Local Tips:

Visit During Happy Hour: Take advantage of any happy hour specials for great deals on wines.

Try the Tapas: The tapas are a perfect match for the wines and make for a satisfying snack.

5. L'Antiquaire

Overview: L'Antiquaire is an elegant cocktail bar known for its classic cocktails and sophisticated ambiance. It offers a refined drinking experience in a stylish setting.

Highlights:

Classic Cocktails: Known for its expertly crafted classic cocktails and sophisticated mixology.

Elegant Decor: Features vintage-inspired decor and a chic atmosphere.

Knowledgeable Staff: Bartenders are skilled in creating traditional and innovative cocktails.

Location: 3 Rue des Capucins, 69001 Lyon, France

Opening Hours:

Monday to Saturday: 6:00 PM – 2:00 AM

Closed on Sundays

Price Range: High-end, reflecting the quality and artistry of the cocktails.

Local Tips:

Order the Classics: The bar is known for its classic cocktails, which are a must-try.

Enjoy the Atmosphere: The vintage decor adds to the overall experience, making it a great spot for a special evening.

Final Tips

Explore Local Wines: Lyon is known for its regional wines, so be sure to sample some local varieties.

Ask for Recommendations: Whether you're at a wine bar or cocktail lounge, the staff can provide valuable recommendations based on your taste preferences.

Consider Reservations: For popular bars, especially in the evenings, it's a good idea to make a reservation in advance to secure your spot.

Lyon's wine and cocktail bars offer a rich tapestry of drinking experiences, from elegant settings and creative cocktails to cozy wine bars and natural wine selections. Whether you're a wine aficionado or a cocktail lover, these establishments provide the perfect backdrop for enjoying Lyon's vibrant drinking culture.

Bars and Nightlife

Lyon's reputation as a gastronomic hub extends to its vibrant wine and cocktail scene. The city boasts a diverse range of bars where you can savor exquisite wines, innovative cocktails, and crafted drinks in stylish settings. Here's a guide to some of the best wine and cocktail bars in Lyon:

1. Les Fines Gueules

Overview: Les Fines Gueules is a chic wine bar offering a curated selection of French wines and an inviting atmosphere. It's known for its knowledgeable staff and comfortable setting.

Highlights:

Wine Selection: Features a broad range of French wines, including rare and local varieties.

Tasting Menu: Offers wine tasting flights and paired snacks.

Atmosphere: Elegant yet relaxed, perfect for enjoying a glass of wine with friends.

Location: 11 Rue des Marronniers, 69002 Lyon, France

Opening Hours:

Monday to Saturday: 5:00 PM – 1:00 AM

Closed on Sundays

Price Range: Moderate to high, depending on the wine selection.

Local Tips:

Ask for Recommendations: The staff is knowledgeable and can recommend wines based on your preferences.

Pair with Small Plates: Enjoy a selection of small plates to complement your wine.

2. Le Verre à Soi

Overview: Le Verre à Soi is a stylish cocktail bar known for its creative cocktails and sophisticated ambiance. It's an excellent spot for cocktail enthusiasts looking for something unique.

Highlights:

Signature Cocktails: Features a menu of innovative cocktails crafted by skilled mixologists.

Ambiance: Modern and elegant, with a focus on creating a refined drinking experience.

Special Events: Hosts cocktail-making workshops and special events.

Location: 20 Rue du Bât d'Argent, 69001 Lyon, France

Opening Hours:

Monday to Saturday: 6:00 PM – 2:00 AM

Closed on Sundays

Price Range: Moderate to high, reflecting the quality and creativity of the cocktails.

Local Tips:

Try the Signature Drinks: Don't miss out on their unique cocktails, which are a highlight of the menu.

Enjoy the Atmosphere: The bar's chic decor and ambiance make it a great place for a special night out.

3. La Cave à Jules

Overview: La Cave à Jules is a charming wine bar with a focus on natural wines and a cozy, rustic atmosphere. It's perfect for a relaxed evening with a focus on quality wines.

Highlights:

Natural Wines: Offers a selection of natural and organic wines from various regions.

Comfortable Setting: Features a warm and inviting environment with wooden interiors.

Cheese and Charcuterie: Accompany your wine with a variety of cheeses and charcuterie.

Location: 7 Rue des Trois Maries, 69003 Lyon, France

Opening Hours:

Tuesday to Saturday: 4:00 PM – 11:00 PM

Closed on Sundays and Mondays

Price Range: Moderate, with a focus on high-quality, natural wines.

Local Tips:

Sample the Cheese Plate: The cheese and charcuterie plates are excellent for pairing with the wines.

Explore Natural Wines: If you're new to natural wines, the staff can help you choose a selection.

4. Le Bistrot du Vin

Overview: Le Bistrot du Vin is a cozy wine bar that offers a relaxed environment and an extensive selection of wines, making it a great spot for casual sipping and socializing.

Highlights:

Wine List: Features a diverse range of local and international wines.

Casual Atmosphere: A friendly and informal setting that's perfect for an easy-going evening.

Small Plates: Offers a selection of light bites and tapas to complement the wine.

Location: 32 Rue de la Charité, 69002 Lyon, France

Opening Hours:

Monday to Saturday: 5:00 PM – 12:00 AM

Closed on Sundays

Price Range: Affordable to moderate, catering to a range of budgets.

Local Tips:

Visit During Happy Hour: Take advantage of any happy hour specials for great deals on wines.

Try the Tapas: The tapas are a perfect match for the wines and make for a satisfying snack.

5. L'Antiquaire

Overview: L'Antiquaire is an elegant cocktail bar known for its classic cocktails and sophisticated ambiance. It offers a refined drinking experience in a stylish setting.

Highlights:

Classic Cocktails: Known for its expertly crafted classic cocktails and sophisticated mixology.

Elegant Decor: Features vintage-inspired decor and a chic atmosphere.

Knowledgeable Staff: Bartenders are skilled in creating traditional and innovative cocktails.

Location: 3 Rue des Capucins, 69001 Lyon, France

Opening Hours:

Monday to Saturday: 6:00 PM – 2:00 AM

Closed on Sundays

Price Range: High-end, reflecting the quality and artistry of the cocktails.

Local Tips:

Order the Classics: The bar is known for its classic cocktails, which are a must-try.

Enjoy the Atmosphere: The vintage decor adds to the overall experience, making it a great spot for a special evening.

Final Tips

Explore Local Wines: Lyon is known for its regional wines, so be sure to sample some local varieties.

Ask for Recommendations: Whether you're at a wine bar or cocktail lounge, the staff can provide valuable recommendations based on your taste preferences.

Consider Reservations: For popular bars, especially in the evenings, it's a good idea to make a reservation in advance to secure your spot.

Lyon's wine and cocktail bars offer a rich tapestry of drinking experiences, from elegant settings and creative cocktails to cozy wine bars and natural wine selections. Whether you're a wine aficionado or a cocktail lover, these establishments provide the perfect backdrop for enjoying Lyon's vibrant drinking culture.

Chapter 13: Day Trips from Lyon

Beaujolais Wine Region

The Beaujolais Wine Region, located just a short drive from Lyon, is a delightful destination for wine enthusiasts and nature lovers alike. Renowned for its picturesque landscapes and exceptional wines, this region offers an ideal day trip opportunity from Lyon. Here's a comprehensive guide on how to make the most of your visit to the Beaujolais Wine Region.

1. Getting to Beaujolais

By Car:

Travel Time: Approximately 1 hour, depending on traffic and your specific starting point in Lyon.

Route: Drive north on the A6 motorway from Lyon, then follow signs to the Beaujolais region. The scenic drive through rolling hills and vineyards is a pleasant experience.

By Train:

Travel Time: Around 30-45 minutes to the town of Villefranche-sur-Saône, which serves as a gateway to Beaujolais.

Train Options: Trains run frequently from Lyon Part-Dieu to Villefranche-sur-Saône. From Villefranche-sur-Saône, you can use local transport or a taxi to reach various wine villages.

By Bus:

Travel Time: Similar to driving, but less flexible. Several local bus services connect Lyon with towns in the Beaujolais region.

Bus Options: Check local schedules and routes for the most convenient options.

By Guided Tour:

Travel Time: Varies depending on the tour provider.

Tour Options: Many tour operators offer day trips from Lyon to Beaujolais, including transportation, guided tours of wineries, and wine tastings.

2. Must-Visit Towns and Villages

Villefranche-sur-Saône:

Overview: The largest town in the Beaujolais region, Villefranche-sur-Saône, is an excellent starting point. It has a charming historic center with shops, cafes, and a lively market.

Highlights: Explore the beautiful old town, visit the Saint-Georges Church, and stroll along the Saône River.

Beaujolais Village:

Overview: A picturesque village known for its wine production, offering a quaint and authentic Beaujolais experience.

Highlights: Visit local wineries, explore the village's charming streets, and enjoy traditional Beaujolais cuisine.

Oingt:

Overview: Often regarded as one of France's "Les Plus Beaux Villages" (Most Beautiful Villages), Oingt offers stunning views and a historic atmosphere.

Highlights: Wander through the medieval streets, admire the traditional stone houses, and enjoy panoramic views of the vineyards.

Villié-Morgon:

Overview: A village known for its excellent wines, particularly the Morgon cru.

Highlights: Visit local vineyards and taste the famous Morgon wines. The village is also home to beautiful landscapes and hiking trails.

3. Wine Tasting and Tours

Local Wineries and Vineyards:

Overview: The Beaujolais region is famous for its Gamay grapes and is renowned for producing light, fruity red wines. Many wineries offer tours and tastings.

Types of Wine: Beaujolais Nouveau (a young, fresh wine released in November), and Beaujolais Crus (from specific appellations such as Morgon, Fleurie, and Chiroubles).

Tour Options:

Guided Winery Tours: Many wineries offer guided tours where you can learn about the winemaking process and taste different varieties.

Wine Tastings: Participate in wine tastings at local vineyards to sample a range of Beaujolais wines. Reservations are often recommended.

Wine Festivals and Events:

Beaujolais Nouveau Day: Held annually in November, this event celebrates the release of the new Beaujolais wine with festivities and tastings.

Local Festivals: Check for local wine festivals and events happening during your visit.

4. Dining and Cuisine

Local Restaurants and Bistros:

Traditional Cuisine: Enjoy regional specialties such as coq au vin, charcuterie, and cheese, which pair perfectly with Beaujolais wines.

Recommended Spots: Many towns have charming bistros and restaurants where you can enjoy a meal with a glass of local wine.

Picnic in the Vineyards:

Overview: Pack a picnic and enjoy it amidst the beautiful vineyards. Some wineries offer picnic areas where you can relax and savor local produce with your wine.

5. Scenic Spots and Outdoor Activities

Hiking and Walking Trails:

Overview: The Beaujolais region offers several scenic trails through vineyards and rolling hills.

Popular Trails: Explore the "Monts du Beaujolais" for panoramic views and peaceful walks.

Cycling:

Overview: Rent a bike and explore the picturesque vineyards and countryside. Cycling routes are well-marked and offer a great way to see the region.

Photography:

Scenic Views: The region's rolling hills, vineyards, and historic villages provide fantastic photo opportunities. Capture the beauty of the landscape and the charm of the local architecture.

6. Practical Tips for Your Day Trip

Weather Considerations:

Seasonal Clothing: Check the weather forecast and dress appropriately. The region experiences all four seasons, with hot summers and cold winters.

Booking in Advance:

Reservations: Make reservations for winery tours and tastings in advance, especially during peak seasons.

Transportation:

Local Transport: If you're not driving, use local taxis or shuttle services to get between towns and vineyards.

Local Etiquette:

Respect Wine Traditions: Follow local customs and etiquette when visiting wineries, including handling wine glasses properly and being courteous to staff.

Language:

French Basics: While many places in the Beaujolais region speak English, learning a few basic French phrases can enhance your experience.

Pérouges

Pérouges, often hailed as one of the most beautiful villages in France, offers a perfect day trip from Lyon. Its medieval charm, cobblestone streets, and historical significance make it a must-visit destination. Here's a detailed guide to help you explore Pérouges and make the most of your visit.

1. Getting to Pérouges

By Car:

Travel Time: Approximately 45 minutes to 1 hour from Lyon, depending on traffic and your exact starting point.

Route: Take the A42 motorway towards Pérouges, then follow local signs to the village. Parking is available at the entrance to the village.

By Train:

Travel Time: Around 30-40 minutes to Meximieux-Pérouges Station.

Train Options: Take a train from Lyon Part-Dieu or Lyon Perrache to Meximieux-Pérouges. From the station, it's a short taxi ride or a 20-minute walk to the village.

By Bus:

Travel Time: Varies, but typically around 1 hour.

Bus Options: Local bus services connect Lyon with the Pérouges area. Check local schedules for specific routes and times.

By Guided Tour:

Travel Time: Varies depending on the tour provider.

Tour Options: Many tour operators offer guided day trips from Lyon to Pérouges, often including transportation, guided tours, and sometimes additional stops.

2. Discovering Pérouges

Overview:

Historical Significance: Pérouges is a well-preserved medieval village with a rich history dating back to the 13th century. Its status as a "Les Plus Beaux Villages de France" (One of the Most Beautiful Villages of France) underscores its historical and aesthetic value.

Atmosphere: The village exudes a timeless charm with its narrow, winding streets, half-timbered houses, and historic buildings.

Highlights:

Medieval Architecture:

Place du Tilleul: The central square of Pérouges, surrounded by charming buildings and historical sites. It's a great place to start your exploration.

Maison des Consuls: A historic building that once served as the town hall. Its Gothic architecture and beautiful façade are notable.

Historic Sites:

Église Sainte-Marie-Madeleine: A lovely church with medieval origins, featuring a simple yet elegant interior.

Remparts: Walk along the old city walls for stunning views of the surrounding countryside and to get a sense of the village's defensive history.

Local Shops and Galleries:

Craft Shops: Explore small shops selling local crafts, souvenirs, and artisanal products.

Art Galleries: Visit galleries showcasing local art and historical exhibitions.

Dining and Gastronomy:

Local Cuisine:

Crêpes de Pérouges: A local specialty, these crêpes are typically filled with sweet or savory ingredients and are a must-try during your visit.

Restaurants and Cafés: Enjoy a meal or a drink in one of the village's quaint restaurants or cafés, which offer traditional French cuisine and local delicacies.

Popular Dining Spots:

Auberge de la Table de Pérouges: A historic restaurant serving traditional French dishes, including the famous crêpes de Pérouges.

Le Café de la Place: A charming café on the central square, perfect for a light meal or a coffee.

3. Things to Do in Pérouges

Walking Tours:

Self-Guided Tours: Wander through the narrow streets and discover the village at your own pace. Maps and information panels are available to help you navigate.

Guided Tours: Join a local guide to learn about the history and significance of various sites in Pérouges. These tours often provide deeper insights into the village's past.

Photography:

Scenic Views: Capture the picturesque streets, historic buildings, and beautiful countryside surrounding Pérouges. The village's well-preserved architecture provides excellent photo opportunities.

Outdoor Activities:

Hiking and Nature Walks: Explore the nearby countryside and enjoy the natural beauty of the region. There are several walking trails and scenic spots around Pérouges.

4. Practical Tips for Visiting Pérouges

Weather Considerations:

Seasonal Clothing: Check the weather forecast and dress appropriately. Pérouges can be visited year-round, but winter can be chilly and summer can be warm.

Parking:

Parking Information: Parking is available at the entrance to the village. It's a short walk from the parking area to the village center.

Local Etiquette:

Respect the Local Culture: Pérouges is a historic village, so be respectful of its heritage. Follow local customs and guidelines, especially when visiting historical sites.

Language:

French Basics: While many locals speak some English, learning a few basic French phrases can enhance your experience and interactions.

Local Events:

Check for Festivals: Pérouges hosts various events and festivals throughout the year. Check local event calendars for any special activities happening during your visit.

Monts d'Or

The Monts d'Or (Golden Mountains) offer a picturesque and tranquil retreat from the bustling city of Lyon. Known for its beautiful landscapes, outdoor activities, and charming villages, this area provides an ideal day trip destination. Here's a comprehensive guide to exploring Monts d'Or.

1. Getting to Monts d'Or

By Car:

Travel Time: Approximately 30-45 minutes from Lyon, depending on traffic and your starting point.

Route: Drive northwest from Lyon on the D306 or D49 roads. The drive offers scenic views as you approach the rolling hills and natural landscapes of Monts d'Or.

By Train:

Travel Time: Around 20-30 minutes to the nearest train stations such as Neuville-sur-Saône or La Tour-de-Salvagny.

Train Options: Trains from Lyon Part-Dieu or Lyon Perrache to Neuville-sur-Saône. From the station, you can use local buses, taxis, or bike rentals to reach your destination in Monts d'Or.

By Bus:

Travel Time: Approximately 45-60 minutes.

Bus Options: Local bus services connect Lyon with towns in the Monts d'Or region. Check schedules for routes and times.

By Guided Tour:

Travel Time: Varies depending on the tour provider.

Tour Options: Many tour operators offer guided day trips from Lyon to Monts d'Or, including transportation, guided walks, and sometimes additional activities.

2. Discovering Monts d'Or

Overview:

Geographical Significance: Monts d'Or is a range of hills located just north of Lyon, known for its natural beauty and outdoor recreation opportunities. The area features rolling hills, forests, and charming villages.

Activities: Popular activities include hiking, cycling, and exploring the scenic countryside.

Highlights:

Outdoor Activities:

Hiking:

Trails: Monts d'Or offers a variety of hiking trails ranging from easy walks to more challenging routes. The trails provide stunning views of the surrounding countryside and Lyon in the distance.

Popular Trails: The "Sentier des Crêtes" is a well-known trail that offers panoramic views and a chance to explore the diverse flora and fauna of the region.

Cycling:

Routes: The region is ideal for cycling enthusiasts, with several marked routes and trails that showcase the natural beauty of Monts d'Or.

Bike Rentals: Rentals are available in nearby towns, and some local services offer bike tours.

Nature Walks:

Scenic Spots: Enjoy leisurely walks through the lush forests and rolling hills. The peaceful environment makes it a perfect spot for nature lovers and those seeking relaxation.

Villages and Local Charm:

Charnay:

Overview: A picturesque village with charming streets and traditional architecture.

Highlights: Explore the local shops, enjoy a meal at a traditional restaurant, and take in the village's serene atmosphere.

Fontaines-sur-Saône:

Overview: A lovely village situated along the Saône River, known for its scenic beauty and historical buildings.

Highlights: Walk along the riverbanks, visit the local market, and enjoy the quaint village ambiance.

La Tour-de-Salvagny:

Overview: A village offering a mix of natural beauty and historical heritage.

Highlights: Explore local landmarks and enjoy the surrounding landscape. The village is also known for its golf course.

3. Things to Do in Monts d'Or

Scenic Views:

Panoramic Vistas: From various viewpoints in Monts d'Or, you can enjoy breathtaking views of the surrounding hills, forests, and the city of Lyon in the distance.

Photography:

Photo Opportunities: Capture the beauty of the rolling hills, charming villages, and natural landscapes. The area is perfect for landscape photography and nature shots.

Local Cuisine:

Dining:

Local Restaurants: Enjoy meals at local bistros and restaurants that offer traditional French cuisine. Many establishments feature outdoor seating with views of the surrounding countryside.

Specialties: Try regional specialties and local wines that complement the rural ambiance of Monts d'Or.

Picnic Spots:

Outdoor Dining: Pack a picnic and enjoy it in one of the scenic spots or parks in Monts d'Or. The peaceful environment makes it an ideal location for a relaxed outdoor meal.

4. Practical Tips for Visiting Monts d'Or

Weather Considerations:

Seasonal Clothing: Dress appropriately for the weather. The region can be quite hot in summer and chilly in winter. Layered clothing is advisable for varying temperatures.

Parking:

Parking Information: Parking is available in the villages and at trailheads. Follow local signs and regulations for parking.

Local Etiquette:

Respect Nature: Follow local guidelines for hiking and outdoor activities. Respect wildlife and keep trails clean.

Language:

French Basics: While many locals speak some English, learning a few basic French phrases can enhance your visit and interactions.

Local Events:

Check for Festivals: Monts d'Or hosts various local events and festivals throughout the year. Check local event calendars for any special activities happening during your visit.

Annecy

Annecy, often referred to as the "Venice of the Alps," is renowned for its stunning lake, picturesque canals, and charming old town. Situated a few hours from Lyon, this idyllic city offers a perfect day trip for those seeking natural beauty, historical charm, and outdoor activities. Here's a comprehensive guide to help you explore Annecy.

1. Getting to Annecy

By Car:

Travel Time: Approximately 1.5 to 2 hours from Lyon, depending on traffic and your exact starting point.

Route: Drive east from Lyon on the A40 motorway. Follow signs to Annecy, with the drive offering scenic views of the French countryside and the Alps.

By Train:

Travel Time: Around 1.5 to 2 hours.

Train Options: Direct trains from Lyon Part-Dieu to Annecy are frequent. The journey provides comfortable seating and beautiful views of the surrounding landscapes.

By Bus:

Travel Time: Approximately 2 to 2.5 hours.

Bus Options: Several bus companies offer services from Lyon to Annecy. Check schedules for specific departure times and routes.

By Guided Tour:

Travel Time: Varies depending on the tour provider.

Tour Options: Many operators offer guided day trips from Lyon to Annecy, including transportation, guided tours, and sometimes additional activities.

2. Discovering Annecy

Overview:

Historical Significance: Annecy is known for its well-preserved medieval architecture and its picturesque setting between the lake and the surrounding mountains. The city has been a popular destination since the 19th century.

Atmosphere: The city combines historical charm with a beautiful natural environment, featuring canals, a lake, and vibrant public spaces.

Highlights:

Lake Annecy:

Overview: Often called the "cleanest lake in Europe," Lake Annecy is a major attraction. The clear blue waters and surrounding scenery make it perfect for relaxation and recreation.

Activities: Enjoy boating, paddleboarding, or a leisurely walk along the lakeside promenades. You can also rent bicycles to cycle around the lake.

Old Town (La Vieille Ville):

Overview: The medieval heart of Annecy is characterized by narrow, winding streets, colorful buildings, and charming canals.

Highlights: Explore the quaint shops, cafés, and historical buildings. Key spots include the Palais de l'Isle and the Château d'Annecy.

Palais de l'Isle:

Overview: A historic building located on an island in the Thiou River. Originally a medieval prison, it now houses a museum.

Highlights: Visit the museum to learn about the history of Annecy and the building itself.

Château d'Annecy:

Overview: A castle overlooking the city and lake, offering panoramic views of the area.

Highlights: Explore the castle's historical exhibits and enjoy the stunning vistas from the ramparts.

3. Things to Do in Annecy

Walking Tours:

Self-Guided Tours: Wander through the Old Town and along the canals at your own pace. Information panels and maps are available to guide you.

Guided Tours: Join a local guide to gain deeper insights into the city's history and architecture. Tours often include highlights such as the Palais de l'Isle and the Château d'Annecy.

Photography:

Photo Opportunities: Capture the beauty of the lake, canals, and medieval streets. Annecy's picturesque setting offers excellent opportunities for landscape and architectural photography.

Dining and Shopping:

Local Cuisine:

Restaurants: Enjoy meals at local bistros and restaurants offering traditional Savoyard cuisine. Try regional specialties such as tartiflette or raclette.

Cafés: Relax at a café by the canal and enjoy a coffee or pastry while taking in the views.

Shopping:

Markets: Explore local markets for fresh produce, cheeses, and crafts. The markets provide a taste of regional flavors and local products.

Boutiques: Browse through unique shops and boutiques in the Old Town for souvenirs and local goods.

4. Practical Tips for Visiting Annecy

Weather Considerations:

Seasonal Clothing: Check the weather forecast and dress accordingly. Summers can be warm, while winters can be chilly, particularly in the surrounding mountains.

Parking:

Parking Information: Parking can be challenging in the city center, especially during peak tourist seasons. Consider parking in designated areas or using public transport where possible.

Local Etiquette:

Respect Local Customs: Annecy is a popular tourist destination, so be courteous to locals and follow any guidelines for public spaces.

Language:

French Basics: While many people in Annecy speak English, knowing a few basic French phrases can enhance your visit and interactions.

Local Events:

Check for Festivals: Annecy hosts various events and festivals throughout the year, such as the Annecy International Animated Film Festival. Check local event calendars for any special activities during your visit.

Geneva

Geneva, renowned for its global significance, stunning lakeside setting, and cosmopolitan atmosphere, is an excellent day trip destination from Lyon. As Switzerland's international hub, Geneva offers a rich blend of cultural landmarks, natural beauty, and refined sophistication. Here's a comprehensive guide to exploring Geneva.

1. Getting to Geneva

By Car:

Travel Time: Approximately 2 to 2.5 hours from Lyon.

Route: Drive northeast from Lyon on the A40 motorway, then cross the border into Switzerland and continue on the A1 towards Geneva. The drive offers scenic views of the French and Swiss countryside.

By Train:

Travel Time: Around 2 hours.

Train Options: Direct trains from Lyon Part-Dieu to Geneva's main train station, Gare Cornavin. The journey is comfortable and provides scenic views of the region.

By Bus:

Travel Time: Approximately 2.5 to 3 hours.

Bus Options: Several bus companies offer services from Lyon to Geneva. Check schedules for specific departure times and routes.

By Guided Tour:

Travel Time: Varies depending on the tour provider.

Tour Options: Many tour operators offer guided day trips from Lyon to Geneva, including transportation, guided tours, and sometimes additional activities.

2. Discovering Geneva

Overview:

Historical Significance: Geneva is known for its role as a center for diplomacy, hosting numerous international organizations, including the United Nations and the Red Cross. The city's historical and cultural heritage is reflected in its landmarks and institutions.

Atmosphere: Geneva is a blend of natural beauty, historical charm, and modern sophistication. The city is situated on the shores of Lake Geneva and is surrounded by the Alps and Jura mountains.

Highlights:

Lake Geneva (Lac Léman):

Overview: One of the largest lakes in Western Europe, Lake Geneva is a focal point of the city. The lake's clear waters and stunning backdrop of mountains make it a prime attraction.

Activities: Take a leisurely boat ride, stroll along the lakeside promenades, or simply enjoy the scenic views. The Jet d'Eau, a famous water fountain, is a must-see landmark on the lake.

Old Town (Vieille Ville):

Overview: Geneva's Old Town is a maze of narrow, cobblestone streets filled with historic buildings, charming cafés, and boutiques.

Highlights: Visit St. Peter's Cathedral (Cathedrale St-Pierre) and climb the tower for panoramic views of the city. Explore the Maison Tavel, Geneva's oldest house, which now serves as a museum.

International District:

Overview: Home to many international organizations, including the United Nations and the World Health Organization.

Highlights: Take a tour of the Palais des Nations (United Nations Office) and visit the Parc des Nations for a glimpse of Geneva's role in global diplomacy.

Parks and Gardens:

Overview: Geneva is known for its beautiful parks and green spaces.

Highlights: Stroll through the Jardin Anglais (English Garden) and admire the flower clock, or visit the Parc des Bastions, a serene park with historical statues and the Reformation Wall.

Museums:

Overview: Geneva boasts a variety of museums that cater to different interests.

Highlights: Explore the Musée d'Art et d'Histoire (Museum of Art and History) for a diverse collection of art and historical artifacts, or visit the International Red Cross and Red Crescent Museum to learn about humanitarian efforts.

3. Things to Do in Geneva

Walking Tours:

Self-Guided Tours: Explore the Old Town and lakeside areas at your own pace. Maps and information panels are available for guidance.

Guided Tours: Join a local guide to discover Geneva's history, architecture, and international significance. Tours often include highlights such as the Palais des Nations and the Old Town.

Photography:

Photo Opportunities: Capture the beauty of Lake Geneva, the Jet d'Eau, and the historic architecture of the Old Town. The city's natural setting and landmarks offer excellent photography opportunities.

Dining and Shopping:

Local Cuisine:

Restaurants: Geneva offers a range of dining options from upscale restaurants to casual eateries. Try Swiss specialties like fondue or raclette.

Cafés: Enjoy coffee and pastries at one of the many charming cafés in the Old Town or by the lake.

Shopping:

Boutiques: Explore Geneva's high-end boutiques and shops for luxury goods and Swiss watches. The Rue du Rhône is a popular shopping street.

Markets: Visit local markets for fresh produce, cheeses, and local crafts.

4. Practical Tips for Visiting Geneva

Weather Considerations:

Seasonal Clothing: Geneva experiences varied weather, with mild summers and cold winters. Check the forecast and dress accordingly.

Currency:

Currency: Switzerland uses the Swiss Franc (CHF). Ensure you have some local currency for small purchases, though credit cards are widely accepted.

Language:

Languages: French is the primary language in Geneva. English is commonly spoken, especially in tourist areas.

Parking:

Parking Information: Parking in central Geneva can be challenging. Consider using public transport or parking in designated areas outside the city center.

Local Etiquette:

Respect Local Customs: Follow local guidelines and be courteous to locals. Geneva is a multicultural city, and respectful behavior is appreciated.

Local Events:

Check for Festivals: Geneva hosts various events and festivals throughout the year, such as the Geneva International Motor Show. Check local event calendars for any special activities during your visit.

Villefranche-sur-Saône

Villefranche-sur-Saône, a charming town located just north of Lyon, offers a delightful blend of historical charm, local culture, and scenic beauty. Known for its picturesque streets, vibrant markets, and proximity to the Beaujolais wine region, Villefranche-sur-Saône makes for an enjoyable day trip. Here's a comprehensive guide to exploring this captivating town.

1. Getting to Villefranche-sur-Saône

By Car:

Travel Time: Approximately 30 to 45 minutes from Lyon.

Route: Drive north from Lyon on the A6 motorway. Follow signs for Villefranche-sur-Saône. The drive offers a glimpse into the beautiful Beaujolais countryside.

By Train:

Travel Time: About 30 to 40 minutes.

Train Options: Direct trains run frequently from Lyon Part-Dieu to Villefranche-sur-Saône. The journey is comfortable and provides scenic views of the region.

By Bus:

Travel Time: Approximately 45 minutes to 1 hour.

Bus Options: Several bus services connect Lyon with Villefranche-sur-Saône. Check schedules for specific departure times.

By Guided Tour:

Travel Time: Varies depending on the tour provider.

Tour Options: Some operators offer guided day trips from Lyon to Villefranche-sur-Saône, including transportation and local guides.

2. Discovering Villefranche-sur-Saône

Overview:

Historical Significance: Villefranche-sur-Saône, founded in the 13th century, has a rich history reflected in its architecture and local traditions. It is an important commercial center in the Beaujolais wine region.

Atmosphere: The town combines historical charm with a lively local culture. Its well-preserved streets, bustling markets, and scenic surroundings make it a pleasant destination.

Highlights:

Old Town (Centre Ville):

Overview: The historical center of Villefranche-sur-Saône is characterized by narrow streets, medieval buildings, and charming squares.

Highlights: Explore the Place des Arts, a lively square with cafés and shops. Visit the Hôtel de Ville (Town Hall) and admire its architectural beauty.

Collegiate Church of Notre-Dame:

Overview: A beautiful Gothic church located in the heart of the town.

Highlights: Visit the church to admire its stunning architecture and serene interior. The church is known for its impressive stained glass windows and historic significance.

Les Halles de Villefranche:

Overview: A vibrant market hall where local vendors sell fresh produce, cheeses, meats, and other local products.

Highlights: Browse the stalls for a taste of regional specialties, including Beaujolais wines, and interact with local vendors.

Beaujolais Wine Region:

Overview: Villefranche-sur-Saône is the gateway to the Beaujolais wine region, known for its red wines and scenic vineyards.

Highlights: Take a short drive or guided tour into the surrounding vineyards to explore local wineries, taste Beaujolais wines, and enjoy the picturesque countryside.

Parc de la Pépinière:

Overview: A local park offering green space and recreational opportunities.

Highlights: Relax in the park, take a leisurely stroll, or enjoy a picnic in this pleasant setting.

3. Things to Do in Villefranche-sur-Saône

Walking Tours:

Self-Guided Tours: Explore the town's historical center and market areas at your own pace. Maps and information panels are available.

Guided Tours: Join a local guide to learn more about Villefranche-sur-Saône's history, architecture, and local culture. Some tours may include wine-tasting experiences.

Photography:

Photo Opportunities: Capture the charm of the Old Town, the beauty of the Gothic church, and the vibrant scenes at the market. The scenic views of the surrounding Beaujolais vineyards are also excellent for photography.

Dining and Shopping:

Local Cuisine:

Restaurants: Enjoy meals at local bistros and restaurants offering regional cuisine. Try local specialties such as Beaujolais wines and traditional French dishes.

Cafés: Relax at a café in the town center and enjoy a coffee or pastry while watching the world go by.

Shopping:

Markets: Visit Les Halles de Villefranche for fresh produce, cheeses, and local goods. The market offers a genuine taste of the region's culinary delights.

Boutiques: Browse through local shops and boutiques for unique gifts and souvenirs.

4. Practical Tips for Visiting Villefranche-sur-Saône

Weather Considerations:

Seasonal Clothing: Check the weather forecast before your visit. Villefranche-sur-Saône experiences mild summers and cooler winters. Dress accordingly based on the season.

Parking:

Parking Information: Parking is available in and around the town center. Look for designated parking areas and be mindful of local regulations.

Language:

Language: French is the primary language spoken in Villefranche-sur-Saône. Basic knowledge of French phrases can enhance your visit, though many people in tourist areas speak some English.

Local Etiquette:

Respect Local Customs: Follow local guidelines and be courteous to residents. Villefranche-sur-Saône is a small town with a friendly atmosphere, and respectful behavior is appreciated.

Local Events:

Check for Festivals: Villefranche-sur-Saône hosts various events and festivals throughout the year, including wine festivals and local markets. Check local event calendars for any special activities during your visit.

317

Chapter 14: Essential Itinerary for First-Timers

Morning: Arrival and Initial Exploration

Arrival:

Airport Transfer: If you're arriving at Lyon-Saint Exupéry Airport, you can take the Rhône Express train to Lyon Part-Dieu station, which takes about 30 minutes and costs around €16. Alternatively, taxis are available for approximately €50-€60.

Hotel Check-in: Check into a centrally located hotel such as Hotel Carlton Lyon, Hôtel Le Royal Lyon, or Mama Shelter Lyon. These hotels are well-rated and provide convenient access to the city's attractions.

Breakfast:

Café du Palais: Located in the heart of Lyon, Café du Palais is perfect for a traditional French breakfast. Enjoy a freshly baked croissant or pain au chocolat with a café au lait. Breakfast typically costs around €7-€10.

Opening Hours: Typically from 7:00 AM to 7:00 PM.

Mid-Morning: Explore Vieux Lyon

Vieux Lyon (Old Lyon):

Highlights: Stroll through the cobblestone streets of Vieux Lyon, a UNESCO World Heritage site. Explore the Renaissance architecture, visit the Lyon Cathedral (Saint-Jean-Baptiste Cathedral), and wander through the traboules (hidden passageways).

Price: Free to explore. Some specific attractions or tours may have an entry fee.

Getting Around:

Walking: Vieux Lyon is best explored on foot. The area is compact, and walking allows you to fully appreciate the architectural details and charming streets.

Afternoon: Museum Visit and Lunch

Lunch:

Les Fines Gueules: Enjoy a delightful lunch at Les Fines Gueules, known for its modern take on traditional Lyonnaise cuisine. A typical lunch might cost between €15-€25.

Opening Hours: Generally from 12:00 PM to 2:30 PM, and then from 7:00 PM to 10:00 PM.

Museum Visit:

Musée des Beaux-Arts (Fine Arts Museum): After lunch, head to the Musée des Beaux-Arts, one of France's largest art museums. It boasts an impressive collection of paintings, sculptures, and artifacts.

Opening Hours: 10:00 AM - 6:00 PM, closed on Tuesdays.

Price: €8 for adults, free for EU residents under 26.

Getting Around:

Metro: Take Metro Line A or B to Hôtel de Ville - Louis Pradel station, which is close to the museum.

Mid-Afternoon: Parc de la Tête d'Or

Visit Parc de la Tête d'Or:

Highlights: This large urban park offers beautiful landscapes, a botanical garden, a zoo, and a large lake where you can rent a pedal boat.

Price: Free entry to the park. Some attractions within the park, like the zoo, are also free, but boat rentals cost around €10-€15.

Opening Hours: Park is open from 6:30 AM to 9:00 PM.

Getting Around:

Tram/Walking: Use Tram Line T1 to reach the park (stop: Tête d'Or - Parc). The park is also accessible by walking if you prefer.

Evening: Dinner and Nightlife

Dinner:

Bouchon Les Lyonnais: Experience authentic Lyonnaise cuisine at a traditional bouchon. Dishes like coq au vin, quenelles, and pâté en croûte are popular here. Expect to pay around €25-€40 per person.

Opening Hours: Typically from 7:00 PM to 10:00 PM.

Nightlife:

L'Antiquaire: For a cocktail or a relaxed evening, head to L'Antiquaire, a stylish bar with a vintage feel. Enjoy a crafted cocktail or a glass of fine wine.

Opening Hours: Usually from 6:00 PM to 2:00 AM.

Getting Around:

Metro/Taxi: Use Lyon's efficient metro system or a taxi to navigate back to your hotel. The metro operates until around midnight.

Getting Around Lyon

Public Transportation:

Metro: Lyon has an extensive metro system with four lines (A, B, C, D). A single ticket costs about €2.00.

Tram: There are several tram lines (T1 to T6) that cover key parts of the city.

Bus: Buses complement the metro and tram networks.

Bike Rentals:

Vélo'v: Lyon offers a bike-sharing system called Vélo'v. Rentals start from €1.50 per hour or €4 for a full day.

Walking:

Pedestrian-Friendly: Lyon's city center is very walkable, especially around Vieux Lyon and Presqu'île.

Day 2: Vieux Lyon and Historical Sites

Morning: Explore Vieux Lyon

Breakfast:

La Boîte à Pain: Start your day with breakfast at La Boîte à Pain, known for its excellent pastries and coffee. Try a quiche or a tartine with your coffee for a satisfying start.

Price: Approximately €8-€12 for breakfast.

Opening Hours: Generally from 7:00 AM to 7:00 PM.

Stroll Through Vieux Lyon:

Highlights: Wander through the Renaissance quarter of Vieux Lyon, which is known for its preserved medieval and Renaissance buildings. Visit key landmarks such as:

Saint-Jean-Baptiste Cathedral: A stunning Gothic cathedral with beautiful stained glass windows.

Traboules: Hidden passageways between buildings used by silk merchants. Notable ones are found around Rue du Boeuf and Rue des Trois Maries.

Place du Change: A picturesque square with historic architecture.

Getting Around:

Walking: Vieux Lyon is best explored on foot due to its narrow, winding streets.

Mid-Morning: Visit the Musée Gadagne

Musée Gadagne:

Highlights: This museum complex includes the Musée d'Histoire de Lyon and the Musée des Marionnettes du Monde. It provides an insightful look into Lyon's history and its famous puppetry tradition.

Opening Hours: 10:00 AM - 6:00 PM, closed on Mondays.

Price: €6 for a combined ticket to both museums.

Getting Around:

Walking: The museum is located in Vieux Lyon, so you can easily walk there from other attractions in the area.

Lunch:

Le Café des Fédérations: Enjoy a traditional Lyonnaise meal at Le Café des Fédérations. This restaurant is famous for its authentic bouchon cuisine, including dishes like andouillette and Lyonnaise salad.

Price: Around €20-€30 per person.

Opening Hours: 12:00 PM to 2:00 PM and 7:00 PM to 10:00 PM.

Basilica of Notre-Dame de Fourvière:

Highlights: After lunch, make your way to the Basilica of Notre-Dame de Fourvière, located on Fourvière Hill. This iconic basilica offers panoramic views of Lyon from its terrace. The interior is richly decorated with mosaics and stained glass.

Opening Hours: 8:00 AM - 6:00 PM.

Price: Free entry.

Roman Theaters:

Highlights: Explore the ancient Roman theaters on Fourvière Hill, including the Grand Theatre and the Odeon. These well-preserved ruins give insight into Lyon's history as the Roman city of Lugdunum.

Opening Hours: Generally accessible throughout the day.

Price: Free to visit.

Getting Around:

Funicular: Take the funicular from Vieux Lyon (station: Vieux Lyon - Fourvière) up to Fourvière Hill. The funicular ride is about €2.00.

Visit Musée des Confluences:

Highlights: This modern museum located at the confluence of the Rhône and Saône rivers showcases exhibitions on science, anthropology, and natural history. The striking building itself is worth seeing.

Opening Hours: 10:30 AM - 6:30 PM, closed on Tuesdays.

Price: €9 for adults, free for under 18.

Getting Around:

Tram: Take Tram Line T1 to the Musée des Confluences stop. The journey from Vieux Lyon takes about 15 minutes.

Dinner:

Le Musée: Situated near the Musée des Beaux-Arts, Le Musée offers classic Lyonnaise dishes in a charming setting. Try local specialties like boudin noir or duck confit.

Price: Approximately €25-€40 per person.

Opening Hours: 7:00 PM - 10:00 PM.

Night Walk:

Place Bellecour: After dinner, enjoy an evening stroll around Place Bellecour, one of the largest squares in Europe. The square is beautifully lit at night and offers a lovely view of the city.

Getting Around:

Walking: Place Bellecour is centrally located, and a walk through the area is a great way to wind down your day.

Getting Around Lyon

Public Transportation:

Metro: Lyon's metro lines can help you navigate between different districts. A single ticket costs around €2.00.

Tram: Trams are convenient for reaching outlying areas, such as the Musée des Confluences.

Bike Rentals:

Vélo'v: If you prefer biking, the Vélo'v bike-sharing system is available throughout the city.

Taxis/Rideshares:

Taxis/Uber: Easily accessible if needed for longer distances or late-night travel.

Day 3: Museums and Parks

Morning: Musée des Beaux-Arts and Parc de la Tête d'Or

Breakfast:

Les Fils à Maman: Enjoy a hearty breakfast at Les Fils à Maman, known for its cozy atmosphere and delicious offerings. Try their eggs Benedict or a classic French breakfast.

Price: Around €10-€15.

Opening Hours: Generally from 8:00 AM to 11:00 PM.

Visit Musée des Beaux-Arts (Fine Arts Museum):

Highlights: Begin your day at one of France's largest and most prestigious art museums. The Musée des Beaux-Arts houses an extensive collection of artworks from ancient times to modern days, including masterpieces by painters like Monet, Van Gogh, and Rembrandt.

Opening Hours: 10:00 AM - 6:00 PM, closed on Tuesdays.

Price: €8 for adults, free for EU residents under 26.

Getting Around:

Walking: The museum is centrally located, so you can walk from your breakfast spot if it's nearby, or use Lyon's metro to reach Hôtel de Ville - Louis Pradel station.

Explore Parc de la Tête d'Or:

Highlights: After the museum, head to Parc de la Tête d'Or, a vast urban park featuring a botanical garden, a zoo, a large lake, and beautiful walking paths. It's an ideal spot for a relaxing stroll or a leisurely boat ride.

Activities: Visit the botanical garden, enjoy a paddle boat ride, or simply relax by the lake.

Price: Free entry to the park. Boat rentals cost around €10-€15.

Opening Hours: The park is open from 6:30 AM to 9:00 PM.

Getting Around:

Tram/Walking: Use Tram Line T1 to get to the park (stop: Tête d'Or - Parc), or if you prefer, walk if you're close by.

Lunch:

Le Bouchon des Filles: Enjoy a delightful lunch at Le Bouchon des Filles, known for its traditional Lyonnaise cuisine. Try dishes like Lyonnaise salad or a hearty stew.

Price: Approximately €20-€30 per person.

Opening Hours: 12:00 PM - 2:30 PM and 7:00 PM - 10:00 PM.

Visit Musée des Confluences:

Highlights: After lunch, head to the Musée des Confluences, a contemporary museum focusing on science, anthropology, and natural history. Its striking architecture and engaging exhibitions make it a must-visit.

Opening Hours: 10:30 AM - 6:30 PM, closed on Tuesdays.

Price: €9 for adults, free for under 18.

Getting Around:

Tram: Take Tram Line T1 to Musée des Confluences stop. The ride from the city center takes about 15 minutes.

Explore La Croix-Rousse:

Highlights: Head to the La Croix-Rousse district, known for its artistic vibe and historic silk-weaving heritage. Walk through the area and discover its famous murals, such as the "Mur des Canuts" and the "Fresque des Lyonnais," which depict scenes from Lyon's history and prominent figures.

Price: Free.

Getting Around:

Metro: Take Metro Line C to Croix-Rousse station.

Evening: Dinner and Relaxation

Dinner:

La Mère Brazier: For a fine dining experience, head to La Mère Brazier, a Michelin-starred restaurant offering refined Lyonnaise cuisine. It's a great place to enjoy a sophisticated dinner.

Price: Approximately €50-€80 per person.

Opening Hours: 7:00 PM - 10:00 PM.

Night Stroll:

Place des Terreaux: After dinner, take a relaxing evening stroll around Place des Terreaux. This lively square is beautifully illuminated at night and features the impressive Bartholdi Fountain.

Getting Around: Walk or use a short taxi ride if needed.

Getting Around Lyon

Public Transportation:

Metro and Tram: Use Lyon's metro and tram system for efficient travel between museums and parks. A single ticket costs around €2.00.

Bike Rentals:

Vélo'v: Utilize the Vélo'v bike-sharing system for a more flexible and eco-friendly way to explore the city.

Taxis/Rideshares:

Taxis/Uber: Convenient for longer distances or if you prefer not to use public transport.

Day 4: Modern Lyon and Cultural Experiences

Morning: Modern Lyon and Breakfast

Breakfast:

Brasserie Georges: Start your day at Brasserie Georges, a stylish spot for a classic French breakfast. Enjoy options like croissants, pastries, or a full breakfast with eggs and bacon.

Price: Around €10-€15.

Opening Hours: Typically from 7:00 AM to 11:00 PM.

Explore Confluence District:

Highlights: After breakfast, head to the Confluence district, known for its modern architecture and urban redevelopment. The area offers a stark contrast to Lyon's historic neighborhoods.

La Sucrière: A former sugar factory now used for contemporary art exhibitions and cultural events. Check for any current exhibitions or events.

Price: Varies depending on the event or exhibition.

Getting Around:

Tram: Take Tram Line T1 to the Confluence district. The ride is about 15 minutes from the city center.

Mid-Morning: Visit the Musée des Confluences

Musée des Confluences:

Highlights: Continue your exploration in the Confluence district with a visit to the Musée des Confluences, known for its futuristic design and diverse exhibits on science, anthropology, and natural history.

Opening Hours: 10:30 AM - 6:30 PM, closed on Tuesdays.

Price: €9 for adults, free for under 18.

Getting Around:

Walking: The museum is located in the Confluence district, so it's easily accessible by walking from other nearby attractions.

Afternoon: Cultural Experiences

Lunch:

Le Gourmet de Sèze: For lunch, enjoy a meal at Le Gourmet de Sèze, which offers modern French cuisine in a sophisticated setting. Try dishes that highlight seasonal ingredients.

Price: Approximately €25-€40 per person.

Opening Hours: 12:00 PM - 2:30 PM and 7:00 PM - 10:00 PM.

Visit the Centre d'Histoire de la Résistance et de la Déportation (CHRD):

Highlights: This museum offers a profound look into the history of resistance and deportation during World War II. It provides an educational and moving experience with exhibits on Lyon's role in the French Resistance.

Opening Hours: 10:00 AM - 6:00 PM, closed on Mondays.

Price: €5 for adults.

Getting Around:

Metro: Take Metro Line D to the station Gare de Vaise, which is near the CHRD.

Mid-Afternoon: Explore the Contemporary Art Scene

Visit the Musée d'Art Contemporain:

Highlights: Explore Lyon's contemporary art scene at the Musée d'Art Contemporain, which features rotating exhibitions of modern and contemporary art by both French and international artists.

Opening Hours: 11:00 AM - 6:00 PM, closed on Mondays.

Price: €8 for adults, free for under 18.

Getting Around:

Metro: Take Metro Line C to the Hôtel de Ville - Louis Pradel station, and walk to the museum.

Evening: Dinner and Cultural Activities

Dinner:

La Table de Suzanne: For a unique dining experience, head to La Table de Suzanne, offering a creative take on traditional French cuisine with a focus on fresh, local ingredients.

Price: Around €30-€50 per person.

Opening Hours: 7:00 PM - 10:00 PM.

Cultural Experience:

Opera National de Lyon: If you're interested in performing arts, check the schedule for the Opera National de Lyon and catch a performance or a concert. The opera house itself is a beautiful example of modern architecture.

Price: Varies depending on the performance.

Opening Hours: Performance times vary; check the schedule in advance.

Getting Around:

Walking: The opera house is centrally located, so a walk from dinner or a short taxi ride might be convenient.

Getting Around Lyon

Public Transportation:

Metro and Tram: Use Lyon's metro and tram lines to travel between modern districts and cultural sites. A single ticket costs around €2.00.

Bike Rentals:

Vélo'v: Rent a bike from the Vélo'v bike-sharing system for a flexible way to explore the city.

Taxis/Rideshares:

Taxis/Uber: Convenient for late-night travel or when you prefer not to use public transport.

Day 5: Day Trip to Beaujolais Wine Region

Breakfast:

Le Café des Artistes: Start your day with a hearty breakfast at Le Café des Artistes. Enjoy fresh pastries, coffee, and a light breakfast to fuel your trip.

Price: Around €8-€12.

Opening Hours: Typically from 7:00 AM to 11:00 PM.

Departure:

By Train: Take a train from Lyon Part-Dieu station to Villefranche-sur-Saône, a central town in the Beaujolais region. The journey takes about 30 minutes and costs approximately €10-€15.

By Car: If you prefer flexibility, consider renting a car for the day. The drive to Villefranche-sur-Saône or other wine towns in Beaujolais takes about 45 minutes.

Mid-Morning: Explore Villefranche-sur-Saône

Explore Villefranche-sur-Saône:

Highlights: Start with a visit to Villefranche-sur-Saône, a charming town often considered the gateway to the Beaujolais region. Stroll through the town center, explore local shops, and visit landmarks like the Saint-Georges Church.

Price: Free to explore.

Getting Around:

Walking: The town center is compact and easily explored on foot.

Late Morning: Wine Tasting in Beaujolais

Visit a Local Winery:

Domaine du Vissoux: One of the renowned wineries in the Beaujolais region. Enjoy a guided tour of the vineyards and wine cellars, followed by a tasting of their excellent Beaujolais wines.

Price: Wine tastings typically cost around €10-€20 per person, with some tours offering more comprehensive experiences at a higher price.

Opening Hours: Generally from 10:00 AM to 12:00 PM and 2:00 PM to 6:00 PM. It's a good idea to book in advance.

Getting Around:

Car: If you have a rental car, driving to various wineries is convenient. Otherwise, check for local wine tour operators who can provide transportation.

Lunch:

Auberge du Vieux Beaujolais: Enjoy a traditional lunch at this local restaurant, which offers classic regional dishes paired with Beaujolais wines. Dishes might include local specialties like coq au vin or charcuterie.

Price: Around €20-€35 per person.

Opening Hours: 12:00 PM - 2:30 PM and 7:00 PM - 9:00 PM.

Continue Wine Tasting:

Château de Pizay: Another great option for wine tasting. This historic château offers tours of its vineyards, cellars, and the opportunity to sample various Beaujolais wines.

Price: Similar to other wineries, tastings range from €10-€20.

Opening Hours: 10:00 AM to 12:00 PM and 2:00 PM to 6:00 PM.

Getting Around:

Car: If you're driving, plan your route to visit multiple wineries. If not, local wine tours often include multiple stops.

Late Afternoon: Explore the Scenic Countryside

Drive Through Beaujolais:

Highlights: Take a scenic drive through the Beaujolais countryside. Enjoy the rolling hills, vineyards, and picturesque villages such as Oingt, recognized for its beautiful medieval architecture.

Price: Free to explore, though some villages may have small entry fees for specific sites.

Getting Around:

Car: A rental car is ideal for exploring the countryside at your own pace.

Evening: Return to Lyon

Dinner:

Le Bouchon des Filles: Upon returning to Lyon, enjoy a relaxed dinner at Le Bouchon des Filles, offering traditional Lyonnaise cuisine. It's a great way to end your day with local dishes and a comforting meal.

Price: Approximately €20-€30 per person.

Opening Hours: 7:00 PM - 10:00 PM.

Return to Lyon:

By Train: Take a train back from Villefranche-sur-Saône to Lyon Part-Dieu.

By Car: Return your rental car if applicable and head back to your accommodation in Lyon.

Getting Around Beaujolais

Public Transport:

Train: Trains connect Lyon to Villefranche-sur-Saône, the main gateway to Beaujolais.

Car Rentals:

Flexibility: Renting a car is highly recommended for exploring Beaujolais, allowing you to visit multiple wineries and enjoy the scenic routes.

Wine Tours:

Organized Tours: Consider booking a guided wine tour that includes transportation, which can enhance your experience and allow you to sample wines without worrying about driving.

Day 6: Arts and Culture

Morning: Musée des Beaux-Arts and Cultural Exploration

Breakfast:

Le Sud: Begin your day with breakfast at Le Sud, a cozy spot offering a range of delicious options from croissants to omelets.

Price: Around €10-€15.

Opening Hours: Typically from 7:00 AM to 10:00 AM.

Visit Musée des Beaux-Arts (Fine Arts Museum):

Highlights: Spend your morning at the Musée des Beaux-Arts, which features an extensive collection of paintings, sculptures, and artifacts spanning from ancient civilizations to modern art. Key highlights include works by Monet, Picasso, and Rembrandt.

Opening Hours: 10:00 AM - 6:00 PM, closed on Tuesdays.

Price: €8 for adults, free for EU residents under 26.

Getting Around:

Walking: The museum is centrally located, so it's convenient to walk from nearby breakfast spots.

Mid-Morning: Explore Place des Terreaux and Hôtel de Ville

Explore Place des Terreaux:

Highlights: After visiting the museum, take a short walk to Place des Terreaux, a grand square known for its impressive Bartholdi Fountain and beautiful surroundings. The square is a hub of activity and a great spot for photos.

Visit Hôtel de Ville (City Hall):

Highlights: Adjacent to Place des Terreaux, the Hôtel de Ville is an architectural gem. While its interior is not always open to the public, the exterior façade and the surrounding area are worth admiring.

Price: Free to explore the exterior.

Getting Around:

Walking: Place des Terreaux and Hôtel de Ville are within walking distance from the Musée des Beaux-Arts.

Lunch:

Le Musée: Enjoy lunch at Le Musée, located near the Musée des Beaux-Arts. It offers a refined menu featuring modern French cuisine.

Price: Around €25-€35 per person.

Opening Hours: 12:00 PM - 2:30 PM and 7:00 PM - 10:00 PM.

Visit Musée d'Art Contemporain:

Highlights: Head to the Musée d'Art Contemporain for a deep dive into contemporary art. The museum hosts a rotating selection of modern art exhibitions from both established and emerging artists.

Opening Hours: 11:00 AM - 6:00 PM, closed on Mondays.

Price: €8 for adults, free for under 18.

Getting Around:

Metro: Take Metro Line C to Hôtel de Ville - Louis Pradel and then walk to the museum.

Visit Théâtre des Célestins:

Highlights: Explore this historic theater known for its stunning architecture and diverse performances. If you're lucky, you might catch a matinee show or take a tour of the theater.

Price: Varies depending on the performance or tour.

Opening Hours: Check for specific tour times or show schedules.

Getting Around:

Walking: The theater is centrally located, so it's easy to walk to from nearby attractions.

Dinner:

Bouchon Les Lyonnais: Experience traditional Lyonnaise cuisine at Bouchon Les Lyonnais. Enjoy regional specialties like quenelles and pâté en croûte in a charming, authentic setting.

Price: Around €25-€40 per person.

Opening Hours: 7:00 PM - 10:00 PM.

Cultural Experience:

Opera National de Lyon: If you enjoy performing arts, consider attending a performance at the Opera National de Lyon. Check their schedule for opera, ballet, or classical music concerts.

Price: Varies depending on the performance.

Opening Hours: Performance times vary; check the schedule in advance.

Getting Around:

Walking or Metro: The Opera House is centrally located. Depending on your dinner location, you might walk or use the metro to reach it.

Getting Around Lyon

Public Transportation:

Metro: Lyon's metro system is efficient and connects you to various cultural sites. A single ticket costs around €2.00.

Walking: Many cultural sites are located close to each other, making walking a convenient option.

Bike Rentals:

Vélo'v: Rent a bike from the Vélo'v bike-sharing system for a flexible way to explore the city.

Taxis/Rideshares:

Taxis/Uber: Use for longer distances or if you prefer not to use public transport.

Day 7: Final Exploration and Departure

Morning:

Activity: Begin your final day in Lyon with a peaceful stroll through the Parc de la Tête d'Or. This large urban park opens at 6:30 AM and is free to enter. It's perfect for a serene morning walk, offering a lake, botanical garden, and even a small zoo.

Breakfast: Enjoy breakfast at **Le Desjeuneur**, located near the park. They offer a variety of pastries, fresh fruit, and coffee. A typical breakfast here will cost around €10-15. They open at 8:00 AM, making it a convenient stop after your early walk.

Getting Around: Use the Lyon City Card for unlimited access to public transportation (metro, tram, bus) and free or discounted entry to various attractions. The card costs €27 for a 24-hour pass.

Mid-Morning:

Activity: Visit the **Musée des Confluences**, a science and anthropology museum located at the confluence of the Rhône and Saône rivers. The museum opens at 10:30 AM and the entrance fee is €9. This museum is not only informative but also architecturally stunning.

Getting Around: Take Tram T1 from the park to the museum, a journey of about 20 minutes.

Lunch:

Place to Eat: Head to **Les Halles de Lyon Paul Bocuse**, an indoor food market offering a variety of local and gourmet foods. You can sample dishes from multiple vendors, ensuring a diverse and authentic Lyonnaise culinary experience. Plan to spend around €20-30 per person. The market opens at 7:00 AM and is open until 7:00 PM.

Afternoon:

Activity: Explore the **Vieux Lyon** (Old Lyon), a UNESCO World Heritage site. Wander through the narrow cobblestone streets, visit the **Cathédrale Saint-Jean-Baptiste** (free entry, donations welcome), and explore the hidden traboules (passageways) that connect the buildings.

Getting Around: Vieux Lyon is best explored on foot to fully appreciate the historic architecture and ambiance.

Mid-Afternoon:

Activity: Take a funicular ride up to **Basilique Notre-Dame de Fourvière**. The basilica offers stunning views over the city and is free to enter. The funicular ride costs about €2 one-way and operates from 7:00 AM to 10:00 PM.

Getting Around: The funicular is accessed from the Vieux Lyon metro station.

Evening:

Activity: Enjoy a leisurely walk along the **Rhône River** banks. The promenades are lively in the evening, with plenty of locals and tourists enjoying the scenery. There are also river cruises available if you prefer a boat ride, with prices starting at around €15 for an hour-long tour.

Dinner:

Place to Eat: Dine at **Restaurant Paul Bocuse**, one of Lyon's most renowned restaurants. Expect exquisite French cuisine and a memorable dining experience. Reservations are highly recommended, and a meal can cost around €150 per person. The restaurant opens at 7:00 PM.

Night:

Activity: Finish your night with a visit to one of Lyon's many wine bars, like **Le Ballon**. Enjoy a glass of local wine or two, and soak in the vibrant nightlife. Most wine bars stay open until midnight or later.

Getting Around: After dinner, use the metro or a taxi to return to your accommodation. The metro operates until midnight on weekdays and 2:00 AM on weekends. Taxi fares within the city center typically range from €10-20, depending on the distance.

Final Tips:

Ensure your Lyon City Card is still valid for transport.

Check the specific closing times for each attraction as they can vary, especially on weekends and holidays.

Confirm your transport to the airport or train station in advance to avoid last-minute stress.

Chapter 15: Practical Information

Safety and Emergency Contacts

Lyon is generally a safe city, but as with any major urban area, it's important to stay aware and take common-sense precautions. Here are some key safety tips for tourists:

Stay Aware of Your Surroundings:

Keep an eye on your belongings, especially in crowded places like public transport, markets, and tourist attractions.

Avoid displaying large amounts of cash or expensive jewelry.

Use Reputable Transportation:

Use official taxis or ride-sharing services like Uber.

If using public transport, be mindful of your belongings, especially during peak hours.

Secure Your Accommodation:

Choose accommodations in safe neighborhoods.

Use hotel safes to store valuables and important documents.

Be Cautious at Night:

Stick to well-lit and populated areas.

Avoid walking alone late at night, especially in unfamiliar areas.

Stay Informed:

Keep up to date with local news and any potential safety advisories.

Familiarize yourself with local customs and laws.

Emergency Contacts

Emergency Services:

Police: Dial 17

Fire Brigade: Dial 18

Ambulance/Medical Emergency: Dial 15

European Emergency Number: Dial 112 (This can be used for any type of emergency and is available throughout the EU)

Tourist Assistance:

Tourist Information Center:

Address: Place Bellecour, 69002 Lyon

Phone: +33 4 72 77 69 69

Hours: Monday to Saturday, 9:00 AM - 6:00 PM; Sunday, 10:00 AM - 4:00 PM

Medical Assistance:

Hospitals:

Hôpital de la Croix-Rousse

Address: 103 Grande Rue de la Croix-Rousse, 69004 Lyon

Phone: +33 4 72 07 17 18

Centre Hospitalier Saint Joseph Saint Luc

Address: 20 Quai Claude Bernard, 69007 Lyon

Phone: +33 4 78 61 81 81

Pharmacies:

Pharmacies are plentiful and many have extended hours. Look for signs saying "Pharmacie de Garde" for those open late or on holidays.

Consular Assistance:

U.S. Consulate General in Lyon:

Address: 1 Quai Jules Courmont, 69002 Lyon

Phone: +33 1 43 12 48 63

British Consulate in Lyon:

Address: 33 Rue de la République, 69002 Lyon

Phone: +33 1 44 51 31 00

Local Law Enforcement:

Police Stations:

Commissariat de Police du 1er arrondissement:

Address: 1 Rue de la Vieille, 69001 Lyon

Phone: +33 4 72 00 14 00

Commissariat de Police du 2ème arrondissement:

Address: 18 Rue de la Charité, 69002 Lyon

Phone: +33 4 72 77 17 50

Embassy and Consulate Websites:

It's useful to bookmark the website of your home country's embassy or consulate in France. They often provide valuable resources and updates regarding safety and emergency services.

Health and Safety Precautions

Healthcare:

Health Insurance:

Ensure you have adequate travel health insurance that covers medical emergencies abroad.

Carry your insurance card and contact information with you.

Emergency Numbers for Insurance:

Many travel insurance companies provide a 24-hour emergency hotline. Make sure you know your policy number and how to contact your insurer in case of an emergency.

Personal Health:

Pharmacies:

In case of minor ailments, visit a local pharmacy. Pharmacists in France are highly trained and can provide advice and over-the-counter medications.

Pharmacies that are open late or on Sundays are marked as "Pharmacie de Garde".

Hospitals and Clinics:

In case of serious illness or injury, visit a local hospital or clinic. Emergency rooms are available 24/7.

Staying Connected:

Mobile Phones:

Ensure your mobile phone works in France and consider getting a local SIM card for easier communication.

Save important numbers (hotel, local contacts, emergency services) on your phone.

Internet Access:

Most hotels, cafes, and restaurants offer free Wi-Fi. Stay connected to keep up with any local safety advisories.

Natural Disasters and Local Hazards:

Weather:

Check the weather forecast regularly, especially if you plan on engaging in outdoor activities.

Lyon can experience sudden changes in weather, so dress accordingly.

River Safety:

If you plan to spend time by the Rhône or Saône rivers, be cautious of strong currents and follow local safety advice.

Cultural Sensitivity

Respect Local Customs:

Language:

Learning a few basic French phrases can be helpful and is often appreciated by locals.

Behavior:

Observe and respect local customs and traditions. This includes dress codes for religious sites and polite behavior in public.

Legal Issues:

Laws:

Familiarize yourself with local laws and regulations to avoid any legal issues.

Remember that drug use, even if legal in your home country, can carry severe penalties in France.

Health and Medical Services

Lyon, as part of France, boasts a high-quality healthcare system known for its accessibility and excellence. The city is well-equipped with hospitals, clinics, pharmacies, and specialized medical services. Here's a comprehensive guide to navigating health and medical services in Lyon as a tourist.

Emergency Medical Services

Emergency Contacts:

Medical Emergency (SAMU): Dial 15

General Emergency (European Emergency Number): Dial 112

Poison Control Center: Dial +33 4 72 11 69 11

These numbers are toll-free and available 24/7.

Hospitals with Emergency Rooms:

Hôpital de la Croix-Rousse

Address: 103 Grande Rue de la Croix-Rousse, 69004 Lyon

Phone: +33 4 72 07 17 18

Centre Hospitalier Saint Joseph Saint Luc

Address: 20 Quai Claude Bernard, 69007 Lyon

Phone: +33 4 78 61 81 81

Hôpital Edouard Herriot

Address: 5 Place d'Arsonval, 69003 Lyon

Phone: +33 4 72 11 11 11

Non-Emergency Medical Services

General Practitioners (GPs):

Maison Médicale de Garde de Lyon (Walk-in Clinic)

Address: 5 Rue Bourgelat, 69002 Lyon

Phone: +33 4 72 33 00 33

Hours: Monday to Friday, 8:00 AM - 8:00 PM

Specialists:

For specialist consultations, it's advisable to seek a referral from a GP or visit a hospital with specialist departments.

Dentists:

Clinique Dentaire Saint Antoine

Address: 15 Rue Saint-Antoine, 69002 Lyon

Phone: +33 4 78 42 99 99

Pharmacies

Pharmacies in Lyon are plentiful and can be found in almost every neighborhood. They provide over-the-counter medications and can also fill prescriptions.

Pharmacie des Célestins

Address: 1 Rue des Archers, 69002 Lyon

Phone: +33 4 78 42 07 52

Hours: Monday to Saturday, 8:00 AM - 8:00 PM

Pharmacie de Garde:

For after-hours service, look for a "Pharmacie de Garde" sign or call the nearest pharmacy for information on the closest open location.

Health Insurance and Costs

Health Insurance:

Travel Insurance:

Ensure you have travel health insurance that covers medical expenses abroad. Carry your insurance card and details of your policy, including contact numbers for emergency assistance.

European Health Insurance Card (EHIC):

If you are an EU citizen, carry your EHIC, which provides access to state-provided healthcare at a reduced cost or sometimes for free.

Medical Costs:

Consultation Fees:

GP visit: Approximately €25-50

Specialist consultation: Approximately €50-100

Emergency room visit: Costs vary depending on treatment but can range from €50-200

Pharmacy Costs:

Over-the-counter medications: €5-20 depending on the type of medication

Prescription medications: Costs vary, but many are subsidized under French healthcare.

Mental Health Services

Psychologists and Psychiatrists:

Centre Médico-Psychologique (CMP)

Address: 5 Rue de la Barre, 69002 Lyon

Phone: +33 4 78 37 39 39

Provides consultations with psychologists and psychiatrists. Some services may require a referral.

Helplines:

SOS Help (English-speaking helpline):

Phone: +33 1 46 21 46 46

Provides emotional support and crisis intervention.

Vaccinations and Health Precautions

Vaccinations:

Ensure routine vaccinations are up to date, including measles, mumps, rubella (MMR), diphtheria, tetanus, and polio.

For specific health advice or vaccinations, consult with a travel clinic or your healthcare provider before traveling.

Health Precautions:

Water:

Tap water in Lyon is safe to drink.

Food:

Follow standard food safety precautions. Lyon is known for its high-quality cuisine, but ensure food is properly cooked and served.

Useful Medical Apps and Websites

Apps:

Doctolib:

A popular app in France for booking medical appointments with GPs and specialists.

Pharmacies de Garde:

Provides information on nearby open pharmacies, especially for after-hours needs.

Websites:

Ameli.fr:

The official website of the French health insurance service, offering information on medical services and reimbursement.

SOS Médecins Lyon:

www.sosmedecins-lyon.fr

Provides home visit services by doctors for non-emergency medical issues.

Travel Etiquette and Customs

Understanding and respecting local customs and etiquette can enhance your travel experience and help you blend in better with the locals. Here's an extensive guide on travel etiquette and customs to keep in mind while visiting Lyon.

General Etiquette

Greetings:

Bonjour/Bonsoir: Always greet people with "Bonjour" (Good morning/Hello) or "Bonsoir" (Good evening) when entering shops, restaurants, or when meeting someone for the first time.

La Bise: The French greeting involves kissing on both cheeks, usually reserved for friends and acquaintances. For tourists, a simple handshake is more appropriate when meeting someone new.

Politeness:

Please and Thank You: Use "s'il vous plaît" (please) and "merci" (thank you) frequently. Adding "madame" or "monsieur" is also appreciated.

Excuse Me: Use "pardon" or "excusez-moi" to get someone's attention or if you accidentally bump into someone.

Dress Code:

Casual Elegance: The French generally dress more formally than in some other countries. Even casual wear tends to be stylish. Avoid wearing overly casual attire like flip-flops, gym clothes, or beachwear unless you are at the appropriate location.

Dining Etiquette

Meals:

Breakfast: Often light, consisting of coffee and a pastry.

Lunch and Dinner: These meals are more substantial, with lunch being the main meal of the day for many. Dinner is typically served later, starting around 7:30 PM or later.

At the Table:

Hands Visible: Keep your hands on the table, not on your lap.

Knife and Fork: The French use the Continental style of eating, with the fork in the left hand and the knife in the right.

Don't Rush: Meals are a social event. Take your time to enjoy the food and company.

Ordering and Tipping:

The Menu: Look for the "menu du jour" (daily special) for a good value meal.

Tipping: Service is included in the bill (service compris), but it's customary to leave small change or round up the bill if the service was good.

Restaurants:

Reservations: Make reservations for dinner, especially on weekends. It's common to reserve a table even for casual dining.

Punctuality: Arrive on time for your reservation. Being late is considered impolite.

Social Customs

Conversation:

Volume: Keep your voice down in public places. Loud conversations can be considered rude.

Topics: Avoid discussing money, politics, or asking personal questions when first meeting someone. Instead, focus on cultural topics like art, food, and travel.

Personal Space:

Respect Space: The French value personal space. Avoid standing too close or touching someone during a conversation unless you know them well.

Queueing:

Lines: Queueing is taken seriously. Do not attempt to cut in line, whether at a bakery, bus stop, or ticket office.

Transportation Etiquette

Public Transport:

Quiet: Maintain a low volume when talking on public transport.

Tickets: Always validate your ticket. Fare evasion is taken seriously and can result in fines.

Priority Seats: Give up your seat for elderly, disabled, pregnant women, or parents with small children.

Driving:

Speed Limits: Adhere to posted speed limits and local driving laws.

Roundabouts: Yield to traffic already in the roundabout.

Parking: Park only in designated areas. Illegal parking can result in fines or your car being towed.

Shopping Etiquette

Stores:

Greetings: Greet the shopkeeper with "Bonjour" upon entering and "Merci, au revoir" (Thank you, goodbye) when leaving.

Handling Goods: Ask before handling items in small boutiques or markets.

Markets:

Bargaining: Unlike some cultures, bargaining is not common in French markets. Prices are generally fixed.

Sampling: It's polite to ask before sampling products.

Cultural Sites and Events

Respecting Venues:

Quiet: Keep your voice down in museums, churches, and other cultural sites.

Photography: Check if photography is allowed, especially with flash. Some places prohibit it.

Events:

Punctuality: Arrive on time for performances, exhibitions, or tours. Late arrivals can be disruptive.

Environmental Etiquette

Littering:

Dispose Properly: Use trash bins provided and recycle when possible. Littering is frowned upon and can result in fines.

Respecting Nature:

Parks and Natural Sites: Stay on marked paths, do not pick flowers, and avoid disturbing wildlife.

Money-Saving Tips

Lyon is a beautiful and vibrant city with a lot to offer, but like any major city, it can also be expensive. Here are some practical money-saving tips to help you enjoy Lyon without breaking the bank.

Accommodation

Book in Advance:

Booking your accommodation well in advance can help you secure better deals. Websites like Booking.com, Airbnb, and Hostelworld often offer discounts for early bookings.

Stay in Budget-Friendly Areas:

Consider staying in areas like the 7th or 8th arrondissement, which are less central but well-connected by public transport and offer more affordable lodging options.

Hostels and Budget Hotels:

Hostels and budget hotels are excellent choices for solo travelers or those on a tight budget. Look for places with good reviews that include breakfast.

Couchsurfing:

Couchsurfing can be a great way to save on accommodation costs and meet locals who can give you insider tips about the city.

Transportation

Public Transport:

Lyon City Card: This card provides unlimited access to public transportation (metro, tram, bus) and free or discounted entry to many attractions. Prices start at €27 for a 24-hour pass.

Bulk Tickets: Purchase a carnet of 10 tickets for a discounted rate (€19.10) instead of buying single tickets (€2.20 each).

Walking and Biking:

Lyon is a very walkable city, especially in the central areas. Take advantage of the Velo'v bike-sharing system for short trips. The first 30 minutes are free, and a day pass costs just €1.50.

Ride-Sharing and Carpooling:

Use apps like BlaBlaCar for intercity travel to save on transport costs.

Sightseeing and Attractions

Free Attractions:

Enjoy the many free attractions such as the Parc de la Tête d'Or, the Basilique Notre-Dame de Fourvière, and the traboules (historic passageways) in Vieux Lyon.

Museum Passes:

The Lyon City Card includes access to many museums and cultural sites. If you plan to visit several, the card can be a great value.

Discount Days:

Many museums offer discounted or free entry on the first Sunday of the month or during specific times. Check their websites for details.

Self-Guided Tours:

Download free walking tour apps or guides to explore the city at your own pace without the cost of a tour guide.

Dining

Affordable Eats:

Bouchons: Traditional Lyonnaise restaurants offer fixed-price menus (menus du jour) that provide excellent value. Lunch menus are often cheaper than dinner.

Markets: Visit local markets like Les Halles de Lyon Paul Bocuse for fresh and affordable food. You can often find delicious, reasonably priced meals from various vendors.

Self-Catering:

If your accommodation has kitchen facilities, consider shopping at local supermarkets and preparing some of your meals. This can be a significant cost saver.

Picnics:

Take advantage of Lyon's beautiful parks and riversides by having a picnic. Pick up some local cheese, bread, and wine from a market or supermarket for a delightful and inexpensive meal.

Happy Hours:

Many bars and cafes offer happy hour specials in the late afternoon and early evening, where you can enjoy discounted drinks and snacks.

Shopping

Sales and Discounts:

Take advantage of the biannual sales in France, known as "les soldes," which take place in January and July. During these periods, you can find significant discounts on clothing and other items.

Markets and Flea Markets:

Shop at local markets and flea markets for unique souvenirs and gifts at reasonable prices. The Marché de la Création and the Puces du Canal are popular options.

Tax Refunds:

If you are a non-EU resident and spend more than €100.01 in a single store, you are eligible for a VAT refund. Keep your receipts and ask for a tax refund form at the point of purchase.

Entertainment

Free Events:

Look out for free cultural events, concerts, and festivals, especially in the summer. Lyon frequently hosts free public events in its parks and squares.

Cinema Discounts:

Cinemas often offer discounted tickets on specific days (like Mondays or Wednesdays). Look for deals at local theaters.

Student Discounts:

If you're a student, carry your student ID to take advantage of discounts on transport, museums, and other attractions.

Language and Communication

Understanding and effectively communicating in the local language can significantly enhance your travel experience in Lyon. While many people in Lyon speak some English, especially in tourist areas, making an effort to speak French can go a long way in building rapport and showing respect for the local culture. Here's a comprehensive guide to help you navigate language and communication during your visit to Lyon.

Basic French Phrases

Greetings and Politeness:

Bonjour (bohn-zhoor) - Hello/Good morning

Bonsoir (bohn-swahr) - Good evening

Salut (sa-loo) - Hi (informal)

Merci (mehr-see) - Thank you

S'il vous plaît (seel voo pleh) - Please

Excusez-moi (ehk-skew-zay mwah) - Excuse me

Pardon (par-doh) - Sorry

Common Questions:

Parlez-vous anglais? (par-lay voo ahn-glay) - Do you speak English?

Où est...? (oo eh) - Where is...?

Combien ça coûte? (kohm-byen sah koot) - How much does it cost?

Pouvez-vous m'aider? (poo-vay voo meh-day) - Can you help me?

Je voudrais... (zhuh voo-dray) - I would like...

Directions:

Gauche (gohsh) - Left

Droite (drwaht) - Right

Tout droit (too drwa) - Straight ahead

À côté de (ah koh-tay duh) - Next to

Dining:

L'addition, s'il vous plaît (la-dee-syon, seel voo pleh) - The bill, please

Un verre de vin (uhn vehr duh vahn) - A glass of wine

Je suis végétarien(ne) (zhuh swee vay-zhay-tah-ree-ehn) - I am vegetarian

Pronunciation Tips

Soft Consonants: French consonants are often softer than English. For example, the 'r' is guttural and pronounced at the back of the throat.

Nasal Sounds: French has several nasal sounds, which are created by letting air flow through the nose.

Silent Letters: Many French words have silent letters, especially at the end (e.g., 'Paris' is pronounced 'Pa-ree').

Communication Tips

Be Polite:

Always start with a greeting (e.g., "Bonjour") when addressing someone.

Use polite forms like "s'il vous plaît" and "merci" frequently.

Speak Slowly and Clearly:

When speaking French, speak slowly and clearly. If the person responds in French and you don't understand, you can politely ask them to repeat or speak more slowly.

Use Gestures:

Non-verbal communication can be very effective. Gestures, facial expressions, and body language can help convey your message.

Carry a Phrasebook or Translation App:

A French phrasebook or a translation app like Google Translate can be very useful for quick translations on the go.

Learn Key Phrases:

Learning a few key phrases in French can be very helpful and is often appreciated by locals.

English-Friendly Places

Tourist Areas:

In tourist-heavy areas like Vieux Lyon, Presqu'île, and around major attractions, many people speak English.

Hotels and Restaurants:

Staff at hotels and restaurants that cater to tourists usually speak English. Menus are often available in English as well.

Tourist Information Centers:

Staff at tourist information centers typically speak multiple languages, including English. They can provide maps, brochures, and advice in English.

Public Transport:

Major train stations and airports have English-speaking staff. Signs are often in both French and English.

Language Resources

Language Apps:

Duolingo: A fun and interactive app for learning French.

Babbel: Offers structured language courses.

Google Translate: Useful for quick translations and includes a conversation mode.

Online Resources:

YouTube: Channels like Learn French with Alexa and FrenchPod101 offer free video lessons.

BBC Languages: Provides free online resources for learning French.

Local Language Schools:

If you plan an extended stay, consider enrolling in a local language school like Alliance Française.

French Meetups and Language Exchange:

Look for local meetups or language exchange groups where you can practice French with locals and other travelers.

Do's and Don't in Lyon

When visiting Lyon, being aware of the local customs and behaviors can help you make a positive impression and enhance your overall experience. Here are some important do's and don'ts to keep in mind:

Do's

Greet People Properly:

Do say "Bonjour" or "Bonsoir" when entering shops, restaurants, or greeting someone. A polite greeting is expected and appreciated.

Enjoy the Local Cuisine:

Do try Lyon's famous dishes like quenelles, saucisson, and cervelle de canut. Visit a traditional bouchon to experience authentic Lyonnaise cuisine.

Explore the Markets:

Do visit local markets such as Les Halles de Lyon Paul Bocuse and outdoor markets like Marché Saint-Antoine. They are great places to sample local produce and delicacies.

Respect Cultural Sites:

Do be respectful in churches, museums, and historical sites. Dress appropriately and keep noise to a minimum.

Learn Basic French Phrases:

Do make an effort to speak some French, even if it's just basic phrases. Locals appreciate when visitors try to speak their language.

Use Public Transport:

Do use the efficient public transport system in Lyon, including trams, buses, and the metro. Consider purchasing a Lyon City Card for unlimited travel and attraction access.

Tip Appropriately:

Do leave a small tip if you've received good service. While service is included in the bill, rounding up or leaving some change is appreciated.

Respect Meal Times:

Do adhere to typical meal times in France. Lunch is usually from 12 PM to 2 PM, and dinner starts around 7:30 PM. Restaurants might be closed outside these hours.

Participate in Local Festivals:

Do join in local celebrations and festivals like the Fête des Lumières in December. It's a great way to experience the culture and community spirit.

Be Environmentally Conscious:

Do recycle and use the correct bins for waste disposal. Lyon is known for its commitment to sustainability.

Don't Speak Loudly:

Don't speak loudly in public places, especially in restaurants and on public transport. The French appreciate a quieter, more reserved public demeanor.

Don't Skip Greetings:

Don't forget to greet shopkeepers, waitstaff, and others with a "Bonjour" or "Bonsoir" before making requests or asking questions.

Don't Touch Produce at Markets:

Don't handle produce at markets without permission. Ask the vendor to help you or indicate what you'd like to purchase.

Don't Expect All Menus in English:

Don't expect all menus to be in English. It can be helpful to familiarize yourself with some food-related vocabulary or use a translation app.

Don't Ignore Dress Codes:

Don't wear overly casual clothing in certain settings. For dining out, especially in finer establishments, dress smartly. Avoid beachwear in the city.

Don't Rely Solely on Credit Cards:

Don't assume all places accept credit cards, especially smaller shops and markets. Carry some cash for small purchases.

Don't Rush Meals:

Don't rush your meal. Dining in France is a leisurely activity meant to be enjoyed. Take your time to savor the food and the experience.

Don't Eat While Walking:

Don't eat while walking down the street. The French generally consider eating to be an activity to be enjoyed sitting down.

Don't Disregard Queues:

Don't cut in line or disregard queues. Whether at a bakery, ticket booth, or public transport, respect the order.

Don't Forget to Validate Transport Tickets:

Don't forget to validate your ticket before boarding public transport. Failure to do so can result in fines.

Chapter 16: Conclusion

Tourist Information Centers

Tourist Information Centers (TICs) are invaluable resources for visitors, offering a wide range of services including maps, brochures, tour bookings, and advice on local attractions. Here are the main Tourist Information Centers in Lyon, along with their services, locations, and opening hours.

Main Tourist Information Centers

Lyon Tourist Office - Bellecour

Location:

Address: Place Bellecour, 69002 Lyon

Services:

- Maps and brochures
- Information on local attractions, events, and activities
- Ticket booking for tours and excursions
- Accommodation information and bookings
- Souvenir shop with local products and gifts

Opening Hours:

Monday to Saturday: 9 AM to 6 PM

Sunday and Public Holidays: 10 AM to 5 PM

Contact:

Phone: +33 4 72 77 69 69

Website: Lyon Tourism

Tourist Information Center - Part-Dieu

Location:

Address: Gare de Lyon Part-Dieu, Place Charles Béraudier, 69003 Lyon

Services:

- Maps and brochures
- Information on transportation options and schedules
- Assistance with accommodation and dining recommendations
- Ticket booking for local attractions and events

Opening Hours:

Monday to Friday: 9 AM to 6 PM

Saturday: 9 AM to 5 PM

Sunday and Public Holidays: Closed

Contact:

Phone: +33 4 72 77 69 69

Tourist Information Center - Saint-Jean

Location:

Address: 6 rue de la Bombarde, 69005 Lyon (Vieux Lyon)

Services:

- Maps and brochures
- Information on historical sites and guided tours
- Ticket booking for cultural events and activities
- Recommendations for dining and shopping in the Vieux Lyon area

Opening Hours:

Monday to Saturday: 9:30 AM to 12:30 PM and 1:30 PM to 5:30 PM

Sunday and Public Holidays: Closed

Contact:

Phone: +33 4 72 77 69 69

Services Provided by Tourist Information Centers

Maps and Guides:

Free maps of Lyon, including public transport maps.

Guides to local attractions, neighborhoods, and historical sites.

Tourist Information:

Detailed information on major attractions like Fourvière Basilica, Parc de la Tête d'Or, and Musée des Confluences.

Updates on current events, festivals, and exhibitions.

Booking Services:

Assistance with booking guided tours, river cruises, and excursions.

Help with purchasing tickets for museums, theaters, and cultural events.

Accommodation and Dining:

Recommendations for hotels, hostels, and bed & breakfasts.

Information on local restaurants, cafes, and bars, including those that serve traditional Lyonnaise cuisine.

Transport Information:

Timetables and routes for buses, trams, metro, and regional trains.

Information on bike rentals and pedestrian routes.

Multilingual Assistance:

Staff proficient in multiple languages, including English, to assist international tourists.

Souvenir Shops:

A selection of local products, souvenirs, and gifts, including regional specialties like silk scarves and Lyonnaise food products.

Special Services:

Tailored recommendations based on specific interests, such as culinary tours, historical walks, or family-friendly activities.

Useful Apps for travelers

In today's digital age, having the right apps on your smartphone can significantly enhance your travel experience. Here are some of the most useful apps for travelers visiting Lyon, covering various needs from navigation and accommodation to language translation and local recommendations.

Navigation and Transport

Google Maps

Description: Provides comprehensive maps, real-time traffic conditions, public transport routes, and directions for driving, walking, or cycling.

Features: Offline maps, nearby places of interest, reviews, and photos.

Availability: iOS and Android

Cost: Free

Moovit

Description: Offers detailed public transportation information, including routes, schedules, and real-time updates for buses, trams, and metro.

Features: Step-by-step navigation, service alerts, and live arrival times.

Availability: iOS and Android

Cost: Free

Velo'v Official App

Description: The official app for Lyon's bike-sharing system, providing information on bike availability and station locations.

Features: Bike availability in real-time, station map, and rental process.

Availability: iOS and Android

Cost: Free

Citymapper

Description: A comprehensive urban transport app that covers all modes of transportation, including public transport, walking, and cycling.

Features: Real-time departures, trip planning, and disruption alerts.

Availability: iOS and Android

Cost: Free

Accommodation and Dining

Booking.com

Description: A popular platform for booking hotels, apartments, and other accommodations.

Features: User reviews, price comparisons, and exclusive mobile deals.

Availability: iOS and Android

Cost: Free

Airbnb

Description: Find unique accommodations, including entire homes, private rooms, and shared spaces.

Features: Filter searches, contact hosts, and book directly through the app.

Availability: iOS and Android

Cost: Free

TripAdvisor

Description: Offers millions of reviews and ratings for hotels, restaurants, and attractions.

Features: Restaurant reservations, tour bookings, and user-generated content.

Availability: iOS and Android

Cost: Free

TheFork (La Fourchette)

Description: Allows you to discover and book tables at restaurants in Lyon.

Features: User reviews, discounts, and online reservations.

Availability: iOS and Android

Cost: Free

Language and Communication

Google Translate

Description: A powerful translation app supporting dozens of languages, including French.

Features: Text translation, voice translation, camera translation, and offline mode.

Availability: iOS and Android

Cost: Free

Duolingo

Description: A fun and interactive language-learning app with bite-sized lessons.

Features: Gamified learning, progress tracking, and multiple languages.

Availability: iOS and Android

Cost: Free with in-app purchases

HelloTalk

Description: Connects you with native speakers around the world for language exchange.

Features: Text, voice, and video chats, language correction, and translation tools.

Availability: iOS and Android

Cost: Free with in-app purchases

Local Recommendations and Experiences

GetYourGuide

Description: Offers a wide range of tours, activities, and experiences in Lyon.

Features: User reviews, instant booking, and mobile tickets.

Availability: iOS and Android

Cost: Free

Like A Local

Description: Provides insider tips and recommendations from locals.

Features: Offline maps, authentic local experiences, and curated city guides.

Availability: iOS and Android

Cost: Free

Eventbrite

Description: Find and book tickets for events, activities, and experiences in Lyon.

Features: Event discovery, ticket purchasing, and event notifications.

Availability: iOS and Android

Cost: Free

Culture Trip

Description: Offers curated content on local culture, attractions, and experiences.

Features: Articles, guides, and recommendations from local experts.

Availability: iOS and Android

Cost: Free

Financial and Currency Management

XE Currency

Description: Provides real-time currency exchange rates and conversions.

Features: Currency charts, offline mode, and rate alerts.

Availability: iOS and Android

Cost: Free

Revolut

Description: A digital banking app offering multi-currency accounts and low-fee international payments.

Features: Real-time exchange rates, spending analytics, and travel insurance options.

Availability: iOS and Android

Cost: Free with premium options

Splitwise

Description: Helps you split expenses with friends and travel companions.

Features: Expense tracking, group payments, and debt calculations.

Availability: iOS and Android

Cost: Free with in-app purchases

Basic Lyonnaise Phrases

When visiting Lyon, knowing a few basic French phrases can greatly enhance your experience. While Lyon is a French-speaking city, there are some local phrases and terms unique to the Lyonnais dialect that might be useful. Here's a list of basic French phrases along with some Lyonnaise expressions that can help you navigate your visit.

General French Phrases

Greetings:

- **Bonjour** (bohn-zhoor) - Hello / Good morning
- **Bonsoir** (bohn-swahr) - Good evening
- **Salut** (sa-loo) - Hi (informal)
- **Au revoir** (oh ruh-vwahr) - Goodbye
- **Bonne nuit** (bohn nwee) - Good night
- **Politeness:**
- **S'il vous plaît** (seel voo pleh) - Please
- **Merci** (mehr-see) - Thank you
- **De rien** (duh ryen) - You're welcome
- **Excusez-moi** (ehk-skew-zay mwah) - Excuse me
- **Pardon** (par-doh) - Sorry

- **Parlez-vous anglais ?** (par-lay voo ahn-glay) - Do you speak English?
- **Où est...?** (oo eh) - Where is...?
- **Combien ça coûte ?** (kohm-byen sah koot) - How much does it cost?
- **Pouvez-vous m'aider ?** (poo-vay voo meh-day) - Can you help me?
- **Je voudrais...** (zhuh voo-dray) - I would like...
- **Directions:**
- **Gauche** (gohsh) - Left
- **Droite** (drwaht) - Right
- **Tout droit** (too drwa) - Straight ahead
- **Près de** (preh duh) - Near
- **Loin de** (lwan duh) - Far from

Dining:

L'addition, s'il vous plaît (la-dee-syon, seel voo pleh) - The bill, please

Un verre de vin (uhn vehr duh vahn) - A glass of wine

Je suis végétarien(ne) (zhuh swee vay-zhay-tah-ree-ehn) - I am vegetarian (végétarienne for female)

Sans gluten (sahn gloo-ten) - Gluten-free

Une carafe d'eau (ewn ka-rahf doh) - A jug of water

Local Lyonnaise Phrases and Terms

Lyonnaiseries:

- **Gône** (gohn) - A term for a child or kid, unique to Lyon.
- **Canut** (kah-new) - Refers to the silk workers of Lyon, historically significant.
- **Traboule** (trah-bool) - Refers to the hidden passageways found in Vieux Lyon.
- **Bugnes** (buh-nyuh) - A type of Lyonnaise pastry similar to doughnuts, often enjoyed during Carnival.

Local Expressions:

- **À la lyonnaise** (ah lah lee-yo-nayz) - In the Lyonnaise style (often used in cooking).
- **Bouchon** (boo-shon) - A traditional Lyonnaise restaurant.
- **C'est la vie à Lyon** (say lah vee ah lee-ohn) - That's life in Lyon (used to describe something typical of Lyon).
- **Gratte-ciel** (graht-syel) - Literally "skyscraper," but locally refers to a specific area in Villeurbanne with notable high-rise buildings.

Common Phrases:

- **Ça roule ?** (sah rool) - How's it going? (informal)
- **Je suis bien ici** (zhuh swee byen ee-see) - I am happy here.
- **On y va ?** (ohn ee vah) - Shall we go?

Politeness Matters:

Always start interactions with "Bonjour" (or "Bonsoir" in the evening) to show politeness. This simple gesture is highly valued in French culture.

Practice Makes Perfect:

Don't be afraid to practice your French. Locals appreciate when tourists make an effort, even if it's not perfect.

Non-Verbal Cues:

Use gestures and body language to complement your spoken French, especially if you're unsure of the pronunciation or vocabulary.

Language Apps:

Use translation apps like Google Translate to assist with more complex phrases or when you're stuck.

Final Tips and Recommendations

To ensure you have a memorable and enjoyable visit to Lyon, here are some final tips and recommendations covering various aspects of your trip:

1. Plan Ahead

Research Attractions: Identify the must-see attractions and plan your itinerary. Key sites include the Basilica of Notre-Dame de Fourvière, Parc de la Tête d'Or, and the Musée des Confluences.

Book in Advance: Reserve tickets for popular attractions and tours ahead of time to avoid long lines and ensure availability.

2. Local Cuisine

Try Lyonnaise Specialties: Don't miss out on local dishes like quenelles, boudin noir (blood sausage), and gratin dauphinois. Lyon is renowned for its culinary heritage, so visiting a traditional bouchon is a must.

Explore Markets: Visit Les Halles de Lyon Paul Bocuse and other local markets to sample fresh produce, cheeses, and pastries.

3. Getting Around

Public Transport: Utilize Lyon's efficient public transportation system, including trams, buses, and the metro. Consider purchasing a Lyon City Card for unlimited travel and discounts on attractions.

Walking and Cycling: Many of Lyon's attractions are within walking distance, and biking is a great way to explore the city. The Vélo'v bike-sharing system is widely available.

4. Cultural Etiquette

Respect Local Customs: Adhere to local customs such as greeting with a "Bonjour" or "Bonsoir," and avoid speaking loudly in public spaces.

Dress Appropriately: Dress smartly, especially when dining out or visiting religious sites. Casual attire is acceptable for most tourist activities, but avoid wearing beachwear in the city.

5. Language and Communication

Learn Basic French Phrases: Familiarize yourself with basic French phrases to help with communication and show respect for the local culture.

Use Translation Apps: If needed, use apps like Google Translate to assist with language barriers.

6. Safety and Health

Keep Valuables Secure: Be mindful of your belongings, especially in crowded areas and public transport. Use a money belt or secure bag for valuables.

Stay Hydrated and Safe: Lyon's climate can be quite warm, especially in summer. Stay hydrated, use sunscreen, and take breaks to avoid heat exhaustion.

7. Money Management

Carry Cash: While credit cards are widely accepted, carry some cash for smaller establishments and markets.

Use Currency Apps: Use apps like XE Currency to keep track of exchange rates and manage your budget effectively.

8. Local Events and Festivals

Check Local Calendars: Lyon hosts various events and festivals throughout the year, including the Fête des Lumières (Festival of Lights) in December. Check local event calendars to see if any coincide with your visit.

9. Emergency Contacts

Know Local Emergency Numbers: Familiarize yourself with local emergency numbers: 112 for general emergencies, 15 for medical emergencies, 17 for police, and 18 for fire.

Locate Nearest Embassies/Consulates: Know the location of your country's embassy or consulate in case of emergencies.

10. Local Etiquette

Dining Etiquette: When dining out, it's customary to keep your hands on the table (but not elbows) and use utensils properly. Tipping is appreciated but not obligatory.

Respect Historical Sites: When visiting historical sites and museums, follow the rules, avoid touching artifacts, and keep noise levels down.

11. Tech Tips

Offline Maps: Download offline maps from apps like Google Maps to navigate without data.

Wi-Fi Access: Many cafes, restaurants, and public spaces offer free Wi-Fi. Look for "Wi-Fi gratuit" signs.

12. Personal Comfort

Pack Light but Wisely: Bring comfortable walking shoes, appropriate clothing for the weather, and a reusable water bottle.

Stay Informed: Keep updated on local news and weather forecasts to adjust your plans as needed.

Made in the USA
Las Vegas, NV
09 December 2024

13744154R00201